AN EPITAPH FOR LITTLE ROCK

AN EPITAPH FOR LITTLE ROCK

---

*A Fiftieth Anniversary Retrospective
on the Central High Crisis*

Edited by John A. Kirk

with a Foreword by Juan Williams

from the *Arkansas Historical Quarterly*

The University of Arkansas Press
Fayetteville
2008

Copyright © 2008 by The University of Arkansas Press

ISBN-10: 1-55728-874-7
ISBN-13: 978-1-55728-874-5

12   11   10   09   08   5   4   3   2   1

Text design by Ellen Beeler

⊝ The paper used in this publication meets the minimum requirements of the American National Standard for Permanence of Paper for Printed Library Materials Z39.48-1984.

Library of Congress Cataloging-in-Publication Data

An epitaph for Little Rock : a fiftieth anniversary retrospective on the Central High Crisis / edited by John A. Kirk.
    p. cm.
  Includes bibliographical references.
  ISBN-13: 978-1-55728-874-5 (paper : alk. paper)
  ISBN-10: 1-55728-874-7 (paper : alk. paper)
  1. School integration—Arkansas—Little Rock—History—20th century.
  2. Central High School (Little Rock, Ark.)—History—20th century. 3. African American students—Arkansas—Little Rock—History—20th century.
  4. African Americans—Civil rights—Arkansas—Little Rock—History—20th century. 5. Little Rock (Ark.)—Race relations—History—20th century.
  6. African Americans—Arkansas—Little Rock—Attitudes. 7. Whites—Arkansas—Little Rock—Attitudes. 8. School integration—Arkansas—Little Rock—Historiography. 9. Central High School (Little Rock, Ark.)—Historiography. I. Kirk, John A., 1970–
  LC214.23.L56E65 2008
  379.2'630976773—dc22

                                              2008003681

Contents

Foreword

Juan Williams

Fifty years ago Little Rock, Arkansas, was the scene of a truly telling moment in American history.

The president of the United States, the governor of Arkansas, and nine black children took center stage for several days as surrogates for Americans caught in the battle over the U.S. Supreme Court's ruling that the nation's schools be racially integrated. That crisis brought federal troops into an American city and sparked fears of a second Civil War.

There was shock on all sides of the events of September 1957. The first shock came with the raw sight of white mobs and the Arkansas National Guard, under orders from Governor Orval E. Faubus, blocking nine black children from entering the city's Central High School. Another shock hit the American body politic when President Dwight Eisenhower sent federal troops, the 101st Airborne, into an American city to protect black people.

The power of these events, filled with so much emotion, has had lasting repercussions over American politics, law, and public education for the last fifty years. Of course, Little Rock also changed the shape of American race relations. The passage of time has confirmed that American history was made in Little Rock much as we now understand the historical power of events at Plymouth Rock, Gettysburg, and Pearl Harbor.

The significance of Little Rock is so accepted that fifty years later the U.S. Mint issued a silver dollar commemorating the event. Statues of the black students are now in place for school children to admire. There is now a museum, run by the U.S. Park Service as a national historical site, dedicated to the events that took place that September at Central High School. College courses are taught about the history of Little Rock and massive resistance to school integration. Most telling of all, the nation still looks back to Little Rock as a critical spark to the modern civil rights movement and an expression of the nation's ideal that all men are created equal.

In fact, the lives of the young black people who integrated Central, the Little Rock Nine, also represent the rapid growth of the black middle class after better schools became open to black people during the 1960s and '70s.

Ernest Green, sixty-five, who became the first black student to graduate from Central High, earned a master's degree in sociology and worked in the Carter and Clinton administrations. Melba Pattillo Beals, sixty-five, chairs the Department of Communications at Dominican University of California and wrote an award-winning book about her experiences at Central High; Elizabeth Eckford, sixty-five, is a probation officer in Arkansas; Gloria Ray Karlmark, sixty-four, moved to Sweden to work for IBM and later founded and edited the magazine *Computers in Industry*; Carlotta Walls LaNier, sixty-four, started a real estate company in Colorado; Terrence Roberts, sixty-five, is a psychologist in California; Jefferson Thomas, sixty-four, fought in Vietnam and worked in government in Ohio for nearly thirty years; Minnijean Brown Trickey, sixty-six, worked in the Clinton administration and is a visiting writer at Arkansas State University; and Thelma Mothershed Wair, sixty-six, became a teacher.

Part of their success comes from their ability to mix easily with black and white people and to comfortably join the social and professional networks that segregation kept from black people. In fact, most of the nine worked in mostly white organizations. And four of the nine married white people (three black women married white men, and one black man married a white woman).

And researchers now confirm that school integration in the mode of Little Rock benefits students, especially minorities. In 2003 the Civil Rights Project at Harvard University collected data on black and Latino students who attended integrated schools indicating that those students "complete more years of education, earn higher degrees and major in more varied occupations than graduates of all-black schools."

Those successes are why fifty years after the Little Rock crisis the nation still uses Little Rock as a measuring stick for the promise of school integration and racial justice. And that measure is why it seems so deflating that American schools are still nearly as segregated in 2007 as they were in 1957.

Recent studies show that nearly three-quarters of African American students, nationwide, are currently in schools that are more than 50 percent black and Latino, while the average white student goes to a school that is 80 percent white. The Civil Rights Project found that twenty-seven of the nation's largest urban school districts are "overwhelmingly" black and Latino, and segregated. The percentage of white students going to school with black students is "lower in 2000 than it was in 1970 before busing for racial balance began," the report said.

And then there is the harsh judgment of what goes on inside schools that claim to be integrated or at least claim to offer every American child the opportunity to rise up based on their intellect, discipline, and desire for the good life. The average black or Latino student graduating from high school "can read and do arithmetic only as well as the average eighth-grade white student," according to a 2005 *New York Times* report. And class divisions are also compounding the racial divide. White children in the nation's elementary schools find about a third of their fellow students qualify for free or low-cost lunches, while the typical black or Latino grade-schooler goes to a school where two-thirds of children are eligible for the reduced-price lunch program.

This trend toward isolation of poor and minority students has consequences—half of black and Latino students now drop out of high school.

And with the Little Rock crisis as a historical marker, federal judges now find themselves frustrated with continued high levels of school segregation and uncertain of what to do about it. Today's federal courts lionize the *Brown* decision as a landmark in the law but write briefs questioning the wisdom of insisting on school integration when American adults continue to display a strong preference for neighborhoods where they isolate themselves by income and race. In 2007 the Supreme Court ruled that even school-integration plans approved on a voluntary basis by locally elected officials in Seattle and Louisville, Kentucky, violated the rights of students to be judged on the basis of their individual merit. The ruling confirmed a political reality: America long ago lost its appetite for doing whatever it takes to integrate schools. Since 1988 racial segregation in public schools has been growing, reversing the trend toward integration triggered by *Brown v. Board of Education* and Little Rock.

And now the battles over racial justice in schools feature proposals for charter schools, magnet schools, and vouchers that allow children to shop for the best schools. President George W. Bush's main domestic legacy will likely be his effort to confront what he calls the "bigotry of low expectations." His plan, called "No Child Left Behind," is an effort to hold schools accountable for student performance regardless of a child's color or family income. Fifty years after U.S. troops had to escort nine black children to school in Little Rock, the issue is still how to take race out of the equation when it comes to educating every American child.

The issues that combined so explosively in Little Rock in 1957 continue to roil American politics and law. That is why Americans continue to study what happened there for some insight into who we really are and where we are headed in this new century.

Acknowledgments

As a current editorial board member of the *Arkansas Historical Quarterly* I am delighted that this volume is able to showcase the journal's vital role in state and regional history. I am grateful to the current editor, Patrick G. Williams, and assistant editor Michael Pierce for running with my idea of a special edition to mark the fiftieth anniversary of the Little Rock school crisis, supporting the project enthusiastically, and doing much of the legwork to get it completed. They were ably assisted in this task by Cody Hackett who worked on retyping pre-word-processor articles and creating the index.

The hidden hand of many editors past who worked with the original manuscripts republished here, and whose keen eye and hard work this book likewise depends upon, is also gratefully acknowledged. The first post-school-crisis editor, Walter L. Brown, served from 1959 to 1990 and published the first article on the crisis by Numan V. Bartley in 1966 while Gov. Orval Faubus was still in office. Jeannie M. Whayne succeeded him from 1990 to 2005, and David L. Chappell guest edited the fortieth anniversary volume in 1997. Gretchen Gearhart served as assistant editor between 1992 and 1999.

The publication of the fiftieth anniversary special edition of the journal to allow it wider circulation and attention was achieved with the help and support of the University of Arkansas Press. Director of the press, Larry Malley, very generously provided me with an office in the McIlroy House while I was on research leave in the autumn of 2007, which allowed me to work closely with those involved in the journal-to-book copyediting process. It was a pleasure to have the benefit of the professional experience and convivial company of the press team: Mike Bieker, David Scott Cunningham, Brian King, Melissa King, Tom Lavoie, Tabitha Lee, Charlie Moss, and Julie Watkins. Thanks are also due to Carol Sickman-Garner for her careful proofreading of the book manuscript.

I am of course grateful to all of the authors whose work is republished in this book, which has influenced my own research on the subject: Numan V. Bartley, David L. Chappell, Tony A. Freyer, Azza Salama Layton, Neil McMillen, Roy Reed, and Lorraine Gates Schuyler. Ben F. Johnson's final essay is a valuable and generous original contribution.

This book is dedicated to the Little Rock Nine, without whose courage and bravery none of this would have been possible. It is also dedicated to the often overlooked contributions of their parents and families, to their NAACP mentors Daisy and L. C. Bates, and to all those who supported them—some of whose stories are known and others whose are yet to be written.

Introduction

The 1957 Little Rock Crisis—
A Historiographical Essay

John A. Kirk

To mark the fiftieth anniversary of a central episode in America's civil rights history, this book brings together a number of the signal works that have been published on the Little Rock crisis in the *Arkansas Historical Quarterly* since the 1960s. These articles represent some of the finest scholarship on the crisis that has appeared anywhere and reflect the wide-ranging concerns that have emerged from its study. The purpose of this introductory essay is three-fold: first, to provide a very brief summary of the events of the crisis; second, to serve as an outline and a guide to published material on the crisis, whether monographs, essays, or articles, that has appeared over the past fifty years, together with radio broadcasts, music, films, and selected unpublished works; and, finally, to contextualize the body of work republished in this collection within the wider historiography of the crisis.[1]

On September 2, 1957, Governor Orval E. Faubus drew national and international attention to Little Rock when, in the name of preventing disorder, he called out the National Guard to block implementation of a court-ordered desegregation plan at Central High School. In defying the local courts and, ultimately, the U.S. Supreme Court's 1954 *Brown v. Board of Education* school desegregation decision, Faubus directly challenged the authority of the federal government as no other elected southern official had since the Civil War. Over the following weeks, frantic negotiations took place between the White House and the governor's mansion that finally led to the withdrawal of National Guard troops. However, when nine African American students—Minnijean Brown, Elizabeth Eckford, Ernest Green, Thelma Mothershed, Melba Pattillo, Gloria Ray, Terrence Roberts, Jefferson Thomas, and Carlotta Walls—attempted to attend classes on September 23, an unruly white mob caused so much disruption that school officials withdrew them from Central High for their own safety. The scenes of violence finally prompted President Dwight D. Eisenhower to intervene by sending federal troops to secure the students' safe passage. Finally, on September 25, the nine completed their first day of classes under armed guard.

Although the admission of the students to the school resolved the immediate constitutional crisis and the media spotlight quickly moved elsewhere, that was not the end of the story. The nine students endured a campaign of harassment by white segregationist students inside the high school. On February 6, 1958, Minnijean Brown was expelled for reacting to provocation by white students, although none of the white intimidators of the nine was ever similarly dealt with. On May 25, 1958, Ernest Green, the only senior among the nine, became the first African American student to graduate from Central High.

As the academic year ended and soldiers were withdrawn from Central, the battle over school desegregation continued. On February 20, 1958, the Little Rock school board had requested a two-and-a-half-year delay in its desegregation plan. On June 21, federal district court judge Harry J. Lemley granted the delay. But on August 18, NAACP attorney Wiley Branton successfully overturned the decision on appeal. The school board then appealed to the U.S. Supreme Court, which on September 12 ordered school desegregation to continue.

In the meantime, Governor Faubus had convened a special session of the Arkansas General Assembly and pushed through six new laws that provided him with sweeping powers to uphold segregation. One of the laws enabled Faubus to close any school integrated by federal order. Voters in the school district could then decide if the school should reopen on an integrated basis. On the day the U.S. Supreme Court ordered integration to proceed in Little Rock, Faubus closed all of the city's high schools. In the referendum held on September 27, 1958, the governor stacked the cards in his favor by offering a stark choice between keeping the schools closed or accepting "complete and total integration." By a margin of 19,470 to 7,561, voters decided to keep the schools closed.

After a brief and failed attempt to run the public high schools as segregated, private institutions, African American and white students were forced to make alternative arrangements for their education while their teachers sat in empty classrooms. In the November 1958 election, Faubus became only the second governor in Arkansas history to win a third term in office. In exasperation, the existing members of the school board resigned, with the exception of segregationist Dale Alford, who soon after left his post to take up a new role as U.S. congressman.

The election of a new school board proved a watershed event. The city's business and professional elite, which had stood on the sidelines since September 1957, was finally spurred into action. Closed schools and the drying-up of outside economic investment convinced them that they had to take a stand to prevent community collapse. Another important factor in their decision to act was the formation of the Women's Emergency Committee to Open Our Schools (WEC), which was composed of the spouses of many of the male elite. The WEC had initially been formed to campaign to keep the city's schools open at the September 27 referendum. Although unsuccessful on that occasion, Adolphine Fletcher Terry, the wife of former Arkansas congressman David D. Terry, persuaded five business candidates to stand against segregationist candidates in the school board election on December 6, 1958. In a close contest, three business candidates and three segregationists won positions on the school board.

A showdown between the businessmen and the segregationists came in May 1959, when segregationists attempted to remove anyone unsympathetic to their cause from the public school system. Blocking each of the measures in turn, the business candidates then withdrew from the meeting so that there would be no quorum to take any further action. However, after they left, Ed McKinley, the segregationist president of the school board, ruled that the meeting could continue as normal. Segregationists proceeded to make a series of arbitrary decisions about the running of the school system. Most dramatic of all was the decision not to renew the contracts of forty-four public school employees, including seven principals, thirty-four teachers, and three secretaries.

On May 8, a group of business and civic leaders met to form Stop This Outrageous Purge (STOP), with the goal of ousting the board's segregationists in a recall election. On May 15, segregationists, similarly intent on recalling business representatives on the school board, joined forces in the Committee to Retain Our Segregated Schools (CROSS). On May 25, the day of the recall election, the vote narrowly went the businessmen's way, with all of their representatives reinstated and all of the segregationists ousted in favor of other business-backed candidates. The new board prepared to reopen the schools. On June 18, the U.S. District Court upheld the NAACP's contention that Faubus's school-closing laws were unconstitutional. In a surprise move designed to limit Faubus's options for further opposition, the new school board announced in July that the next school term would begin a month early, on August 12. The schools successfully opened on a token integrated basis without trouble.[2]

For those interested in archival materials on the crisis, the best starting point is Michael Dabrishus's essay on the subject.[3] There are, in addition, a number of published primary sources that serve as a good introduction. One of the earliest and most accomplished of these is *Little Rock, U.S.A.,* compiled by a husband-and-wife team, Wilson Record and June Cassels Record, in 1960. Its first section contains an impressive collection of press accounts, while its second section consists of opinion pieces, some of which were specially commissioned for the project. The superlative *Eyes on the Prize* documentary series on the civil rights movement, which has now received a much-welcomed re-release, devotes half of one episode to the Little Rock crisis. The collection of oral histories and the document collection that accompany the series are also useful. Well worth a listen is a radio documentary made by the Southern Regional Council, *Will the Circle Be Unbroken?,* which includes five programs on Little Rock, before, during, and after the crisis.[4]

One of the most striking things about the specialist secondary literature on the Little Rock crisis is the panoramic view it provides of a white southern community in the mid-1950s. Several historians, most notably Karen Anderson, David Chappell, Pete Daniel, and C. Fred Williams, have examined the competing tensions and factions that existed among whites. Chappell's republished article represents that work in this collection.[5]

From a local perspective, Governor Faubus has garnered the most attention as a key figure in events. Early accounts presented him as a demagogue who either contrived or manufactured the crisis for his own political gain.[6] Later analyses, notably the work of Roy Reed, whose essay on the subject is republished in this collection, provide a more nuanced picture of a politician who was the son of a Socialist and who entered Arkansas politics by way of the progressive administration of Governor Sidney S. McMath (1949–53). These studies argue that a set of concerns more complex than simple naked political ambition weighed on Faubus's decision to call out the National Guard.[7]

Faubus's own reflections on the crisis were often guarded and evasive. His first book ignored the events altogether and instead recounted his wartime army service overseas. Two subsequent volumes, *Down from the Hills* and *Down from the Hills, II,* were little more than press collages from his time as governor. A further book, on the various dogs and the menagerie of other pets that Faubus owned as governor, is willfully obscure. Faubus did, however, late in life produce a short self-published booklet, which came closest to a written account and explanation of his actions. In addition, he offered candid accounts to historians when he was interviewed. Yet to his death in 1994, Faubus remained unwilling to accept that he had any politically viable alternatives to the course of action he took.[8]

If Faubus dictated political developments in Little Rock, the chief architect of public school policy was the city's superintendent of schools, Virgil T. Blossom. In 1955, Blossom drew up a plan for school desegregation that provided for some, albeit very closely guarded and controlled, integration in city schools. The merits and demerits of the so-called Blossom Plan have met with varying interpretations. Elizabeth Jacoway has given the school board its most sympathetic hearing, claiming that, in taking a gradualist approach to the problem of school desegregation, its members did the best job they could under pressure from segregationists and widespread community opposition. Numan V. Bartley flagged the many inherent flaws of the Blossom Plan in one of the earliest scholarly studies of the crisis, and the first to appear in the *Arkansas Historical Quarterly,* which is republished in this collection. Yet Bartley still attributed the plan's eventual downfall to "an accumulation of failures by well-meaning leaders." My work has been the most critical of Blossom's intentions, arguing that his call for "minimum compliance" with the *Brown* decision was in fact just another, if more subtle, form of resistance to school desegregation.[9]

Despite the fact that Little Rock became a focal point for massive resistance, prior to the events of September 1957 it was regarded as a moderate Upper South city in a progressive Upper South state. Contributing to this image was Congressman L. Brooks Hays. Hays's story is a case study of the dilemmas faced by southern moderates in the post-*Brown* political landscape. Before the crisis, Hays had a distinguished record of service, which included holding Arkansas's Fifth Congressional District seat in the U.S. House of Representatives since 1942. In September 1957, Hays attempted to conciliate between Faubus and Eisenhower through his friend Sherman Adams, Eisenhower's chief of staff. But Hays's efforts to help proved his undoing. Running for reelection in 1958, he found himself facing a "write-in" campaign from Little Rock optometrist, school board member, and segregationist Dale Alford. Alford pulled off a shock victory that ended Hays's career as an elected politician. Hays's defeat only added to the clamor among other southern candidates to take the most extreme segregationist position possible in political contests.[10]

One of the ironies of Hays's defeat was that he, like all of Arkansas's congressional delegation, had signed the "Southern Manifesto" in 1956, which condemned the U.S. Supreme Court for handing down the *Brown* decision. The fact that U.S. senator John McClellan and U.S. House of Representatives members Oren Harris, E. C. Gathings, Wilbur D. Mills, and W. F. Norrell all signed the manifesto was not surprising, given their previous staunch support for the preservation of segregation. However, U.S. senator J. William Fulbright and Representative James W. Trimble, along with Hays, were all considered moderates on the race issue who, although often ambivalent about the prospect of racial change, did not look to actively oppose it. Fulbright, the most eminent of Arkansas's political moderates, has received the most criticism for bowing to segregationist pressure. Trimble had a more plausible defense for signing: he was badgered in his hospital bed for three hours by Orval Faubus, accompanied by Oren Harris and Brooks Hays, before finally doing so. Tony Badger argues that the signatures of political moderates on the

Southern Manifesto, in Arkansas and elsewhere, helped to undermine calls for compliance with *Brown* and gave the upper hand to the segregationists in the battle over school desegregation.[11]

It was not just Brooks Hays's political background but also his religious beliefs that marked him as a moderate. Hays served as president of the Southern Baptist Convention in 1957–58. Although by no means uniform in sentiment, as Mark Newman has observed, some members of the Southern Baptist Convention and the Arkansas Baptist Convention were prepared to speak out for accepting school desegregation. As sociologists Ernest Q. Campbell and Thomas F. Pettigrew have noted, this muted support for desegregation was reflected in other denominations and, as Carolyn Gray LeMaster points out, in other faiths as well.[12] David Chappell argues that divisions over integration reflect the wider reality that organized religious opposition to *Brown* was weak across the South, although Jane Dailey has questioned that conclusion, maintaining that if religion was not always an overt part of resistance to segregation, it was often integral to it.[13]

Another source of moderation was Little Rock's business and professional elite, which had successfully steered the community toward economic, political, and social progress in the postwar period. That elite had helped to create an industrial zone on the outskirts of the city to lure northern investment, secured the location of a federal air base nearby, and just a year before the crisis organized a Good Government Committee in a successful bid to reform the way that city government was run. But when it came to school desegregation, the elite proved flat-footed in dealing with an issue that would strike at the very heart of the city's progress. The reasons for this have been a matter of debate. Elizabeth Jacoway argues that the city's elite was "taken by surprise" by events that quickly escalated beyond their control, although she contends that the crisis did ultimately lead them to realize that racial progress was necessary for economic progress, which in turn forced a reordering of their priorities. By contrast, Tony Badger emphasizes the limits of businessmen's moderation. He finds striking, in Little Rock and elsewhere, the "persistent determination of businessmen that economic change should not lead to racial change"—a point Ben F. Johnson III amplifies in a new essay included in this volume.[14]

The most visible advocate of moderation in Little Rock during the crisis was the city's leading newspaper, the *Arkansas Gazette*, whose opinions reflected those of its executive editor Harry S. Ashmore. A seasoned journalist and a war veteran, Ashmore was a supporter of southern political, social, economic, and racial progress. He continually criticized the reckless actions of Governor Faubus and called for a more enlightened approach to school desegregation. In 1958, he won a Pulitzer Prize for his editorials, but he was forced to leave the city a year later because of segregationist harassment.

Ashmore published several books on race in the South and the United States, and there are a number of collections of *Gazette*-related materials.[15] For the prosegregation position of the city's rival newspaper, the *Arkansas Democrat,* see the collection of articles published by columnist Karr Shannon.[16]

Those who see the failure of the moderates in Little Rock, whether politicians, public policy makers, or businessmen, as pivotal to the crisis that befell the city cite as grist to their mill the apparent weakness of the opposition they faced. In Little Rock, and throughout Arkansas, the most active segregationists were not respected figures of great social standing, as they were in many other southern states, but were instead the socially, economically, and politically marginalized, who found in the segregation issue a way to transform, if only temporarily, their circumstances. Several articles by Graeme Cope have profiled segregationists in Little Rock, and Neil McMillen has examined the activities of the White Citizens' Councils in the state in an essay republished in this collection, which is part of a larger work on the Citizens' Councils in the South. As McMillen notes, Citizens' Council membership in Arkansas was just one-tenth that of neighboring Mississippi.[17]

Segregationists in Little Rock were, however, bolstered by the regionwide movement of massive resistance, which, as Jeff Woods and George Lewis have noted, also rode the tide of post-McCarthy-era anticommunism. In Arkansas, Attorney General Bruce Bennett attempted to cash in politically on that bandwagon, but without much success. He did nevertheless push a number of harassing measures through the Arkansas General Assembly, including Act 10, which required state employees to list their political affiliations, and Act 115, which outlawed public employment of NAACP members.[18]

Beyond the state borders, Joseph P. Kamp wrote *The Lowdown on Little Rock and the Plot to Sovietize the South,* which began by comparing Eisenhower's decision to send troops into the city to Hitler's use of storm troopers, before going on to assert that, in fact, Eisenhower was less justified in his actions. On the opposite end of the political spectrum, James Jackson's conclusion that Little Rock represented an "opening wide of the doors to great new initiatives of struggle to advance, under the leadership of the working-class, along the whole social frontier," sounded almost as misdirected, given the composition of those opposing school desegregation in Little Rock.[19]

Little has been written about the ongoing military operation at Central High School after September 1957. Federal soldiers remained on patrol inside the school for only a short time before being replaced by federalized National Guard troops. Robert W. Coakley's fairly plaintive military overview of the operation provides some useful information about how the mission was run, but it is Elizabeth Huckaby, a white vice principal at Central, who gives the most vivid insider account of events at the school. Huckaby's book served as the basis for the first cinematic dramatization of events, in *Crisis at Central*

High. Phoebe Godfrey's work has touched upon what was happening inside the school by looking at Faubus's attempts to discredit federal soldiers by claiming that they were loitering around the girls' locker rooms. Godfrey also examines the prominence of discourses of race, gender, and sexuality, focusing on miscegenation in Little Rock segregationists' rhetoric.[20]

The so-called Lost Year of 1958–59, when Little Rock's high schools were closed, has been the subject of much recent attention. Beth Roy has conducted a study based on a number of interviews with white students, and Sondra Gordy has written about the experiences of teachers. Much of this work is imbued with a sense of loss, regret, and more than a tinge of nostalgia. As important as it is to recognize that all of the city's teachers and students were the victims of closed high schools, it must also be remembered that it was the predominantly white electorate that voted to keep the schools closed rather than to integrate them. That electorate presumably included the parents of many of the white children who were left without an education. In that sense, the year was less lost than tossed—given away.[21]

Alongside the detrimental effects of closing the schools, it was the drying-up of outside economic investment that finally prompted the city's elite to mobilize against the segregationists. The economic impact of the crisis on the city was documented by Gary Fullerton in a 1959 article in the *Nashville Tennessean,* and it is the subject of studies by James C. Cobb and Michael Joseph Bercik.[22]

A good deal has been written on the campaign to reopen Little Rock's schools, with the preponderance of work examining the efforts of the Women's Emergency Committee to Open Our Schools. There are several good studies of the WEC and its members, including Lorraine Gates's piece republished in this collection.[23] There are also a short documentary film on the subject and firsthand accounts by Sara Murphy and Vivion Brewer.[24] Irving Spitzberg's study provides a good overview of the formation of STOP, and Henry M. Alexander provides a useful account of the recall election in which segregationist members were ousted from the school board and a business slate of candidates was installed.[25]

There is a long list of other white characters in the Little Rock crisis whose actions have been touched upon by scholars or chronicled in memoirs. Mayor Woodrow Mann, who was left a lame duck by the reforms to city government voted in 1956, urged Eisenhower to intervene to quell the growing disorder in the city. Assistant Chief of Police Eugene E. Smith valiantly tried to uphold law and order at Central High in the period between Faubus abdicating responsibility for events and Eisenhower sending the soldiers in. Nat Griswold, executive director of the Arkansas Council on Human Relations (ACHR), an affiliate of the Atlanta-based Southern Regional Council, attempted to keep lines of racial communication open in the city. Another member of the ACHR, Professor Georg Iggers, a German-Jewish immigrant to the United States, taught at Philander Smith, an African American college in Little Rock, and was one of the few white members of the city's NAACP branch.[26] Osro Cobb, U.S. attorney for the Eastern District of Arkansas, was the federal government's all too anonymous chief law-enforcement officer in the city and was responsible for liaison with the Justice Department. Governor LeRoy Collins of Florida publicly criticized Faubus for his actions as the crisis unfolded and urged a more moderate approach to school desegregation by state officials.[27]

In contrast to the rich and detailed portrait available of the white community, Little Rock's African American community has been relatively poorly served in the historiography of the crisis. Most attention has focused on Daisy Bates, the president of the state's NAACP conference of branches and, along with her husband, L. C. Bates, owner of the city's and state's leading African American newspaper, the *Arkansas State Press*. As an important study written by two African American sociologists, Tilman Cothran and William Phillips Jr., points out, Daisy Bates was unquestionably the key local African American figure during the crisis years. Bates's account of events, *The Long Shadow of Little Rock,* first published in 1962, for a long time remained the sole voice of the African American community on the crisis. Several articles have touched upon Bates's life and career since, but only recently have fully fledged biographies begun to appear, with the most accomplished to date being Grif Stockley's account. Stockley makes the case for giving due credit to L. C. Bates for his leadership in the crisis, which has remained neglected.[28]

There is surprisingly little substantive literature on the Little Rock Nine, the African American students who were at the very heart of the events. One of them, Melba Pattillo Beals, has written two autobiographical accounts, but beyond personal detail, neither work really moves the story of the crisis much beyond Bates's book. Ernest Green's story has received the Disney treatment on film, and Minnijean Brown has spoken about events in two published oral histories and a documentary film on her life. Several profiles of the nine have appeared over the years, the best being the series of articles by African American journalist Ted Poston published in the *New York Post* in October 1957. Although a number of scattered oral histories and interviews exist, the history of the crisis still cries out for a uniform collection of stories of the nine, both as individuals and as a collective group of ordinary people thrust into extraordinary circumstances.[29]

My own work, as the article republished in this collection demonstrates, has sought to contextualize the experiences of Bates and the Little Rock Nine within the unfolding struggle for African American freedom and equality in the state. The interaction among local, state, regional, and national activists and organizations played a prominent role in that struggle.[30] In the Little

Rock crisis, all were bound together in the *Aaron v. Cooper* (1956) lawsuit, which was launched by the local NAACP branch, before being taken over by the national NAACP's Legal Defense and Educational Fund lawyers. Under the title *Cooper v. Aaron* (1958), it became a landmark case in the civil rights struggle when the U.S. Supreme Court ruled that violence and disorder could not be used as excuses for delaying school desegregation. Tony Freyer explores the legal and political dimensions of the crisis in his article republished in this collection.[31] Several excellent studies frame the lawsuit and the Little Rock crisis within wider developments in the courts.[32]

Did the Little Rock crisis represent a victory for the NAACP or for massive resistance? From a regional perspective, this has proved a key question. Adam Fairclough succinctly sums up the arguments in his short opinion piece for a special issue of the *Arkansas Historical Quarterly* commemorating the fortieth anniversary of the crisis.[33] Those pointing toward a victory for massive resistance can plausibly contend that Eisenhower only sent troops to the city as an ad hoc response to events and that his actions did not immediately pave the way for further strong executive action in defense of civil rights. Neither did it prevent Faubus from closing the city's high schools the following year. If *Cooper v. Aaron* represented a triumph for the NAACP, another court decision the same year, *Shuttlesworth v. Birmingham Board of Education* (1958), simultaneously upheld the use of pupil placement laws that significantly slowed school desegregation. These laws permitted school boards to assign school places to students based on a number of criteria other than race, but in practice they were often used simply to perpetuate segregation. The NAACP proved vulnerable to attack, and its branches in Arkansas and across the South were decimated by the late 1950s. Thus, scholars such as Michael Klarman have argued that *Brown* actually helped to strengthen white resistance more than it aided the cause of African American advancement.[34]

Nevertheless, Fairclough argues, Little Rock was ultimately a triumph for the NAACP. It forced the issue of school desegregation and moved both the president and the Supreme Court, however reluctantly, to act. Segregationists viewed the episode as a defeat yet failed to unite in a common strategy of opposition. The enduring lessons of Little Rock, Fairclough asserts, were the futility of directly defying court orders, the folly of closing schools, and the social and economic costs of racial turmoil. Few other governors tried to emulate Faubus's stand, and few other business communities wanted to risk the costs of racial conflict. *Brown* may not have delivered all that many hoped it would, but it did expose a legal Achilles heel for segregation that paved the way for successfully challenging other aspects of Jim Crow. In demonstrating the futility of violent resistance, the Little Rock crisis encouraged segregationists to take to state legislatures and the courts rather than to the streets, thereby reducing the potential casualties of change. It also brought international pressure to bear on the United States to tackle the problem of racial inequality.

From a national perspective, President Dwight D. Eisenhower's response to the *Brown* decision has been viewed as one of the major blights on his otherwise popular presidency. Eisenhower was reluctant to voice support for *Brown* in public, and he disparaged the Supreme Court's decision in private. It was with much reluctance that he eventually sent federal troops into Little Rock, and then only when Governor Faubus issued a direct challenge to his executive authority.[35] But there were more enlightened and progressive figures in Eisenhower's presidential administration who sought to take a stronger stand for civil rights, foremost among them Attorney General Herbert Brownell and Arthur B. Caldwell, the latter a native Arkansan and assistant to the assistant attorney general for the Civil Rights Division of the Department of Justice, which was established in 1957.[36]

The images of the Little Rock crisis that flashed around the world were some of the earliest and most dramatic of the unfolding civil rights movement. Despite being one of the movement's first major televised events, some of the most memorable visual images of the crisis came from photographs. *Arkansas Democrat* photographer I. Wilmer Counts's published collection is an excellent starting point for these, and it includes the famous photograph of white student Hazel Bryan hurling abuse at Elizabeth Eckford, an image that has become one of the most enduring emblems of the crisis.[37]

So iconic were events in Little Rock that they instantaneously became a reference point for popular culture, with an influence that stretched into theater, poetry, music, and intellectual debate. In September 1957, in a New York City suburb, a young actress found herself playing a character with an unfortunate-sounding name from a woe-betide place in the musical *South Pacific*— Nellie Forbush from Little Rock, Arkansas—that brought a halt to the performance because of the ferocity of the jeers that it prompted. African American poet Gwendolyn Brooks wrote "The *Chicago Defender* Sends a Man to Little Rock," included in her 1960 collection of poems *The Bean Eaters,* which vividly portrayed the violence and hatred displayed by the white mob in the city. Her muse was African American journalist L. Alex Wilson, whom the mob turned upon and beat during the first day of integrated classes at Central High. Wilson was the editor and general manager of the Memphis-based *Tri-State Defender,* the *Chicago Defender's* southern affiliate. German American political theorist Hannah Arendt stoked controversy with her essay "Reflections on Little Rock," which questioned whether schools were in fact the best place to begin the process of desegregation.[38]

African American jazz musician Charles Mingus composed the music and wrote the lyrics for a song called "Fables of Faubus," which lambasted the Arkansas governor, labeling him, among other things, a "Nazi Fascist supremist." Columbia Records felt the lyrics too controversial and would only release the track as an instrumental on Mingus's 1959 album *Mingus Ah Um*. The following year, Mingus recorded the song with a different label, this time with lyrics, as "Original Faubus Fables," for his album *Charles Mingus Presents Charles Mingus*. The song proved a favorite with Mingus and his audiences over the years, and in 1973, in the midst of the Watergate scandal, he trans- formed it into "Fables of Nixon." It has been covered by a number of other artists since, the most recent version being the Normand Guilbeault Ensemble's "Fable of (George Dubya) Faubus," released in 2005.[39]

Another jazz great, Louis Armstrong, abandoned a planned government- sponsored trip to Moscow because of events in Little Rock. Described by the U.S. State Department as "perhaps the most effective un-official goodwill ambassador this country ever had," Armstrong told the press that "the way they are treating my people in the South, the Government can go to hell." He called Faubus "an uneducated plow-boy" and insisted that, if he had to choose, he would rather play in Moscow than in Arkansas, because Faubus "might hear a couple of notes—and he don't deserve that."[40]

As the Armstrong incident illustrates, from an international perspective, the Little Rock crisis was a public relations disaster for a country engaged in an effort to win hearts and minds in the Cold War. Several historians have written about Little Rock's global impact in recent years, with the crisis featur- ing most prominently in the work of Azza Salama Layton and Mary Dudziak. Layton's work is represented in an article republished in this collection. Dudziak labels Little Rock "a crisis of such magnitude for worldwide percep- tions of race and American democracy that it would become a reference point for the future." Newspapers around the world reported events in Little Rock, critics of the United States pointed to the crisis as evidence of the country's disregard for human rights, and federal officials wrung their hands over the damage done. In later years, the U.S. Information Agency tried to claim Little Rock as a victory by holding it up as a triumph of presidential action in sup- port of civil rights.[41]

The Little Rock crisis has continued to linger indelibly in historical mem- ory. Several studies by firsthand participants in events have updated the ongo- ing story of school desegregation and the accompanying court litigation since 1957. Each gives a snapshot of the different stages of that process over the years.[42] In a new piece written especially for this collection, Ben F. Johnson III provides one of the first scholarly reflections on school desegregation in Little Rock since the crisis. He suggests the need to look beyond the 1959 triumph- of-moderation narrative for a better sense of the decided limits of that process. By his account, some of the elements of the business community who were embarrassed by what massive resistance had done to their community were the very same people who had pursued development strategies that purposefully kept African Americans and whites apart. My own work on public housing has similarly suggested the need to attend to broader social and economic developments that circumscribed the political and legal victories won for civil rights.[43]

In addition to the ongoing impact of the crisis, commentators' reflections on the actual events of 1957–59 and their wider significance for the city and the South have continued to be published, clustering around landmark anniversaries.[44] Indeed, these reflections and memories have become subjects of study in their own right.[45] With the opening of the Central High Museum and Visitors Center in 1997, the Little Rock crisis has become part of a growing heritage industry in the South devoted to the civil rights movement.[46]

The Little Rock crisis has provided an inspiration for many writers, poets, musicians, and filmmakers over the past fifty years. Such has been its grip on the scholarly, artistic, popular, and public imagination that it will surely continue to fascinate and to attract attention for many more years to come.

LOOKING BACK AT LITTLE ROCK

Numan V. Bartley

Relatively progressive Upper South capital city Little Rock, Arkansas, was among the first communities below the Potomac to make preparations for compliance with the 1954 *Brown v. Board of Education* Supreme Court decision.[1] The percentage of Negro students in Little Rock public schools was less than that of Wilmington, Delaware; Louisville, Kentucky; St. Louis, Missouri; Nashville, Tennessee; Charlotte, Greensboro, or Winston-Salem, North Carolina, cities that had abandoned Jim Crow educational facilities or were in the process of doing so in the fall of 1957.[2] Already Little Rock had made inroads on caste inequities in several fringe areas, including seating arrangements on city buses.

While segregation remained the rule and the vast majority of Little Rock's white citizenry preferred it that way, the community had no record of political extremism on the race question. In November 1956, almost half of the city's voters opposed a White Citizens' Council–sponsored constitutional amendment "nullifying" the *Brown* decision.[3] When white supremacy advocates directly challenged Little Rock's token desegregation plan in March 1957 school board elections, extremists were soundly defeated by moderate candidates.[4]

Yet, in the fall of 1957, Little Rock became the epitome of state resistance. While sharpening political antagonisms in the South, the Little Rock upheaval provided a decisive test not only of the federal government's resolve but also of the national will to enforce Negro rights.[5]

This essay first appeared in the summer 1966 issue of the *Arkansas Historical Quarterly*.

Thus far the debacle at Little Rock has been pictured in terms of a deliberate conspiracy, originating either when Deep South racists persuaded Governor Orval E. Faubus to thwart the creeping advance of integration or when Faubus himself decided to manufacture a racial crisis for political gain.[6] The significance of Little Rock, both to the "massive resistance" phase of southern politics and to the course of race relations generally, makes the origins of that conflict worth further reexamination.

One day after the May 17, 1954, school desegregation decision, the Little Rock school board instructed Superintendent of Schools Virgil T. Blossom to draw up a plan for compliance.[7] Although unenthusiastic about the change, neither Blossom nor any board member suggested defiance of the high court ruling. Later in May 1954, school authorities made public their decision, announcing that planning would begin immediately.[8]

During the following year, Blossom formulated and reformulated desegregation arrangements. Originally conceived as a plan for substantial integration beginning at the grade school level, the Little Rock Phase Program that emerged in May 1955 provided for token desegregation starting in September 1957 with one senior high school. The second phase would extend tokenism to junior high schools by 1960, with the final step, desegregation on the elementary level, tentatively scheduled for the fall of 1963.[9] A transfer provision permitted students to escape from districts where their race was in the minority, thus assuring the heavily Negro Horace Mann High School zone would remain segregated. A rigid screening process eliminated most of those remaining colored students who were eligible and who wanted to attend the formerly white high school.[10]

Although devoting enormous time and energy to the creation and promotion of the Phase Program, Blossom showed questionable wisdom in his approach to the problems of desegregation.

The plan contained a central flaw. Desegregation was delayed until 1957 specifically to allow time for construction of Hall High School, Little Rock's third center of secondary education. With the exception of limited facilities for technical training, Little Rock had traditionally operated two senior high schools, one for Negroes and one for whites. Upon completion, Hall, located in the western part of the city, enrolled students from the Pulaski Heights region, the status residential area and home of many of Little Rock's most influential people. Central, the old white high school and the one to be desegregated, was left with pupils drawn primarily from the city's lower and middle classes. Thus, the Phase Program insured that much of Little Rock's civic leadership was effectively isolated, while those white citizens most likely to hold strong racial prejudice were immediately involved. This arrangement added an element of class conflict to the racial controversy and allowed segregationist spokesmen to charge that integrationists were sacrificing the common citizen while protecting the wealthy. More important, it amputated the center of white moderation from direct involvement.[11]

In addition to creating this Achilles heel, Blossom and the school board did little to construct a solid foundation of public support. Compared to some southern cities, Little Rock had a relatively flourishing moderate community, whose sentiments were given voice by institutions such as the *Arkansas Gazette* and the Greater Little Rock Ministerial Alliance and by individuals such as Winthrop Rockefeller, Sidney McMath, and Brooks Hays. Yet Blossom made no effort to enlist affirmative support from these sources. When, for example, the Ministerial Alliance offered to endorse publicly desegregation plans, Blossom successfully opposed the action.[12] Similarly, school authorities encouraged city news media to play down events concerning the Phase Program, although both daily newspapers—the *Gazette* and the *Arkansas Democrat*—supported the plan.[13]

Blossom did, of course, undertake a program of community education. He delivered some two hundred speeches, addressing any group that would provide a rostrum. In these talks, the superintendent often pointed out his own and the board's disapproval of integration, explaining that there was no alternative to some desegregation and that the Phase Program would insure gradual change. Many Negro observers were soon "convinced that Superintendent Blossom was more interested in appeasing the segregationists by advocating that only a limited number of Negroes be admitted than in complying with the Supreme Court's decision."[14]

Basically, school authorities regarded desegregation as a problem in school administration, and from this assumption flowed a negative approach. Early in the planning stage, Blossom and his staff sampled public opinion, concluding that prevailing sentiment was to respect the law while delaying social change as much as possible. They also discovered that white parents with small children seemed more committed to segregation than those with high-school-age children.[15] As a practical administrator dependent upon public support, Blossom devised a functional plan tailored precisely on these findings and went about explaining it to the community. Since many of his speeches were delivered before service clubs, businessmen's groups, and church organizations, he spent a disproportionate amount of time among people of higher socioeconomic standing, some of whom could send their children to Hall High School anyway, and thus he encountered little hostility. With everything going smoothly, the superintendent apparently saw no reason to muddy the waters with a more vigorous program of community preparation.

When opposition to desegregation developed during the summer of 1957, the school administration had no reservoir of public support. The moderate position was based on acquiescence to the inevitable rather than commitment, making it psychologically easy for many of the city's more responsible citizens to ignore the school board's growing dilemma. Further-more, Blossom and his staff sacrificed to community sentiment an educator's plan to begin desegregation on the grade school level, where problems of scholastic inequality and developed race consciousness were minimal, and then failed to prepare teachers for the problems of adjustment to a biracial student body. Compared to Louisville or St. Louis, Little Rock was singularly unprepared for integration.

Contributing substantially to Little Rock's headaches was the discredited lame-duck status of the city government. Mayor Woodrow Wilson Mann headed an unsuccessful administration that had been effectively repudiated at the polls in November 1956, when voters chose to replace the mayor-alderman system with a city-manager form of government. Mann's tenure did not end, however, until after the election of city directors in November 1957.

For all practical purposes, Mann turned desegregation arrangements over to Blossom to deal with as another educational problem. City officials took virtually no advance precautions. Little Rock police faced near-riot conditions without benefit of mob-control training, although concerned citizens had suggested this step well in advance.[16] Apparently not until August 1957 did city officials formulate even a meager and—considering the circumstances—inadequate concrete plan for maintaining order in the Central High School area.[17] Given the mayor's lack of confidence in Chief of Police Marvin H. Potts, this negligence was particularly surprising.[18] Similarly, during the weeks prior to school opening, when a forceful statement warning that the city would not tolerate disorder was obviously called for, the mayor issued no policy statement at all.

The impotency of Mann's administration was not fully revealed until September 20, when Governor Faubus removed the National Guard and left Little Rock to rely upon its own resources in coping with opposition to deseg-regation. Mann attempted to support the school administration, but by this time his authority had collapsed. The police department refused to escort Negro children to Central High School.[19] The fire department balked at pro-viding hose equipment, although, Mann later noted, "police officials had made it clear that success in mob control depended largely on the supple-mentary use of water."[20] The mayor could only plead with the Eisenhower administration for federal troops to restore order.

Well before the first jeering crowd appeared, the Capital Citizens' Council, later assisted by the Mothers' League of Central High School, was aggressively promoting public opposition. While a member of the Arkansas Association of Citizens' Councils, the Capital chapter was a local movement, drawing its greatest popular support in working-class districts but enjoying sympathy from lower- and middle-class white Little Rock. Ministers, lawyers, and occasional independent businessmen were most prominent among the organization's leadership, with ministers, mainly of Missionary Baptist faith, probably the most active single group.[21] Robert S. Brown, publicity director for a Little Rock radio-television station, was chapter president during 1957, but most observers credited Amis Guthridge, an attorney and states' rights political figure, as the council's de facto head.

Neither the Capital Citizens' Council nor the Mothers' League, which was created only two weeks before the National Guard intervened at Central High School, enjoyed large membership, and neither succeeded in enlisting support from Little Rock's traditional civic leadership. Nonetheless, segregationist influence could be easily underestimated. The Capital Citizens' Council undoubtedly voiced the prejudices of large numbers of white residents. As a local political party, organized segregationists polled 35 percent of the city vote in March 1957, and almost 50 percent in November of the same year.[22]

In the spring of 1957, the Capital Citizens' Council launched an intensive propaganda campaign, disseminating leaflets and sponsoring advertisements attacking integration, holding rallies (three times with out-of-state speakers), initiating letter-writing campaigns aimed at Governor Faubus, spreading (perhaps originating) rumors about impending violence, and organizing crowds to disrupt public meetings of the school board. Above all, segregationists demanded that Faubus intervene to prevent violence and preserve dual school systems in the state capital.[23]

The appearance of Georgia governor Marvin Griffin and states' rights champion Roy V. Harris at a council dinner on August 22 was one of the most publicized events in the summer-long war of nerves. Assuring listeners that Georgia would not allow school integration, the two featured speakers called upon Arkansas to join in defense of segregation.[24]

That night, Griffin and Harris stayed at the executive mansion, and the following morning, they breakfasted with Faubus. Reportedly, the breakfast conversation concerned topics other than segregation. As Harris explained, "We thought he was so far on the other side that we didn't even speak about it."[25] Despite considerable speculation, no valid evidence has yet contradicted this version of the affair.

Griffin and Harris were frequent orators on the Citizens' Council circuit throughout the South. Little Rock segregationists were seeking big-name speakers to lure patrons to a fund-raising banquet, and, in Griffin's words, "they knew me and Roy would attract a crowd."[26] It was logical that the Capital Citizens' Council should consider the two well-known racists, and it was equally logical that Griffin and Harris, when invited, should offer their support to white supremacy in Little Rock.

On August 20, two days prior to the dinner, Faubus telephoned Griffin requesting that he refrain from advocating violent action while in Arkansas.

When Griffin gave assurances, the Arkansas governor invited the visiting Georgia governor to stay overnight in the executive mansion.[27]

The Georgians' visit proved to be one of several effective Capital Citizens' Council propaganda strokes. "People are coming to me," Faubus testified shortly afterward, "and saying if Georgia doesn't have integration, why does Arkansas have it?"[28]

"The integration of Central High School," Blossom wrote in his memoirs, "was no longer a local, administrative problem."[29]

None of these factors—lack of preparation, absence of city leadership, rise of militant opposition—was in itself fatal to desegregation. Little Rock remained basically a moderate community, and most citizens assumed that preparations for token integration were proceeding on schedule.

The situation did have a vital effect on the actions of the school administration, however. Fearing difficulties and perhaps becoming aware of their exposed position, school authorities began a desperate search for support.

During the summer of 1957, Blossom conferred frequently with Chief of Police Potts. Although promising to maintain law and order, Potts, who was opposed to desegregation, showed faint enthusiasm and was apparently hesitant to make concrete commitments.[30] The superintendent and school board president, William G. Cooper Jr., decided to seek assistance elsewhere.[31]

Blossom appealed to federal district judge John E. Miller, asking for a public pronouncement pointing out to potential troublemakers the consequences of obstructing court-approved desegregation plans. The judge refused.[32]

Blossom then turned to Governor Faubus. The superintendent sought from the governor a public statement promising to maintain order and to permit no obstruction to integration, thus making the state responsible for peaceful desegregation in Little Rock. Faubus steadfastly refused. Beginning in early August 1957, Blossom, accompanied twice by school board secretary Wayne Upton and three times by the entire school board, tirelessly pressed the governor for a commitment.

Anxious to justify their request, school spokesmen probably exaggerated the dangers of public disorder, reiterating fears that outside agitators might converge on Little Rock to disrupt desegregation. On at least three occasions, Blossom related to Faubus threats of impending violence, once, for example, retelling a story about the existence of a secret society that intended to halt desegregation by armed terror.[33] "The more the tension mounted late in August," Blossom later wrote, "the more anxious the school board was to persuade Governor Faubus to issue a formal statement."[34] Little Rock insisted upon making Faubus part of its troubles.

Prior to his intervention in Little Rock, Faubus sought more or less consistently to avoid involvement in the school desegregation question, holding that it was a local problem best solved on the community level.

Raised in the isolated hill country of Madison County, where the Negro population was negligible, Faubus was not a racist by personal conviction. After being elected governor in 1954, he oversaw the integration of Negro members into the state Democratic Party machinery and the dropping of racial barriers on the undergraduate level at state colleges.[35] During his early period as chief executive, he rarely commented on school desegregation. Even when the northern Arkansas community of Hoxie became involved in a much-publicized integration controversy, Faubus ignored the event.

Segregation was a topic too fraught with emotional appeal to remain buried, and Faubus was too much a politician not to shift with the political winds. Early in 1956, he endorsed a committee composed of East Arkansas spokesmen studying problems posed by the Supreme Court ruling. The committee recommended two proposals, a locally administered pupil assignment measure and a protest interposition resolution. With Faubus's backing, both measures became law by initiative petition.[36] Then came the 1956 gubernatorial primary, the tone of which was set by the governor's chief opponent, who conducted a blistering display of racial demagoguery. In a campaign that developed no other issue, Faubus turned to a more positive defense of segregation. Similarly, when faced with pressure from East Arkansas lawmakers during the 1957 legislative session, Faubus supported and signed four additional anti-integration bills.[37]

Through all these maneuvers, Faubus continued to insist that desegregation "is a local problem which can best be solved on the local level."[38] During his renomination campaign, Faubus pledged that "no school board will be forced to mix the races in schools while I am governor."[39] Yet, at a press conference on July 17, 1957, when asked about his support of segregationist legislation, Faubus responded that "everyone knows . . . state laws can't supersede federal laws," adding that he would not attempt to nullify federal authority with state legislation.[40]

A central thread of logical consistency marked the governor's tortured path. All administration-sponsored racial legislation was written by a member of the governor's advisory committee and carried out a basic strategy designed to block desegregation in communities where white race feeling ran high and to limit it within the bounds of community acceptance elsewhere. The program centered around the pupil placement act, which delegated to district school authorities the task of assigning pupils to schools according to certain criteria. Among various other legal stratagems were irresponsible and potentially dangerous laws to intimidate the National Association for the Advancement of Colored People. None of these measures penalized integration, and the governor and his advisors consistently rejected nullification theories. This approach allowed Faubus to uphold local autonomy while promising to prevent forced integration.

In practice, the state followed a laissez faire policy prior to the fall of 1957, leaving each district to work out its own racial problems. Under this arrangement, five Arkansas communities desegregated, and five more were planning to do so in 1957. One of these—Van Buren—was acting under court order.[41]

Little Rock, however, interrupted the state's policy of drift. Here, school authorities and organized segregationists—the effective voices of both the proponents and the enemies of desegregation—insisted that the governor take action to preserve order.

Faubus found himself in a dilemma. He had promised not to force integration upon an unwilling community—a pledge that the Mothers' League reminded him of in a petition late in August; and he had indicated an intention not to subvert federal law with state action.[42] Although political expediency eventually overrode executive responsibility, Faubus, rather than a conniving politician coolly manufacturing a crisis, was more correctly a much-worried man fearful of being pushed to the unpopular side of a major racial controversy.

During the last days of August 1957, as time ran out for laissez faire, Faubus maneuvered to avoid taking a stand at Little Rock.

The governor first invited the Eisenhower administration to accept the burden. The Justice Department responded to Faubus's telephone inquiry by sending Arthur B. Caldwell, head of the Civil Rights Division, to Arkansas on August 28. Faubus, expressing fear of violence, questioned the Justice Department representative about federal assistance in the event of trouble. Caldwell could only explain that the Eisenhower administration did not wish to get involved and would assume no advance responsibility for maintaining order.[43]

In fact, of course, the national government had no plans for dealing with opposition to desegregation, relying instead upon a vague hope that the problem would go away.[44] At a time when many southern leaders were loudly and belligerently championing "massive resistance" and when recalcitrance at the University of Alabama and in Mansfield, Texas, was a part of the immediate past, such lack of forethought bordered on the incredible.

The indecisiveness of national leadership became clear during the following weeks. After Faubus called out the National Guard on September 2, Eisenhower responded the next day at a press conference, explaining that "you cannot change people's hearts merely by laws," adding that desegregation must be "executed gradually" since "there are strong emotions on the other side."[45] Not until September 5 did the president make a firm statement that the Constitution would be upheld.[46]

Even then, the statement was followed by little action. For three weeks, from September 2 to September 20, National Guard troopers defied federal authority, while the president refused to take the simple expedient of federalizing the soldiers and changing their orders. After Faubus removed the guard on September 20, Little Rock officials begged for assistance from federal marshals, a plea the Justice Department denied.[47] The Eisenhower administration did, of course, intervene decisively on September 23, but only after opportunities for preventing or minimizing the crisis had been rejected.

Following the conference with Caldwell, the governor had attempted a legal gambit to free himself from the perils of social change in Little Rock. He helped initiate and testified in support of a Mothers' League petition asking an Arkansas chancery court to enjoin school authorities from carrying out planned desegregation. Faubus informed the court that violence was likely if immediate integration was attempted in the tense city. Relying heavily upon the governor's testimony, the chancery court judge issued the injunction on August 29; on the next day a federal district court injunction voided the chancery court order.[48]

With the date for school opening fast approaching, Faubus had to choose. Given the suppositions from which the governor approached the problem, his decision was perhaps predictable. He feared a leaderless city was slipping into violence. He felt that political considerations and past commitments prevented his underwriting peaceful desegregation. There remained only one alternative, even this not an enviable one for a cautious politician who had never shown a desire to fan racial discord or to alienate Negro voters.

On September 1, the governor announced publicly that he had no plans concerning Little Rock and privately indicated that he intended to let the city officials deal with the problem.[49] That night he had a long talk with Blossom, who impressed upon Faubus the necessity for state support. When the governor remarked during the discussion that desegregation could likely be accomplished by local officials, Blossom answered, "We will succeed if only you will issue a statement that you will not tolerate defiance of the law."[50] Faubus refused to make the commitment, hinting instead that he might intervene to block the school board's plans.[51]

The governor did act the next day, ordering the guard, which had been alerted earlier, to prevent desegregation in Little Rock.[52] Appearing on television that night, he explained that the mission of the soldiers was "to maintain or restore order and to protect lives and property of citizens."[53] During the emotion-packed weeks that followed, Faubus insisted that he was not interposing or attempting to defy any court order. He reiterated that he was neither opposing integration nor defending segregation. In fact, he often pointed to Arkansas's progress toward racial equality and bragged that "my only child . . . is now attending classes in a state-supported integrated college."[54]

Having committed himself nonetheless to a segregationist course—and finding that he rode the crest of a wave of popularity—Faubus found his range of political choice sharply narrowed. He became increasingly demagogic and even more irresponsible, almost criminally so on September 20, when he precipitously removed the National Guard, leaving Little Rock to struggle with the dangerously tense situation that the governor had done so much to create.

Little Rock in the fall of 1957 became the hub of the South's resistance to racial integration. The strategy of massive resistance, as well as the phrase itself, had emerged from the patrician state of Virginia, where Harry Flood Byrd, William Old, and James Jackson Kilpatrick had formulated a careful scheme to defend "the southern way of life" and yesterday's Constitution, to protect the rights of states and the rights of white men. Arkansas's commoner in the state house would hardly have recognized the paternalistic pattern Virginia purported to defend. Unconcerned with state sovereignty concepts, massive resistance strategy, or even the sanctity of segregation, Orval Faubus threw up sudden, crude barricades against national law, creating a major constitutional crisis.

Three governments—local, state, and federal—failed to avert a debacle that reasonable planning and a modicum of responsible leadership could have halted at several stages of its development.

THE WHITE CITIZENS' COUNCIL AND RESISTANCE TO SCHOOL DESEGREGATION IN ARKANSAS

Neil R. McMillen

It is one of the ironies of southern history that Hoxie and Little Rock, Arkansas, have become synonyms for white resistance to desegregation in the era of the "Second Reconstruction." In May 1954, when the Supreme Court handed down its decision in the school segregation cases, few suspected that in the troubled years ahead Arkansas would provide Deep South intransigents with the battle cry "Remember Little Rock"—a slogan that recalled for some segregationists the invocation of the long-dead patriots who remembered the Alamo. Indeed, Arkansas's preeminent stature among the defiant states in the first decade of desegregation is as undeserved as it was unexpected. In 1948, the "Land of Opportunity" became a pioneer among southern states in bi-racial higher learning when the University of Arkansas lowered its racial barriers without court order and without popular turmoil. Arkansas was also the first of the former Confederate states to begin complying with the Court's ruling.

Even before the rendering of the so-called second *Brown* decision, the implementation decree of May 30, 1955, four school districts in the state either desegregated their classrooms or moved in that direction.[1] Furthermore, while it can hardly be said that state officials were enthusiastic, their reactions

---

This essay first appeared in the summer 1971 issue of the *Arkansas Historical Quarterly.*

to the nullification of the state's separate-but-equal education statutes were among the region's most positive. In vivid contrast to the defiant mood of Deep South governors, Governor Francis A. Cherry summarized the position of his administration with a terse observation on May 18, 1954: "Arkansas will obey the law. It always has."[2] Nor did the election of Orval E. Faubus signal a shift in official attitude. In his inaugural address in January 1955, Cherry's successor failed even to mention segregation. Similarly, in the legislature, then in its regular sixty-day biennial session, a pupil assignment law designed to preserve segregation in public schools died in the senate.[3] Little wonder, then, that an NAACP field secretary during the spring of 1955 could pronounce the state "the bright spot of the south."[4]

The very paucity of the Negro population itself was a major force working to point the state in the direction of a relatively easy adjustment to desegregation. In 1954, fully 184 of the state's 432 school districts and fifteen of its seventy-five counties had no Negro students at all. Moreover, Negroes constituted 1 percent or less of the total population in twenty-five upcountry counties, and 10 percent or less in twelve more.[5] But there were areas in Arkansas where the density of the nonwhite population approached that of black belt counties in the Deep South. East of the state's fall line, in the lowlands that sweep flat in an alluvial plain toward the "delta" counties along the river, cotton flourished on vast tracts of rich land, much as it did on the opposite shore in Mississippi. Here the great majority of Arkansas's Negro population resided, as did much of its Deep South racial attitudes.

Quite in keeping with patterns already established in the states of the Lower South, organized white resistance to school desegregation in Arkansas began in the black belt. White America, Inc., the first group of its kind in the state, emerged during March 1955 in Pine Bluff, the seat of Jefferson County, one of only seven Arkansas counties where the black population either equaled or exceeded the white. Patterned after such Deep South "protective societies" as the Citizens' Council, this ineffective but noisy group of segregationists languished in obscurity until the following September, when it joined other organized white militants in a concerted effort to resegregate the schools in Hoxie.[6]

A rural trading center in the northeastern portion of the state, Hoxie was an unlikely scene for racial turmoil. Although most whites in this Lawrence County village of some two thousand inhabitants were opposed to racial integration, they took comfort in the knowledge that in the county at large Caucasians outnumbered Negroes nearly ninety-nine to one. Not remarkably, then, when economy-minded School District No. 46 moved to consolidate its dual education system by integrating Hoxie's twenty-six Negro pupils with more than eight hundred whites in July 1955, there was some criticism but no untoward action from the community.[7]

But in the aftermath of the three-page photo story of Hoxie's successful desegregation in *Life* magazine, July 25, 1955, white supremacists both inside and outside the state began to stir.[8] Racist literature bearing the imprint of Deep South Citizens' Councils and other resistance groups was mailed to Hoxie residents, placed under their doors, and put in their cars.[9] Herbert Brewer, a local soybean farmer and part-time auctioneer, began organizing local dissidents into the Citizens' Committee Representing Segregation in Hoxie Schools. Soon thereafter, angry parents began to picket and boycott the village schools. In mid-August, following a segregation rally sponsored jointly by White America and Brewer's committee, the Hoxie school board suspended classes for the fall harvest—fully two weeks ahead of schedule.[10]

During September, the Citizens' Committee and White America were joined by a third organization, the White Citizens' Council of Arkansas, newly formed by former state senator James D. Johnson of Crossett, a recently defeated candidate for state attorney general, and Curt Copeland, former publisher of a small Hot Springs newspaper. Johnson rapidly assumed the lead in a campaign to insure that when Hoxie reopened its schools as scheduled in October, it would do so on a segregated basis.

Typical of Johnson's efforts was his use of a fraudulent tape recording as a recruiting aid. First employed at a rally in nearby Walnut Ridge, this recording was presented as a live tape of an address given by Professor Roosevelt Williams of Howard University to an NAACP audience in Mississippi. Supplied by the Association of Citizens' Councils of Mississippi, this recording left little to the imagination about the "real" motives behind the Negro's quest for social equality. According to a Council newspaper, the tape proved that "the NAACP and their insolent agitators are little concerned with an education for the 'ignorant nigger'; but, rather, are 'demanding' integration in the white bedroom." Somewhat later this spurious document was exposed when a country editor from Georgia revealed that "Professor Williams" was known neither to Howard nor to the NAACP—but not before it had been used by Council organizers to inflame white sentiment in more than half a dozen southeastern Arkansas towns.[11]

Despite such techniques, organized resistance failed in its first venture in Arkansas. The local school board sought and obtained a temporary injunction restraining the three segregationist groups from further interference with the operation of the Hoxie public schools. On October 24, after the harvest recess, the schools reopened as they had closed, on an integrated basis.[12]

The setback at Hoxie was critical for the resistance movement in Arkansas. Providing dramatic proof of the great diversity of the southern region, the incident demonstrated that in the Upper South, particularly in areas where few Negroes resided, organized racism would not enjoy the success it was then experiencing deep in Dixie. Further demonstration of this point came during that same autumn in the southeastern county of Lincoln, where 53 percent of the population was Negro. There, in Star City, the county seat, White Citizens' Council organizers were prevented from holding a rally after white residents petitioned against it. Expressing the view of many residents of the county, the sheriff declared: "We're getting along fine without anybody stirring up trouble."[13]

Undeterred, the advocates of organized resistance persevered. During the following year, the most significant groups merged, including the White Citizens' Council of Arkansas, White America, and the Hoxie Citizens' Committee. Under the leadership of Jim Johnson, unsuccessful candidate in the gubernatorial primary in July, segregationists from some twenty-one counties gathered in Pine Bluff in September 1956 to form the Association of Citizens' Councils of Arkansas (ACCA). L. D. Poynter, a local railroad official and founder of White America, became president and acting executive secretary.[14] Although Poynter was well into his sixties, his new responsibilities could not have been burdensome, for the activities of the ACCA were never more than limited. Unlike many state associations, it was never vital enough to sustain a regular publication for its membership. Even *Arkansas Faith,* published during 1955 by the White Citizens' Council of Arkansas, did not survive the merger.

In time, the state association acquired more-or-less active local affiliates in such counties as Arkansas, Crittenden, Drew, Jefferson, and Lonoke, as well as in the western cities of Texarkana and Van Buren.[15] Generally, however, the movement possessed little strength in these localities. Groups were formed to meet the exigencies of a local desegregation crisis, but once racial tensions subsided, popular interest in organized racism faded.

Because membership lists have never been released, it is difficult to estimate Council strength in any state, and in Arkansas it is particularly hazardous. Unlike many state Council associations, the ACCA seldom quoted membership figures to the press. But in August 1957, it did report that there were organizations in thirty-two of the state's seventy-five counties, a figure that appears to be exaggerated.[16] Similarly, the Southern Regional Council, an Atlanta-based civil rights agency that frequently overestimated resistance group strength, suggested twenty thousand as "the maximum realistic figure" for the ACCA's total membership.[17] In light of the available evidence, this too seems highly inflated.

By far, the most viable affiliate of the ACCA was the Capital Citizens' Council (CCC) of Little Rock. Originally organized in 1955 as an affiliate of White America, the CCC became the largest and most vocal segregation group in the Upper South.[18] But it too was small by Deep South standards. At peak strength, the organization could boast of only some five hundred dues-paying members, and fewer than three hundred of these actually resided in the capital city.[19] Moreover, public rallies rarely attracted large crowds. Nor did it enjoy the support of the city's "substantial" middle class; and, unlike those of many another southern urban center, the organization's officers were not drawn from the city's traditional civic leadership. Indeed, on the eve of the Little Rock school desegregation crisis, the organization's limited standing in the community was underscored during a school board election when voters rejected a pair of Council-endorsed candidates—one of whom was the CCC president—in favor of two others pledged to uphold the board's desegregation plan. To make matters worse, Council membership was seriously fragmented in September 1958, when Robert E. Brown, a former CCC president and one-time executive secretary, led a group of dissidents out of the organization to form the States' Rights Council of Little Rock.[20]

But however much it lacked in size, stature, and stability, the Capital Citizens' Council was a force to be reckoned with. Its strength may probably be better measured by its considerable contribution to the polarization of public sentiment in Little Rock than by the number of its members. Given the troubled course of public school desegregation in the capital city, it seems likely that the CCC's extreme position appealed to a far greater audience than its comparatively small membership would indicate. Moreover, because it possessed the advantage of established organization and leadership, the CCC constituted what one writer on Little Rock politics has aptly described as "the most vocal and potent group within the community."[21] As the events surrounding the desegregation of Central High School in September 1957 would prove, its disruptive capacity could be considerable.

To many observers, the confrontation between state and federal forces in Little Rock and the protracted disorder that followed were wholly unexpected. For, if mere long-range planning were a valid index to peaceful desegregation, the city's submission to the dictates of the *Brown* decision would have been accomplished without incident. While its program of preparedness was neither as well conceived nor as effectively executed as those in the South's border cities of Louisville and St. Louis, the Little Rock school board began preparing for desegregation immediately after the Court's ruling. On May 18, 1954, the board instructed Superintendent Virgil T. Blossom to formulate a plan for compliance. Unenthusiastic though he was, Blossom set to work and within a year presented a functional blueprint for tokenism at the high school level beginning in September 1957.[22]

Although failing to utilize fully the leadership of the flourishing moderate community within this Upper South capital city, Blossom undertook a constructive program of public education. In some two hundred addresses to service clubs, businessmen's organizations, and church groups, he emphasized that there was no practical alternative to desegregation. Perhaps because, as one NAACP spokesman believed, "Superintendent Blossom was more interested in appeasing the segregationists by advocating that only a limited number of Negroes be admitted than in complying with the Supreme Court's decision," significant opposition to Blossom's Little Rock Phase Program did not materialize until the summer of 1957.[23] When that opposition did materialize, its vanguard was occupied by the CCC.[24]

The opening salvo in the campaign to prevent desegregation at Central High came when CCC president Robert E. Brown addressed an open letter to Governor Faubus in the late spring of 1957. Reminding Faubus that Governor Allan Shivers had successfully flouted a federal court order and prevented desegregation in Mansfield, Texas, Brown observed that "in order to preserve domestic tranquility" he could block the school board's program. "As the sovereign head of a state," Brown added, "you are immune to federal court orders."[25] As Superintendent Blossom later recalled, this letter became "the basis of hundreds of thousands of circulars and many full-page newspaper advertisements."[26] But the governor was apparently unmoved. As late as mid-July, he indicated that he would have nothing to do with defiance. "Everyone knows no state law supersedes a federal law," he told a press conference. "If anyone expects me to try to use them to supersede federal laws they are wrong."[27]

Quite obviously, the use of state laws for such purposes was precisely what some segregationists had in mind. Throughout the summer, the CCC's efforts to sabotage the desegregation plan continued. Whether creating disorder at open meetings of the school board, organizing letter-writing campaigns to urge the governor to invoke police powers, or urging defiance through an avalanche of propaganda, the organization managed to keep the sensitive issue in the public's eye. Typically, the organization sought to exploit the white community's darkest fears about racial comingling. "If you integrate Little Rock Central High in September," one CCC-sponsored newspaper advertisement inquired of the school board, "would the negro boys be permitted to solicit the white girls for dances?"[28] Other CCC advertisements, "exposing" the "plot" between Blossom and the NAACP, urged parents to "disrupt [the] vile schemes" of a "small clique of white and Negro revolutionaries."[29] Repeatedly, segregation leaders linked "the Blossom race-mixing plan" with black militants, and at one CCC rally a speaker suggested that it might even have been drafted by the "hidden hand which is the invisible world government."[30]

Persistent rumors of impending violence, fed by the ominous predictions of the extremists, served to cloud the issue still further. Amis Guthridge, a furniture dealer and lawyer who served as the CCC's most articulate spokesman in Little Rock, gravely warned that desegregation at Central High School could only be followed by "hell on the border."[31] The Reverend J. A. Lovell, a Dallas radio minister imported by the CCC for a midsummer public meeting, warned that "there are people left yet in the South who love God and their nation enough to shed blood if necessary to stop this work of Satan." Quickly affirming its nonviolent principles, the Council denied that Lovell's statement meant that the organization would condone physical resistance, and Guthridge even publicly advised members that expulsion would follow any act of violence. Nevertheless, the organization's resolute commitment to segregation at any price contributed to widespread uneasiness within the city as the first day of school approached.[32]

The acme of the summer-long crusade came late in August with the appearance at a Council fund-raising dinner of Georgia's governor, Marvin Griffin, and its former speaker of the house, Roy V. Harris. Prior to the engagement, Governor Faubus, fearful lest their visit spark disorder, telephoned Griffin in Atlanta to express his apprehensions. Although the Georgia governor replied that "I was gonna give 'em hell on the Constitution and Roy was gonna give 'em hell on the civil rights thing," he offered his assurances that there would be no inflammatory statements. Thus satisfied, Faubus hospitably invited the pair to be his guests at the governor's mansion during their stay in Little Rock.

To be sure, these roving ambassadors of resistance did not incite angry whites to riot. But their defiant speeches left little doubt that when and if the Court ordered Georgia to desegregate, there would be no peaceful submission. Amid tumultuous applause, the vow was made that as a last-ditch measure, the Griffin administration would summon "every white man in Georgia" to defend "our cherished institutions."[33]

These intimations were clear not only to Little Rock's militant segregationists but to Faubus as well. Soon after his guests departed, the governor reported that "people are coming to me and saying if Georgia doesn't have integration, why does Arkansas have it?"[34] Certainly the appearance of Harris and Griffin had a galvanic effect. Until their arrival, Superintendent Blossom believed "we had a chance of getting people to accept the gradual integration plan." But afterward, popular opposition solidified.[35] In his testimony at an August 29 hearing at Pulaski County Chancery Court, where segregationists sought an injunction against Little Rock school desegregation, and again in a nationwide broadcast early in September, Faubus expressed agreement. Sentiment in the city had undergone a profound change, he said, and Griffin had "triggered" it.[36] Griffin himself was inclined to view his role as catalytic. Soon after Faubus called out the state militia, ostensibly to prevent "tumult, riot and breach of peace"—but also to bar the admission of nine Negro students to Central High—the Georgian conceded: "I think my visit did make a little contribution to the unity of the people."[37]

Less certain was the degree to which the arch-segregationists influenced Faubus's own decision to follow the destructive route of defiance. Almost until the very moment of his September 2 proclamation activating the National

Guard, the governor had been vilified by white militants. Indeed, there was little in the record of this upcountry politician to suggest that he would become the hero of the resistance movement. Raised in Negro-sparse Madison County, he recognized early the advantages accruing from a discreet cultivation of the state's growing number of black voters. Following his first-term election in 1954, he became the first Arkansas governor to appoint Negroes to the state Democratic central committee. During the Democratic gubernatorial primary campaign of 1956, he courted and won a majority of the state's Negro voters to gain a second nomination over the opposition of segregationist candidate James Johnson. When racist ire was raised over desegregation at Hoxie, he ignored all pleas for intervention to preserve all-white schools in that troubled village; and even at the very peak of the crisis at Little Rock, he recalled with pride that peaceful desegregation of the state colleges had occurred during his tenure.[38]

Precisely because his generally constructive attitude of compliance invited favorable comparison with other moderate South governors, notably Frank G. Clement of Tennessee and Luther H. Hodges of North Carolina, Faubus became the target of the extremists. From its first issue in November 1955, *Arkansas Faith* lampooned "Governor Orval 'Fabalouse'" (also "Awful Faubus"), whose anxieties to "appease" the integrationists had made him "unable to remember whether he received his college training at the communist Commonwealth College or at a mule barn."[39] Even as late as the fund-raising banquet at the Hotel Marion, Griffin and Harris felt obliged to apologize for accepting the governor's hospitality. As Harris reassuringly explained, "Having us two there at the mansion's the worst thing could happen to Faubus. It'll ruin him with the integrationists and the liberals."[40]

But however moderate his previous record, Faubus chose to bend with the current of racial extremism. Perhaps to his own consternation, he was swept along into the very vortex of massive resistance. Having deployed the National Guard to block the execution of a federal mandate, the governor flirted with armed rebellion for seventeen days. Only after a series of complicated maneuvers involving President Dwight David Eisenhower, the Department of Justice, and a federal judge—and the issuance of a federal injunction against further obstruction—did he withdraw the guard on September 20.[41]

Three days later, when Negroes at last gained admission, an unruly mob gathered outside the school. Just three and a half hours after their appearance, apprehensive school and city administrators, fearful lest there be bloodshed, ordered the removal of the black students by a side exit.[42] That same day, President Eisenhower issued an emergency proclamation urging the angry crowd of whites to disperse. When the jeering throng appeared for a second day, the president federalized the Arkansas National Guard and ordered in a battle group of one thousand men from the 101st Airborne Division.[43] For nearly a month, while a sullen calm settled over the city, the nine Negro children attended school with a troop escort. On November 27, the last of the regular army forces were withdrawn, leaving a shrinking detachment of federalized guardsmen in control until the commencement of the summer recess on May 29, 1958.

Although the Capital Citizens' Council heralded the day the troops left Little Rock as "Liberation Day," there is little reason to believe that the occasion was particularly joyous for the organization.[44] Since desegregation had been achieved, the CCC's preoccupation had been the creation and maintenance of an atmosphere so unrelentingly hostile that a permanent federal garrison would be required to keep the peace. During a return engagement in mid-January 1958, Roy Harris, this time in the company of Robert Patterson, founder of the original Citizens' Council in Mississippi, expressed well the mood of Little Rock's CCC members. "Little Rock has Ike over the barrel," he informed more than one thousand segregationists assembled in the city's largest hotel ballroom. "If the people of Little Rock stand pat and he is forced to keep troops here from now on he soon will be the laughing stock of the nation and the world." In similar language, the Mississippi spokesman encouraged militants to persist in their defiance: "Little Rock has proved that forced integration is impractical if not impossible."[45]

To insure that integration would remain impractical at best, the organized segregationists met the entrance of Negroes at the all-white school with a vow of eternal resistance. Having urged whites to "peacefully and prayerfully assemble," the CCC may be at least partially credited for the appearance of the milling throngs of people that appeared so often around the high school during the month of September.[46] An additional manifestation of its approval of mob action came when it formed the "Freedom Fund for Little Rock" and toured the Deep South for contributions to defray the legal expenses of the seventy-five persons arrested during the disorders.[47] In its persistent harassment of school officials, the organization endeavored unsuccessfully to bring charges of malfeasance and nonfeasance against Blossom and members of the school board. Failing here, it supported a recall election law in hopes of effecting their removal by other means.[48]

Through it all, the CCC continued its inflammatory efforts to equate communism and the NAACP with school desegregation. During December 1957, it circulated a broadside charging that the state president of the NAACP, "'Mrs.' Daisy Bates, Little Rock's 'Lady' of the Year," was the "unofficial 'principal' in charge of lecturing white students at Central High who 'cross' any of her 'brave' nine negro students." The circular, which carried police photographs of Mrs. Bates and a transcript of her "record" ("failure to register the NAACP," "gaming," and "contempt of court"), indicated that "iron-clad censorship" and even "prison-like fear" prevented white pupils from telling even their parents of the horrors of student life inside the integrated school.[49] With similar disregard for credibility, state Council leader James Johnson advised members of the Mothers' League of Central High School that an "active Communist cell in your own community" was "pulling the strings" throughout the summer and fall of 1957. Given sufficient time, the former state senator promised the prosegregation organization that he could even produce the "card numbers" of Little Rock's "Communist Organizers."[50]

Tactics such as these contributed substantially to a crystallization of white attitudes against continued compliance. Evidence that the extremists had gained support in the wake of the military and legal proceedings that ended with federal troops at Central High School came on November 5, 1957, in a citywide government election. Although decisively defeated in a school board election the previous spring, the militant element made a surprisingly strong showing in the election of Little Rock's first seven-member city manager board. Only one of the candidates endorsed by the CCC was elected, but the voting was extremely close. The narrow margin of victory for the six moderate candidates came in wards where Negro voting was heaviest and in Pulaski Heights, the "silk stocking" section of the city.[51]

Undoubtedly encouraged by this mood of mounting intransigence, Faubus responded to a Supreme Court reversal of a lower court decision granting Little Rock a two-and-a-half-year "tactical delay" without further desegregation by closing the city's high schools for the 1958–59 academic year.[52] Hailing Faubus's action as a major blow for "racial integrity and states' rights," Little Rock's segregationists began planning immediately for the reopening of the high schools on a private basis. Although the governor endorsed the plan and declared it not only "sound and workable" but beyond the reach of the "so-called 'law of the land,'" a federal court intervened to prevent the transfer of public school facilities and the diversion of public revenue.[53]

Nevertheless, the newly formed Little Rock Private School Corporation opened tuition-free T. J. Raney High School late in October 1958 in a two-story, thirty-two-room former orphanage. Not officially a Capital Citizens' Council project, the Private School Corporation was in everything but name a CCC enterprise. Among its six incorporators were to be found such stalwarts of the organization as Amis Guthridge and the Reverend Wesley Pruden. Its treasurer was Dr. Malcolm G. Taylor, an osteopath who became the president of CCC in January 1959.[54] Moreover, the Private School Corporation was a chief beneficiary of Citizens' Council philanthropy. The October 1958 issue of the *Citizens' Council,* the monthly organ of the South-wide Council movement, carried a front-page appeal for "CONTRIBUTIONS TO LITTLE ROCK." To simulate generous giving, Little Rock Council spokesmen—occasionally in the company of Faubus himself—made solicitation tours to several southern cities.[55]

The returns were impressive. In its November 1958 issue, the *Citizens' Council* reported that "the Little Rock Private School Corporation is receiving financial support from people in every Southern state and many parts of the North." Paced by the Morehouse Parish, Louisiana, Citizens' Council, which collected $11,000 in a "Four Blocks for Little Rock" campaign to ring the courthouse with silver dollars, American segregationists and their sympathizers from as far away as South Africa contributed generously to Arkansas's lily-white private school. Before the drive was a month old, the corporation's president could boast the collection of $175,000 of the estimated $600,000 necessary to operate the private academy for a year.[56]

Meanwhile, the embattled school board remained the focus of the controversy. During the months following the school closing, the Mothers' League of Central High joined the CCC in a campaign to recall the five moderate board members. But when the sixth and favored member, Dr. Dale Alford, defeated incumbent representative Brooks Hays in a write-in, or "paste-in," campaign for the Fifth District congressional seat, the moderates resigned in recognition of "the utter hopelessness of our present position." When the new board was elected in early December 1958, three of its members carried the endorsement of the CCC, and three represented a so-called businessmen's ticket, which the Council branded as "integrationist."[57] With the board thus equally divided, Faubus's supporters in the state legislature introduced a bill to permit the governor to appoint three additional members. Opposed by Little Rock PTA groups and the Women's Emergency Committee to Open Our Schools, a one-thousand-member moderate counterpart to the Central High Mothers' League, the board-packing measure failed to pass.[58]

Defeated but unruffled, Faubus and the Council-endorsed board members joined the city's organized segregationists in demanding the removal of the principal of Central High, his two vice principals, and the principal of all-Negro Horace Mann High School. The issue came to a head after months of rumors about a mass purge of school personnel in a meeting of the school board early in May. Following a fruitless morning of deadlock over the renewal of teacher contracts, the moderates withdrew. In their absence, the pro-Faubus trio voted to replace Superintendent Terrell E. Powell, Blossom's successor, with T. H. Alford, father of Congressman Dale Alford, and to discharge forty-four teachers and administrators for "integrationist" activity.[59]

The outcry was instantaneous. No sooner had the purge been announced than the Little Rock Classroom Teachers Association declared the action illegal. The following day, PTA groups held mass protest rallies in at least five schools. In a statement of censure, the Little Rock PTA Council urged citizens to "carefully consider all legal measures allowed by Arkansas law to achieve recall of officials who use their positions to jeopardize our public school system." Within a week, seventeen of the city's twenty-five PTA chapters endorsed the central council's demand for a recall, and the committee to Stop This Outrageous Purge (STOP) was organized by 179 prominent business and civic leaders to promote the effort.

Fighting back, the racists organized a committee and a recall campaign of their own. The CCC and the States' Rights Council united with the Central High Mothers' League in the formation of CROSS, the Committee to Retain Our Segregated Schools. With opposing petitions of recall filed and the election date set for May 25, both camps campaigned vigorously. Limiting itself to the issue of the purge and excluding any specific stand on desegregation, STOP waged a dignified battle. CROSS, on the other hand, indiscriminately identified all those who protested the firings as not only "integrationists" but "left-wingers," "fellow travelers," and "Communists."[60] Echoing CROSS, CCC leaders labeled such open-school advocates as the Little Rock Chamber of Commerce and the PTA as "communist fronters" and pawns in a "race-mixing conspiracy." Congressman Dale Alford, joined by Mississippi's congressman John Bell Williams, spoke at CROSS rallies, as did Faubus, who made two appearances on local television in support of the purge and the recall of the moderates.[61]

On May 25, the voting was heavy and the margin narrow, but STOP emerged the victor. With the purgers themselves purged by the voters and the moderates exonerated, the always neutral *Southern School News* could report that "for the first time since September, 1957, there was widespread opposition to Faubus at Little Rock on a school matter." In less measured tones, a jubilant *Arkansas Gazette* proclaimed: "The air is clearer today and the future brighter."[62]

Unquestionably, the future of public education was brighter in the months after the recall election. In June, a federal court struck down Arkansas's school-closure statutes and ordered the Little Rock school board to proceed with its original desegregation plan. For its part, a reconstituted school board expunged the action taken during the rump session of May 5 and prepared for the reopening of the city's four high schools.

With the public institutions slated for reopening, the already hard-pressed private schools began to fold. Baptist High School, able to register only twenty-two students by mid-July, scuttled its plans for reopening as a permanent "Christian Academy." About the same time, Trinity (Episcopal) Interim Academy advised its pupils to enroll in the public schools and closed its doors. By the end of the month, only T. J. Raney High School, the largest of the private institutions, was preparing to open its classrooms in the fall. Despite a projected enrollment of more than twelve hundred students and plans for a twenty-eight-room addition to its physical plant, even Raney was foundering. Ineligible for state aid and unable to repeat its spectacular fund raising of the previous year, the theretofore free school announced early in the summer that it would charge a monthly tuition of fifteen dollars. Then in August, to the surprise of friend and foe alike, the corporation declared its insolvency and terminated its operations.[63]

No less suddenly, the city school board, perhaps maneuvering to foil any plans the governor might have had for a special legislative session, announced on August 4 that city high schools would reopen on August 12, nearly a month early. The CCC met the move with a long statement condemning the "cowardly yellow quiters [*sic*]." Dr. Taylor, its president, taking note of the sharply rising incidence of poliomyelitis in Arkansas during the past year, charged that "our schools are in the hands of reckless daredevils who are willing to open schools in the height of a polio epidemic in order to force integration." Failing to arouse public indignation here, Council leaders accused downtown merchants of prointegrationist sentiment and called for a "buyers' strike" to commence the day before school opened. They failed again. According to the Federal Reserve Bank, Little Rock department stores enjoyed a sales increase of 1 percent that week.

Having exhausted every other means of resistance, the organized segregationists turned to the streets. On the morning the schools reopened, the Council participated in a mass segregation rally on the state capitol grounds. Although some one thousand people attended, only about two hundred heeded the call of Robert J. Norwood, president of the States' Rights Council, to march on Central High, fifteen blocks away. Chanting "two, four, six, eight, we don't want to integrate," the demonstrators were intercepted and dispersed by city police, led by Chief of Police Eugene Smith. When twenty-one were arrested, Guthridge and Pruden condemned the use of "Hungarian Gestapo tactics" by police officers and offered the services of the Council's attorney.[64]

With some disorder, then, but without major mishap, Central High School was once again desegregated. All remained peaceful until Labor Day, the second anniversary of the appearance of the National Guard at the school. Then the calm of the sultry summer night was shattered by a series of dynamite explosions—one damaging the school board office, another the front of the building in which the mayor maintained an office, and a third a city-owned automobile parked in the driveway of the chief of the fire department. A fourth and unsuccessful bombing attempt was made on the office of a member of the city manager board. The culprits were readily apprehended, and during the course of the trial in November, testimony revealed that the dynamitings had been planned at a Ku Klux Klan meeting. But it was E. A. Lauderdale Sr., a member of the CCC's board of directors, the owner of a Little Rock lumber company, and a twice-defeated candidate for the city manager board—and not a Klan leader—who was charged as the originator and mastermind of the bomb plot. Convicted and sentenced to three years in prison, Lauderdale did not begin serving his term until February 1961. Scarcely six months later, Faubus granted him a pardon.[65]

Midway between Lauderdale's conviction and his imprisonment, the Council in Arkansas was linked yet another time with violence and the hooded legion. During July 1960, Emmett E. Miller—who had served the cause of segregation in various capacities, most notably as founder and president of the Crittenden County Citizens' Council and, more recently, as Klan recruiter— was charged with planting thirty sticks of dynamite in a classroom at all-black Philander Smith College in Little Rock. Perhaps coincidentally, several hours after the attempt at the Negro campus, a warehouse owned by the Little Rock school district was partially destroyed by an unknown bomber.[66]

Although available evidence does not suggest CCC complicity in these violent acts, the resort to dynamite by those associated with the Council served further to discredit the organization. With its vein of potential lawlessness thus laid bare and its pretensions to respectability stripped away, the organization rapidly ceased to be a significant factor in the city's political life. A measure of its declining influence in Little Rock and across the state was the overwhelming defeat in November 1960 of a proposed constitutional amendment providing for the closing of schools by local option in order to prevent desegregation. Despite the Council's declaration that a negative vote was a vote for racial amalgamation and Governor Faubus's last-minute endorsement, the measure failed to carry even a single county and was defeated by a margin of three to one.[67] Having once tasted the bitter fruit of defiance, Arkansans clearly wanted no more of it.

By 1960, even the Association of Citizens' Councils of Arkansas had begun to recognize the inevitability of at least token compliance with the Court's mandate. After a noisy and often unseemly yearlong battle to block the court-ordered desegregation of the Dollarway School District, on the very doorstep of the organization's state headquarters in Pine Bluff, ACCA leaders urged popular acceptance of the school board's admission of six-year-old Delores Jean York to an all-white Dollarway elementary school. As ACCA president L. D. Poynter conceded, school officials had exhausted their every recourse for delay; no other avenue of nonviolent resistance remained open. When school reconvened at Dollarway on September 7, 1960, Arkansas enjoyed its first statewide peaceful school opening in four years. What the ACCA had repeatedly called the "gateway to southeastern Arkansas" was thrown open to desegregation, and when a single Negro girl marched in, the organization retreated.[68] Two years later, the school board in Pine Bluff itself admitted five Negro children to three previously segregated schools. It did so without court order and without significant opposition from the Citizens' Council.

Perhaps more telling than even the desegregation of the Council's home-town was the defection of Orval Faubus from the ranks of the massive resisters. Unerringly playing his role as barometer for popular sentiment in the state, the governor demonstrated his consummate political virtuosity by moving full circle by 1962. Opposed by Representative Dale Alford for an unprecedented fifth two-year term, the erstwhile hero of the organized resist-ance movement ignored the race issue, condemned extremists on either side, and unabashedly posed for the voters as an apostle of moderation. Although the CCC did not openly endorse Alford, its most articulate spokesman waged a radio campaign against Faubus, charging that he had joined the "ranks of the gutless." But Arkansas voted for Faubus, as it would do once again two years later.[69]

The campaign against Faubus was the Council's political swan song in Arkansas. To be sure, the organization's impress on public policy outside Little Rock had never been great. Until the governor's unexpected emergence as a champion of massive resistance in 1957, its most influential patron, James D. Johnson, could claim only the most dubious political credentials. Defeated in successive bids to be the state attorney general (1955) and governor (1956), the former state senator was without a public forum until his election to a seat on the state supreme court in 1958. And in the end, Johnson proved no more constant than Faubus. He too could sense a shift in the popular mood. In 1962, he endorsed Faubus and, much to the displeasure of militant segre-gationists, played a conspicuous role in his campaign. Having lost a governor and a supreme court justice, the organized resistance movement had as its sole remaining friend of even marginal public prominence Representative Alford, the defeated gubernatorial candidate who was soon to lose his con-gressional district through reapportionment and thus to return to the politi-cal obscurity whence he came.

The loss of its few tenuous links with the power structure was more symptom than cause of the Council's rapid decline in Arkansas. Most of its rank-and-file support had already deserted. Following the confrontation between state and local governments at Little Rock, white Arkansans had become aware of the inevitability of some desegregation. In the face of seem-ingly irresistible pressure for compliance, the vast majority was making at least token adjustments to the nation's changing pattern of race relations. Undesirable though even limited social change may have been, all but the most intractable segregationists clearly evinced a preference for the new order over the chaos that last-ditch defiance would surely bring. Amid such a cli-mate of accommodation, a program of resistance at any price could have little appeal.

Politics and Law in the Little Rock Crisis, 1954–1957

Tony A. Freyer

On the morning of September 3, 1957, the world learned that Governor Orval Faubus of Arkansas had blocked the federally mandated integration of Little Rock Central High School. The governor's action initiated a confrontation between state and federal authority that persisted for two years.[1] Proponents of integration believed that political ambition was behind Faubus's decision to obstruct integration.[2] Supporters of segregation, however, traced the controversy to the community's stand for states' rights against an impending Communist threat and the unconstitutional use of federal judicial and executive power.[3] Other analyses have stressed the need to understand the complex factors giving rise to and perpetuating the Little Rock crisis, emphasizing a failure of leadership in the national government and on the local level to adequately prepare the city of Little Rock for integration.[4]

Recognizing that the origins of the crisis were complex, this study examines the role of law as a political and social force influencing the course of events leading up to the fateful day of September 3. The examination shows that both supporters and opponents of integration developed justifications for their positions based upon the value of the rule of law. This reliance upon legalism increasingly became absorbed in political considerations, which in turn created uncertainty as to the constitutional basis of integration. The interplay of law and politics shaped decisions concerning integration that resulted in confrontation and conflict.[5]

This essay first appeared in the autumn 1981 issue of the *Arkansas Historical Quarterly*.

The integral connection between federal judicial action and local politics began in 1954 with the Supreme Court's landmark *Brown* decision. While unanimously and clearly holding that racial segregation in public schools was unconstitutional, the Court also ordered further argument concerning the decision's implementation. The Court considered this issue during the spring of 1955. In order to give thorough consideration to wide-ranging factors involving compliance, the Court invited the states affected to submit briefs on the situations in their public schools and local communities. These briefs pressed upon the Court the need for attention to local circumstances in the enforcement of *Brown*. On May 31, the Court responded to these pleas by ordering that integration should proceed "with all deliberate speed." The intent of the 1955 decision (known thereafter as *Brown* II) was to give localities maximum flexibility while obligating them to a "prompt and reasonable start" toward integration. In practical terms, this meant, however, that state officials, local school boards, and federal district judges had been given an ambiguous mandate that could be interpreted to justify delay and gradualism.[6]

Local political considerations influenced the drafting of the brief filed by Arkansas during the hearings preceding the *Brown* II decision. Even though the state's attorney general was nominally in charge of drawing up the brief, its contents and approach were formulated by Richard B. McCulloch, an attorney from the East Arkansas community of Forrest City. East Arkansas included the Mississippi delta region, where plantation agriculture was predominant. In this region, a majority of the state's blacks lived, outnumbering whites in some areas. Delta blacks also provided vital labor for the area's economy. McCulloch, a graduate of Harvard Law School and recognized among members of the state's bar as a leading constitutional lawyer, had been hired by several delta school districts to represent their interests as Arkansas moved toward compliance with the Supreme Court's overruling of segregation. Regional alignments of counties dominated legislative and gubernatorial politics in the state. The delta counties represented a major political force; elected and appointed officials from the region were influential in the state's public schools administration. Through this influence, McCulloch was given an instrumental role in putting together the Arkansas brief for *Brown* II.[7]

McCulloch's basic approach to the Supreme Court's integration decision stressed the need for local flexibility and gradual compliance. "We want . . . plenty of elasticity," he said. "What I *don't* want is for the Supreme Court to fix a definite deadline for the completion of integration in all the schools." This assumption suffused the Arkansas argument presented to the Court during the spring of 1955. The state's position acknowledged that limited integration would occur immediately (in fact, two Arkansas communities had brought a few blacks into the public schools following the *Brown* decision of 1954). All school boards across the state would make a "prompt start" toward

compliance by formulating long-range desegregation plans. In general, however, integration would proceed gradually, with most schools remaining segregated for the indefinite future. Local school boards would take maximum
advantage of pupil assignment laws. These laws gave boards great discretion in
the placement of students in local school districts so long as race was not the
basis for transfers. (The Supreme Court did not consider the legal standing of
pupil assignment provisions in *Brown* or *Brown* II; for years these measures were
used by Arkansas and other states to justify limited or no integration.) Finally,
the three federal district courts in Arkansas would monitor the progress of integration plans as they were formulated.[8]

The Supreme Court's *Brown* II opinion seemed to sanction Arkansas's
gradual approach to integration. The Court's decision occurred only days after
Little Rock, the largest public school district in the state, announced significant changes in its integration plan. Immediately following the *Brown* decision of 1954, Little Rock's school board had assigned School Superintendent
Virgil Blossom the responsibility of drawing up a desegregation plan. Although
Blossom and the school board generally favored improved, but segregated,
black schools, they were willing to comply with the Court's decision because
it was the law of the land. The initial approach proposed substantial integration beginning quickly and extending to all grades within a matter of years.
By May 1955, however, this proposal was replaced by one that was more in
line with the minimum standards worked out in McCulloch's brief. The new
approach, thereafter designated the Blossom Plan, would start in September
1957 with token integration of one high school, Little Rock Central. A second
phase would open up the junior high schools to a few blacks by 1960. The
final stage would involve limited desegregation of the city's grade schools at
an unspecified time, perhaps not until 1963. The Blossom Plan also took full
advantage of pupil assignment procedures. This meant that Horace Mann
High School, in predominantly black east Little Rock, and Hall High School,
in predominantly white west Little Rock, would remain segregated. A screening process also greatly restricted the number of blacks eligible to attend
Central.[9]

The new plan was not without problems. Implementation was delayed
until 1957 in order to permit completion of the new high schools of Hall and
Horace Mann. The location of Hall meant that it would serve the west side of
town, including Pulaski Heights, where many of the city's prominent and
influential people lived. Hall, of course, was not to be integrated. Central
High, Little Rock's oldest, most respected, and (under the Blossom Plan) first
and only integrated school, was located in a predominantly working-class
neighborhood. Placing the responsibility for integration on the shoulders of
white working-class families, while the more influential had no such duty,
generated inevitable class tensions. More importantly, perhaps, Blossom and

the school board failed to tap the influential moderate support that had given Little Rock a well-deserved reputation as a progressive city in race relations. Interracial groups such as the Urban League and the Ministerial Alliance; nationally prominent political and business leaders such as Winthrop Rockefeller, Brooks Hays, and Sidney McMath; and the respected Little Rock *Arkansas Gazette* indicated that the capital city possessed a significant moderate constituency. When, however, it was suggested that the moderates should be brought into the process of developing the integration plan, Blossom rejected the idea. The superintendent did give over two hundred speeches promoting his plan throughout the city, but most of these were to business groups whose members had little direct involvement with the public schools.[10]

Despite such problems, there was reason for optimism concerning integration in Little Rock. The Blossom Plan was consistent with the gradual, token approach set out in the Supreme Court's decision of 1955. Also, Governor Orval Faubus had not taken a direct stand on integration in general or on the Little Rock plan in particular, but his reputation as a moderate and his apparent willingness to withstand the criticism of ardent segregationists suggested that he would not interfere with the school board's efforts. Another ground for hope was that the legislature in the session of 1955 had rejected several prosegregation measures submitted by East Arkansas representatives. The measures passed the lower house but were defeated on the floor of the senate through parliamentary maneuvering. This defeat revealed the disunity of the segregationist interests in the state and suggested the influence in the legislature of the representatives of Little Rock's fifth and first wards. The fifth ward included many of the city's influential and prestigious whites, while the first ward was predominantly black. The second and third wards were composed of predominantly white working-class neighborhoods. In local and state elections, voter turnout in the white working-class wards was usually low. The turnout in the first and fifth wards was generally more substantial, and on issues touching race relations, whites and blacks from these areas tended to vote together. Probably responding to the politically active constituencies, state senator Max Howell of Little Rock led the opposition to the East Arkansas–sponsored measures.[11]

Guarded optimism seemed further justified when the school board's plan was upheld by the federal district court in the summer of 1956. The local branch of the NAACP had initiated the suit earlier in the year. Immediately after the *Brown* decision of 1954 and during the first part of 1955, the NAACP responded favorably to the school board's early integration proposals. But as the school board retreated to its more limited plan, a group within the black civil rights organization urged litigation. For some time, the membership of the local branch was divided over the issue. Eventually, however, agreement was reached that nothing but litigation could bring about integration of all public schools within the near future. The branch challenged the gradualness of the Blossom Plan, its failure to state precisely when integration would occur throughout Little Rock's public schools, and the burden it placed on black young people who would have to attend schools outside their neighborhoods. The NAACP's legal brief rested upon these points. The suit was prepared with the aid of counsel from the regional and national offices of the NAACP, but most of the work was done by Wiley Branton, a black attorney from Pine Bluff, Arkansas.[12]

When the suit was filed, the school board responded with a strategy designed both to contest the NAACP suit and to strengthen public support for the Blossom Plan. The board retained lawyers from five of Little Rock's leading law firms. The personal opinions of the five attorneys on integration ranged from moderate to firmly segregationist. By employing these noted attorneys whose views were known to be both favorable to and opposed to the Supreme Court's *Brown* decision, the board hoped to demonstrate the practicality and wisdom of its plan. Led by the school board's regular counsel, A. F. House, the "attorney group" built a case that stressed the extent to which the Blossom Plan was consistent with the gradual and limited standards (vague though they were) established in *Brown* II.[13]

The suit came to trial in the summer of 1956 before federal district judge John E. Miller. Neither side disputed the token character of the Little Rock integration plan. The NAACP's carefully prepared case was ruined, however, by a misunderstanding between the visiting attorney from the regional office and the local counsel. The regional lawyer, without consulting local attorneys, went beyond the narrow contentions set out in the brief and argued that the Blossom Plan was unconstitutional. Since the constitutionality of the plan had not been at issue, Judge Miller rejected the NAACP's argument and upheld the plan on grounds argued in the school board's brief. The judge then retained jurisdiction of the suit in the event that further questions might arise during the course of the plan's implementation. The NAACP appealed.[14] Local response to Miller's decision indicated, however, that there were those in the community who were pleased that the plan had overcome its first legal challenge.

The city's two major newspapers, which often disagreed on integration matters, reflected this cautious optimism. The *Arkansas Democrat* proclaimed that the decision was a "momentous victory": "Common sense, social order and local school authority stand triumphant [upholding] . . . gradual integration." While considering the decision in a somewhat broader context, the *Gazette* stated a similar view concerning its meaning and impact. Its editorial noted that "extremists" both for and against integration were "fated" to "attack" the Little Rock plan because it provided "a minimum of integration" spread out over a period "that may run as long as 10 years." But despite extremist criticism, the paper observed that the "program has the support of a considerable majority of the citizens of Little Rock of both races, who accept it as a practical solution to a difficult problem." The paper also suggested the judicially sanctioned plan might "well set a pattern for the Upper South and point a way out of the dilemma that now faces many Southern communities. It takes into account the social problems inherent in any such transition, and the emotional climate in which school officials must function. But it turns away from the futile course of defiance of the legal process . . . which is being urged across the Deep South."[15]

The *Gazette* editorial also noted, ominously, that Miller's decision occurred during a "disturbed" period. During the months preceding the argument and decision of the Little Rock suit, conditions emerged that gradually undermined the moderate support for the integration plan. A major factor was the increased solidarity of the ardent segregationists, those who opposed any and all integration. Following defeat of the prosegregationist measures during the legislative session of 1955, the state's segregationists gradually resolved various disagreements among themselves and formed a united front. The coalescing began during the summer of 1955 in response to the integration of public schools in the small East Arkansas community of Hoxie, where segregationists attempted to coerce the local school board into reversing its decision to voluntarily bring twenty-five black children into a previously all-white school. A unified statewide effort was not clearly evident, however, until December. At that time, a federal district judge, especially appointed to hear the case, upheld the Hoxie school board's efforts in the face of strong segregationist opposition. Hoxie was important in part because it received national attention as the first integration case in which the Justice Department intervened directly. An investigation of segregationist activities in the small town by the Federal Bureau of Investigation raised the threat of "foreign" federal intervention. Segregationists also perceived danger in the case because it might have established a precedent for the integration of the schools of the entire delta region.[16]

The Hoxie controversy helped make integration a major issue during the gubernatorial primary campaign of the spring and early summer of 1956. The issue came to the fore, however, in the form of a states' rights doctrine known as interposition. Interposition offered the idea that state authority could prevent enforcement of the *Brown* decision until such time that the states passed an amendment to the U.S. Constitution giving Congress the power to implement or to deny implementation of integration. The idea of interposition had had no legal credence in American constitutional jurisprudence since at least the time of the Civil War. But to many white southerners wrestling with the fears, prejudices, and uncertainties aroused by integration, the idea had great appeal. While many proponents used interposition largely to rationalize tactics of delay and obstructionism, others fervently believed in it.[17]

After the Hoxie decision, segregationists began clamoring for a special session of the legislature to consider the integration question. Governor Faubus, who under the state's constitution had sole authority to call a special session, resisted this pressure. James Johnson—a lawyer, a former state senator, and a vocal segregationist—then began a campaign to get an interposition proposal on the ballot for the general election in November using the state's initiative procedure. In the early summer, the segregationists chose Johnson as a candidate for governor, and he campaigned in the Democratic primary largely on the interposition issue. Johnson proposed an amendment to the federal Constitution that would in effect nullify *Brown* until Congress acted on the constitutionality of integration. Johnson's successful efforts at getting interposition on the November ballot and his race for governor forced Faubus to respond. Until the spring of 1956, Faubus had successfully maintained his reputation as a moderate. Faced with Johnson's challenge, however, he appointed a committee composed largely of East Arkansas residents (including Richard B. McCulloch) to investigate and formulate interposition proposals. The committee studied interposition laws from other states, visited Virginia (where such laws were quickly passed after *Brown*), and made recommendations based upon pupil assignment procedures and attendance zones. These recommendations adopted an approach to interposition that was considerably weaker than that embodied in Johnson's referendum measure. Faubus adopted these recommendations and used his office to mobilize support to get them, too, on the November ballot. These moves helped win him the Democratic primary and certain election as governor for a second term.[18]

Faubus's support of interposition tarnished his image as a moderate. The *Southern School News* of April 1956 ran the headline, "Governor of Arkansas Inclines to Segregation." Faubus's transition was no doubt motivated by a desire to ensure his nomination for a second term, but this narrow motivation was enmeshed in larger considerations. Faubus had been brought into state politics as a part of liberal Sidney McMath's administration. The McMath administration had pushed programs for increased industrialization and improved social services for a state whose civic backwardness was well-known. As governor, Faubus made this program his own; to carry it out, however, increased taxes were essential. Failure to win the nomination for governor threatened the tax program so vital to the state's development. Thus, so far as Faubus was concerned, the politics of the gubernatorial race, interposition, and the need to develop Arkansas were entwined.[19]

During the summer and early fall of 1956, interposition was the subject of heated debate. As the November election and referendum neared, Faubus worked to convince the people of the state that his interposition proposals were more moderate than the Johnson measure. At the same time, he maintained a solid base of support among black voters by increasing social services for the poor; favoring integration of public transit facilities; moving to bring the salaries of black teachers up to levels comparable with whites; and, most importantly, giving blacks representation on the state Democratic Party committee

(Arkansas was the first state of the old Confederacy to do this in the post-*Brown* era). By October, tension heightened when the federal court of appeals upheld integration in Hoxie. In November, majorities in both the city of Little Rock and the state voted in favor of Faubus's proposals and in favor of the Johnson measure, which further confused the issue.[20]

In late August, Judge Miller's integration decision in the NAACP case seemed to reflect a general acceptance, at least in Little Rock, of gradual integration. The fact that nearly half of the city's voters opposed interposition two months later indicated that people's attitude toward the legal basis of integration was quite ambiguous. This ambiguity deepened after the new year. During a Little Rock school board election in March 1957, three out of four prosegregation candidates were narrowly defeated. On April 29, the federal court of appeals upheld Miller's decision; the NAACP did not appeal the federal ruling because it feared that the Supreme Court might sustain as a "model" for the Upper South a plan that was too gradual and limited.[21]

At the same time, the political interplay between Faubus's tax program and interposition reflected growing segregationist influence. The interposition measures voted on in November required enabling legislation to be passed in the next legislative session, beginning in February 1957. In the same session, Faubus introduced a tax plan that would, if passed into law, represent the largest tax increase in the state's history. Representatives from the state's three major urban areas, those from West Arkansas, and miscellaneous others, including a representative from Faubus's own county, opposed the increase. The largest single bloc favoring the governor's program came from the East Arkansas delta region. The region's votes, however, came at a price: Faubus must support the enactment into law of not only those proposals passed in November but also legislation establishing a state sovereignty commission.[22]

Faubus conceded to the East Arkansas interests on the interposition legislation, and consequently his tax plan passed too. Victory in the legislature combined with defeat in federal court fired increased segregationist activity during the summer of 1957. A heavy advertising campaign, well-publicized meetings, and regular mass rallies increased the public's awareness of the segregationists' position. A steady barrage of phone calls, letters, and telegrams to Governor Faubus demanded that he take a strong stand against the integration of Central High. As tensions grew, Wayne Upton, an attorney and member of the school board, decided that it might be useful to consider another course of action. On August 13, he appeared before Judge Miller's court in Fort Smith as part of a pretrial hearing having nothing to do with integration. After the hearing, he told Miller that he believed a suit would be filed in state court requesting delay of integration until such time as interposition legislation was found to be illegal. Miller replied that, if such a case did

develop, the school board should come to him and he would consider ordering a stay until there was a final determination of the validity of the interposition laws.[23]

Soon thereafter, Upton discussed with Blossom the meeting with Miller.
On the morning of August 15, Upton and Blossom talked with Faubus in very
general terms about the same subject. That evening, the attorney and the
school superintendent met with William J. Smith, a legal adviser to the governor, at Blossom's home. Blossom hoped that a court test of the interposition laws would make it easier for Faubus to make a public statement to the
effect that he recognized the need to comply with the integration order. But
nothing conclusive came out of the meetings with Faubus and Smith. The
next day, however, a suit was filed in the local chancery court by William F.
Rector, a Little Rock businessman, requesting a judgment on the constitutionality of the interposition measures. Except for Upton, the members of the
school board seemed not to have been aware that this suit was going to be
initiated. Upton probably knew the suit was being contemplated but apparently was not directly involved with it. On Sunday, August 18, Blossom,
Upton, and Harold J. Engstrom (another member of the school board) went
to Fort Smith to meet with Judge Miller. They discussed with Miller the newly
filed litigation; he suggested that another procedural approach (an injunction) might better serve the school board's purposes. The three returned to
Little Rock and informally discussed Miller's advice. Finally, they decided
against pursuing further this particular course of action. Several local ministers filed a suit in federal district court challenging the constitutionality of the
interposition laws on August 20, but this seems to have been an independent
action.[24]

The situation soon acquired a sharper focus. On August 22, Governor
Marvin Griffin, a well-known segregationist from Georgia, spoke at a White
Citizens' Council meeting in Little Rock. Griffin contended in vague but
inflammatory terms that Georgia was using interposition to nullify the *Brown*
decision. The idea that Georgia was able through legal means to circumvent
the Supreme Court's mandate had an electrifying effect on segregationist
efforts in the city. Although Griffin's contention was a distortion of the operation of interposition in Georgia, extremists used the claim to build up still
more public pressure. The pressure became so great that Faubus increasingly
came to question whether integration should be allowed to take place on
September 3.[25]

Concerned over the growing intensity of the segregationist protest,
Blossom, in private conversations, repeatedly urged the governor to make a
public statement in support of integration. Faubus refused, arguing in part
that the interposition laws passed earlier in the year had given him a mandate supported by a large majority of the people of Arkansas. Failure to enforce

this mandate would have significant political ramifications for Faubus and his policies. The governor said that no public statement was possible until the interposition legislation had been judged by the courts. He also said that Griffin's speech had generated a major change of opinion in the city, from a position that was resigned to the acceptance of integration to one that was opposed. This change could, he feared, lead to violence if black children entered Central High School as scheduled.[26]

Faubus decided that a delay was essential. He arranged to have a suit filed in Pulaski County chancery court on August 27 asking for a temporary injunction against the school board. The governor hoped that the suit would force the school board to request a postponement of integration at least until the constitutionality of the interposition legislation was determined. On August 28, he met with an attorney from the Department of Justice to find out what action the federal government intended to take if violence developed in the city. He was disappointed to learn that the federal authorities had no plan to intervene. The next day, the chancery court heard his suit, with the governor appearing as a witness. In his testimony, Faubus repeated his fears that violence was likely. When questioned as to the basis for his fears, he replied in vague and evasive terms. The chancery court then granted an injunction against the implementation of the integration plan. That evening, the governor called a meeting of his advisors to discuss the Little Rock integration situation. At the meeting, Faubus repeated his concern about possible violence but again mentioned no specific basis for such concern. The next day, the school board went to federal district court and was granted an injunction against the enforcement of the chancery order. Following the federal court order, the governor met again with his advisors, but nothing concrete about the integration problem was discussed. After the federal court's action, there were still more private exchanges between Faubus and Blossom.[27]

By the evening of September 2, members of the school board, Blossom, the NAACP, and the people of Little Rock did not know what to expect when the schools opened the following day. The governor appeared on television with an important announcement. He reviewed the state's progress toward integration over the preceding years, emphasizing his role as a moderate. He said that until Griffin's speech, public opinion in Little Rock was resigned to accepting integration, but that Griffin had created a climate in which a majority of the city's population was now unsure as to whether the state was bound to follow the Supreme Court's *Brown* decision. This uncertainty existed in part, he said, because Griffin had stressed the ability of interposition legislation to supersede the Supreme Court's authority.[28]

Faubus noted that majorities in Little Rock and across the state had voted in favor of the interposition measures during the November election. He noted too that the legislature had passed legislation implementing the measures. As governor, he was bound to enforce these laws until they were declared unconstitutional. Faubus insisted that violence would occur if Central was integrated the next day (though he gave no specific proof supporting this claim). He explained that "one of the greatest reasons for the unrest and for the imminence of disorder and violence" was the uncertainty over whether the interposition statutes or the Supreme Court's opinion constituted the law of the land. Until this uncertainty was cleared up "by the proper authorities," the state law was supreme. In order to preserve the peace and order of Little Rock, black children would not be allowed to enter Central High. The order would be enforced, Faubus said, by units of the state's National Guard that had been stationed around the school.[29]

During the fall of 1957, Little Rock became the focus of international attention as Governor Faubus challenged first the authority of the federal district court and then that of President Dwight D. Eisenhower. The governor's challenge resulted in Eisenhower's decision that regular U.S. Army troops were necessary to enforce the federal court's integration order. Throughout the rest of the school year, attention turned to the plight of the handful of black children attending integrated classes at Central. Despite the best efforts of the school administration and the school board, the children suffered relentless harassment from segregationists in Little Rock and across the South. By the spring of 1958, concern over the deterioration of educational standards was such that the school board requested from the federal district court a two-and-one-half-year delay in the implementation of the integration order. Publicly, the school board argued that the delay would provide a cooling-off period, after which conditions might be more receptive to change. Privately, however, the reason given for the board's move was that in two and one half years, Faubus's two-year term as governor would be at an end.[30]

In June 1958, federal district court judge Harold E. Lemley granted the delay, but the NAACP appealed at once. After a series of procedural maneuverings, the court of appeals overturned Lemley's decision. The school board then appealed to the U.S. Supreme Court. The Supreme Court announced it would review the appeals court's reversal in a special term (only the third such term in modern history). In August, the Court considered the appeal, unanimously rejected the plea for delay, and ordered immediate compliance with the integration order given by Judge Miller in 1956.[31]

The governor and the state legislature responded to the Supreme Court's ruling by closing all of Little Rock's high schools for the 1958–59 academic year. They then attempted to develop a plan whereby the state would fund, with taxpayers' money, segregated private schools. The Supreme Court's decision and the state's response crystallized opposition among several influential Little Rock business groups. These groups mobilized enough community support to win a special school board election in May 1959. This election led to the return of the schools to local public control on a limited integrated basis. This victory broke the governor's power over Little Rock's public school system. In the fall of 1959, despite continued resistance from Faubus and segregationists, all of Little Rock's high schools opened with at least a few blacks attending classes.[32]

Tracing the local response to integration from the Supreme Court's *Brown* decision in 1954 to the outbreak of trouble in the fall of 1957 shows that the confrontation between state and federal authority set off by Faubus's actions was partially rooted in the vague standards of compliance formulated by the Court in *Brown* II in 1955. In drafting Arkansas's response to the order for briefs detailing local conditions, McCulloch hoped that the Court would establish criteria allowing maximum flexibility and gradualism. The imprecision of "deliberate speed," along with the Court's silence concerning the validity of the pupil assignment laws, in effect sanctioned McCulloch's position. This sanction gave legal support to a more restricted approach to integration than had in fact emerged in Little Rock by the beginning of 1955. During the hearing of *Brown* II before the Supreme Court, the school board changed its plan from one proposing substantial integration beginning in 1956 to one that opened up only one school in 1957, with more integration stretched out over as much as ten years or more. Various reasons were given for this change at the time, but a major rationale was that it allowed a minimum of integration consistent with the law.[33]

This position, although intended to attract moderate support, actually established a basis for opposition to integration. In the legislative session of 1955, the state senator from Little Rock was able to stall segregationist measures proposed by representatives from East Arkansas. During the same time and for months after, Governor Faubus perceived no political risk in refusing to answer segregationist charges that he was in favor of integration. This indicated, in part, a lack of vocal and active public support for those opposing any and all integration. It also suggested that many Arkansans were apathetic or perhaps even shared a moderate attitude toward the race question at least through the summer of 1955. By this time, several developments began to converge, however, that complicated the integration issue. The school board's changed approach publicized the idea that there was considerable flexibility in the standards of compliance established by the Supreme Court. The imprecision of *Brown* II was further revealed when the NAACP announced its decision to challenge the revised Blossom Plan. Condemning the failure of the new plan to establish specific dates for the phased approach, the NAACP drew attention to the fuzziness of "deliberate speed."[34]

In response to the Hoxie controversy and subsequent litigation, segregationists were able to establish a more unified front against integration. This growing unity occurred during the same time as the increased discussion over the question of what constituted proper compliance with the Supreme Court's decision. At this juncture, Johnson introduced his interposition measure. Despite its incompatibility with the main tenets of American constitutional law, interposition strongly appealed to the fears and doubts of those confronted with what was becoming an increasingly unclear legal justification for integration. The apparent sanction of McCulloch's approach to integration in *Brown* II, the school board's change in policy that was consistent with this approach, and the NAACP's suit that publicized this change reinforced a general uncertainty among Arkansans over what was in fact the law of the land.[35]

In the context of this uncertainty, Johnson's measure had significant political ramifications. The ease with which the lawyer succeeded in his campaign to get interposition on the November ballot revealed widespread popular support for some legal way to avoid integration. It also became apparent that Johnson could use the interposition issue to challenge Faubus for the nomination for governor in the upcoming primary of 1956. To head off this threat, the governor responded with his own more moderate interposition proposals, stressing the pupil assignment and attendance zone measures. Faubus's move assured him the nomination, but it also gave credence to the idea that it was possible through constitutional means to avoid integration. This undermined the appeal of the justification for integration that rested upon complacent obedience to "the law."

The symbolic and political force of interposition increased in 1957. Faubus was firmly committed to a program of economic development for Arkansas. This program required, however, the largest tax increase in the state's history. Passage of the tax measures depended upon the votes of East Arkansas representatives; they were willing to give their support in return for more interposition legislation. The political trade took place privately, so that the public was unaware of the connection between the passage of the tax program and the interposition laws. It was understandable that the success of interposition was generally interpreted as another segregationist victory. During the spring and summer, in their mounting publicity campaign, the segregationists emphasized that the legislation gave state government (particularly the governor) the means to avoid enforcement of the Supreme Court's integration order. The climax of the campaign was the appearance and presentation of Governor Griffin of Georgia on August 22. Griffin's contention that Georgia was using interposition to escape compliance with integration through constitutional means further clouded the already confused public mind as to what in fact the legal basis of integration was. This confusion contributed to heightened tension in the city.

The events surrounding Upton's efforts further revealed the significance of the interposition issue. Amid the growing tension, the effort to ascertain

Miller's course of action if a suit testing the interposition laws was filed no doubt seemed appropriate. In practical terms, the effort was made in order to get Faubus to make a public statement that he would back compliance with the federal court's integration order. But the incident is most useful in explaining several of the governor's actions following Griffin's speech. During the interview on August 28 with the Justice Department attorney, Faubus stated that he had "arranged" a suit to temporarily block the integration of Central. While the extent to which Faubus knew the details of Upton's initiative is unclear, it is certain that he was aware that some sort of litigation was being considered by the school board because he discussed the possibility with Blossom and Upton on August 15. Then, the day following, two suits were filed challenging the interposition laws.

These events placed the Faubus-backed suit of August 27 in a new light. Faubus told the Justice Department attorney that he had initiated the suit in order to force the school board to request delay in the integration of Central. When the delay was granted, he hoped that the school board would then challenge the interposition laws. This would, he explained, get him "off the hook" of having to enforce the segregation measures. Considering the suit of August 27 in light of the Upton initiative also suggests why Faubus, in the proclamation of September 2, emphasized the uncertainty generated by the interposition laws as a significant cause of possible violence. In his address, the governor exclaimed that he was bound by the laws until their validity was determined by the "proper authority." The statement was quite possibly another attempt to "force" the school board to act and to thereby lift from his shoulders the responsibility to get involved with integration.[36]

This analysis supports the view that the Little Rock crisis, in part, had its origins in failures of local civic and political leadership. A full understanding of these failures, however, must take into account the extent to which the interaction between law and politics was a significant factor shaping events prior to the opening of Central on September 3. Beginning with its public response to the announcement of the *Brown* decision in 1954, the school board emphasized that its voluntary integration plan was being developed largely out of a practical necessity to comply with the new law of the land. This same justification was used during the spring of 1955 when the school board retreated from its original, more progressive integration plan.

No doubt virtually everyone could appreciate a justification for integration based upon the realistic necessity to·obey the law. Such a rationale ignored, however, the degree to which a precise meaning of "the law" was subject to differing interpretations. Thus, when proponents of interposition and the NAACP challenged the Blossom Plan, they not only were attacking its substantive character but were also undermining the persuasive appeal of a justification for change based solely upon a reluctant deference to legal compulsion. Governor Faubus's increasing reliance upon interposition further undermined the school board's principal rationale for integration. By the summer of 1957, integration was enmeshed in the issue of interposition. Like the school board before him, Governor Faubus no doubt viewed his reliance upon legalism as a sound move that would create public support. But in this legalism lurked unanticipated ambiguity. Confronting this ambiguity, the governor and the school board found they had sown the wind and reaped the whirlwind.

ORVAL E. FAUBUS

Out of Socialism into Realism

Roy Reed

Orval E. Faubus was reared a liberal. His father, Sam Faubus, was a Socialist who detested capitalism and bigotry with equal fervor. The son's critics, myself included, have accused him through the years of selling out the beliefs of his father on both race and economics. The story may be less straightforward than that.

Orval Faubus came to power in Arkansas after World War II when two things were happening:

First, the old populist revolt that had inflamed the hills for several generations was burning itself out.[1] The end of Faubus's own radicalism coincided almost perfectly with the decline of radicalism among his people, not only in the Ozarks but right across the southern uplands. Prosperity, meager as it was, finally intruded into the hills and nudged out not only the Socialists like his father but also the intellectually tamer populists who had used their hill-country base to shower invective on the delta planters and their establishment cohorts in banking, business, and industry. Resentment slowly began to give way to the other side of the populist coin, hope. Hope and appetite and a vestigial populist belief still current: that our fellow hillbilly Sam Walton made it, and with a little luck, I can make it, too.

Second, a national phenomenon with far-reaching consequences was coming to a head during the 1950s. The racial equilibrium of the South was being

---

This article first appeared in the spring 1995 issue of the *Arkansas Historical Quarterly*.

extraordinarily disturbed, not merely by local agitation but more importantly by external forces that eventually would sweep away the entire breastwork of white supremacist defenses. The liberal Faubus might have thrown in with the national mood, a growing impatience with southern heel-dragging. Realistically, however, how much can he be blamed for choosing to be seen as defender of the local faith, no matter how little he shared that faith? What would have been the fate of a governor who chose the other side? Some of my heroes have argued that he could have exerted leadership for the rights of blacks and survived. Or that, at the least, he could have died an honorable political death.

Maybe so. But Orval Faubus had seen quite enough of honorable struggle for lost causes in his boyhood home. And there was something else. By the time he was grown, he had seen enough fear, loss, and death to last a lifetime.

Literally from the beginning, Orval Eugene Faubus's life was threatened. He weighed two and one-half pounds when he was born the night of January 7, 1910, and was so frail that the midwife expected him to die before morning. One night when he was a year old, he caught the croup and stopped breathing. His father rushed him outside into the cold air and plunged a finger into his throat to save his life. The toddler was just learning to talk when he wandered from the house and fell into a deep spring of water and somehow did not drown but climbed out just as his mother got there.

Danger continued to surround him as he grew and became part of the community. The year he was seven, one playmate died of diphtheria and another was crushed to death by a falling tree. During another year, flux swept the community and killed two children in a neighboring family.

Life was not only perilous at Greasy Creek; it was also hard. Southern Madison County was like most of the Ozarks at that time. The residents scraped by. The towns had a small prosperity, but the countryside provided little more than subsistence. Rural people like the Faubuses raised almost all their food. Shoes and coats were practically luxuries because they had to be bought with cash, and cash was pitiably scarce. Even kerosene for the lamps was so dear that, after John D. Rockefeller cornered the market and raised the price, young Orval had to walk behind the wagon and carry the filled can the two miles from Combs to Greasy Creek, so as not to spill any—or so he recollected in 1964 when Rockefeller's grandson Winthrop tried to wrest the governorship of Arkansas from him.

Even granted that poverty and fear may be goads to ambition, it still seems extraordinary that a youngster could rise from such circumstances in such a place to be governor of his state, to keep the job longer than any other person, and to become a public figure known around the world.

Greasy Creek was, in every sense, the end of the road. Orval had to walk twelve miles to his first job across mountain trails; no roads went there from his home. Communication was primitive. News in Greasy Creek—that is, any report that reached beyond Madison County and the community grapevine—was limited to what certain elders deemed worth passing on from the occasional mail subscription to the *Kansas City Weekly Star* or the even rarer subscription to the *Arkansas Gazette* or the *Daily Oklahoman*. Politics was conducted almost entirely face-to-face, man-to-man, in a kind of slow-motion pulsation radiating from the county seat at Huntsville. Politics was also an important diversion, and there we have a clue to Faubus's escape and survival.

From his earliest years, young Orval carried a double burden of shyness and pride. He was not strong enough to excel in physical competition. He turned to the private world of words and found that he had a talent not only for language but also for retaining information. Through reading magazines and books, he learned of a world far different from the hillside farm of his father. He dreamed of entering that world.

There were two ways out for a young man of his background and temperament: teaching and politics. His mother and father together pushed the shy son toward the first. His father pushed him, perhaps unwittingly, toward the second.

John Samuel Faubus was anything but shy. He came from a large, loud, sometimes boisterous family of fifteen children, counting step-siblings. He claimed to have a fourth-grade education, but that was a flexible interpretation of the record. He once confessed that he had attended only three or four months of school by age eleven and that he did not learn to write until he was twenty, about the time he married. But before the last of his seven children was born, Sam Faubus had become known as one of the best-informed people in his part of Arkansas. The same year Orval was born, Sam took the lead in one of the most baffling political movements in the history of the state. He and two friends signed up most of the voting-age population on Greasy Creek as members of the Socialist Party.

Not that socialism itself was baffling, although many people do not appreciate how significant a hold it had on Arkansas at that time. The southwestern states of Oklahoma, Louisiana, Texas, and Arkansas provided a substantial vote for the Socialist Party candidate for president, Eugene V. Debs, in the election of 1912. The mystery is how Marxian socialism penetrated to the fastnesses of Greasy Creek, twenty-five miles from the nearest county seat, seventy years before the first pavement would be laid on the one dirt road to the place. The best guess is that it was imported by a gentlemanly old bachelor from the North, probably from Illinois, one O. T. Green. After a sojourn in a boarding house at Combs, where his socialist views caused a few embarrassing arguments, Green settled on a small farm near Sam Faubus's place. He raised goats and peacocks, corresponded with Socialist acquaintances in other states, and befriended the young neighbor whose inquiring mind intrigued him.[2]

From whatever source, Socialist publications began to appear in the Faubus household.[3] And Sam, once convinced that the big corporations controlled the American economy and that capitalism was his enemy, became an outspoken advocate of the socialist system. He and his friend Arch Cornett, a teacher, wrote eloquent letters to the editor of the Huntsville newspaper denouncing the entrenched interests.[4] Their concern spread to political reform; Sam circulated petitions calling for woman's suffrage, old-age pensions, and abolition of the vote-restricting poll tax.

In May 1910, Sam and his friends formally established the Mill Creek Local of the Socialist Party. The charter from the state committee was addressed to "the comrades of Combs" and carried the names of ten men, four of them named Faubus. Whoever copied the names apparently inverted Sam's initials so that he is listed as S. J. Faubus. The post of secretary, carrying with it the responsibility of chief organizer, went to him. Arch Cornett, O. T. Green, and Sam Faubus became the most devoted members of the south Madison County local.[5]

As many as thirty people, including some from neighboring communities, might have been members of the Mill Creek Local at one time. The party had a majority of the adult residents of the Greasy Creek community. The local was large enough to provide the swing vote in district election contests between the Democrats and Republicans.[6] Madison County had at least two other thriving Socialist locals, one at Witter and the other at Kingston. Several other locals sprang up across the Ozarks.[7]

Sam and Arch joined other Socialists in opposing World War I. They almost went to prison for their troubles. Just before the war ended, the two men were arrested for distributing literature protesting the war. The charge was serious: violating the Sedition Act of 1918. Only the timely end of the war and the help of a good lawyer kept them out of the penitentiary. Sam has been referred to in recent years as an "old-time mountain Socialist." The designation suggests that people like Sam Faubus were too innocent to fully understand the implications of socialism. The old man would be indignant at that condescension if he were alive. It is probably true that the Socialists of the Southwest were less rigorous in the faith than their comrades in the industrial East. But they were apparently earnest in their attempt to change capitalism in the United States. Their hatred of Wall Street and capitalism was as intense as that of their hero Debs and any of the eastern Marxists.

Sam's interest in public affairs rubbed off on his eldest child. Orval read the Socialist Party literature that came to the house. He even joined his father on at least one occasion when the two of them debated the merits of socialism with a pair of teachers at nearby St. Paul.

In 1935, after he was married and had been teaching several years, Orval indulged in his most serious flirtation with the political Left. He hitchhiked to Commonwealth College, a labor self-help school near Mena, with the intention of gaining there the college education that he had not been able to afford elsewhere. The college comprised Socialists, Communists, labor organizers of various persuasions, and a smattering of unaffiliated idealists. They apparently had in common a conviction that the American economic system, then in collapse, was basically flawed.

How long Faubus remained on the campus has been disputed, but he was there long enough to give a May Day speech and be elected president of the student body. He says he never formally enrolled but simply took part in campus activities in what sounds like a walk-on role.

Whatever the case, there is little doubt that young Faubus about that time began to develop a streak of political realism that was largely missing in his father. He shook the dust of Commonwealth from his feet after a few weeks or at most a few months. Instead of turning him into a crypto-Communist, as some of his later enemies put it about, the close encounter with Marxism seems to have left him eventually disenchanted. It might be argued that the Commonwealth experience, far from producing a Communist subversive, was actually the beginning of a slow swing to the right that would send him into the conservative orbit more than twenty years later.

Back at Greasy Creek, Sam continued to urge socialism on his son. But Orval understood early that if he wanted a future in politics, a minority party with a radical reputation was not the way to go. And he was definitely interested in a political career.

Luckily, he was offered an alternative by national developments. Franklin D. Roosevelt was elected president in 1932. The New Deal, with its extensive social programs, co-opted some of the Socialist Party's more appealing ideas. Orval became a New Dealer. Eventually, so did Sam.

Orval remained a Democrat, at least nominally, throughout his long career. He remained a liberal of declining intensity until his second term as governor.

Faubus entered public life just as his part of America, the South, was starting to revive after three-quarters of a century of lassitude. In the language of economics, the South was entering the takeoff stage in 1940—just when young Faubus was proving himself in county politics and entering his own takeoff stage.[8] He had been elected circuit clerk of his county in 1938 and had hopes of moving up to county judge—or even higher, with a little luck. Along with his growing success in politics, it would be his fate to come to maturity while his region was seeing its first real love affair with capitalism. The affair would bring greater prosperity to more people than the South had ever seen. It would also bring the evils of make-it-fast go-getterism: industrial pollution, runaway greed, corruption of institutions, and what is probably misnamed as conservatism in politics. As governor during the 1950s and 1960s, Faubus would preside over his state's immersion in all this, the good and the bad.

For starters, he plunged headily into the race for industrialization. He saw that the only way that backward Arkansas could ever catch up with the rest of the country was to build a base of industrial production to balance the state's traditional and always uncertain agricultural base. He induced the conscience-ridden Baptist playboy Winthrop Rockefeller, who had fled to Arkansas to escape a disastrous marriage and his family's disapproval, to head up Arkansas's program for attracting industry. They made a good team, the compassionate capitalist and the Socialist-reared hillbilly. Steadily, out-of-state industry moved into the state and enriched its payroll. Faubus later estimated that 125,000 industrial jobs had been added during his twelve-year administration. The new industry also, in many cases, exploited the state's resources and fouled its air, water, and forests. Not much thought was given to regulation of industry in those days. A people who had never had any easy factory jobs—easy compared to subsistence farming—was not concerned with unfortunate consequences. Neither was the governor, except for a few notable instances when his Ozarks upbringing asserted itself, as it did, for example, when he threw in with the environmentalists and stopped the Corps of Engineers from damming the Buffalo River.

The business establishment of Little Rock was openly contemptuous of the country boy from Madison County when he first became governor. He swallowed his pride and set out to win them over. Within a year, he had made peace with many of the capital's go-getters, including some who had held him up as a figure of amusement at posh cocktail parties. Even after he had made peace with them, many of the country-club set continued for years to poke fun at his country speech and country ways.

Faubus never became a country clubber. He built his own set of affluent friends and associates. At the center of his set was another self-made man, a country boy who took his own revenge against the city sophisticates by simply piling up a larger fortune than any of them had. W. R. (Witt) Stephens was already a behind-the-scenes power in Arkansas politics when Faubus became governor. He and Faubus quickly formed an alliance of mutual benefit.

For Stephens, the alliance provided friendly, profitable treatment from state agencies and administration allies in every institution from banks to the state legislature to scores of courthouses and city halls across the state. Early in 1957, when the state supreme court struck down a lucrative pricing arrangement for Stephens's Arkansas Louisiana Gas Company (ARKLA)—one that Faubus's complaisant Public Service Commission (PSC) had approved—the legislature, equally complaisant, overruled the court and passed a law reinstalling the pricing arrangement. The entire exercise, from the court decision to the governor's signature on the new law, took only a week. Stephens got the same friendly reception when his various enterprises needed official help on other matters. For example, bonds for municipalities, school districts, and other public bodies were almost always handled through Stephens, Inc., or one of its allies.

For Faubus, the alliance provided vital support during the increasingly expensive election campaigns that he was obliged to run. Stephens not only contributed heavily to Faubus's campaigns, but he also cajoled, conned, and arm-twisted his many wealthy friends around the state and persuaded them to throw their collective weight behind Faubus. With the wealth of the Stephens combine behind him, Faubus became almost unbeatable. Faubus spread the benefits to his friends. An ally who headed the state Democratic Party became the lawyer for a large Stephens gas company in Fort Smith.[9] A number of Faubus administration officials, including members of the governor's staff, became owners of cheap ARKLA stock before the stock price, inspired by action of the PSC, increased substantially.[10]

Among the most reluctant power bases to come around to Faubus was the Arkansas Power and Light Company (AP and L). AP and L had had its way with the state's politics for many years. Governor Francis A. Cherry had been the latest in a long series of public figures who had been in the utility's debt. He found the association so congenial that he raised no objection when AP and L, with customary arrogance but uncharacteristic ineptness, raised its electric rates during the 1954 election campaign. Faubus leapt on the issue. He had already come to the utility's attention as a gnatlike irritant several years earlier when he had had the gall to editorialize in his *Madison County Record* against the company and in favor of publicly owned electric cooperatives. Now that he was governor, Faubus knew that he could expect no favors from the power company.

The flexible Witt Stephens had become a Faubus man in a matter of hours after the voters turned out his man Cherry in the Democratic primary. The men who ran AP and L were more stiff-necked. It took a while for them to absorb the new reality. Within one eighteen-month period during Faubus's first term, the Public Service Commission—not yet dominated by Faubus, but certainly alert to his growing power—granted two rate increases to Stephens's gas company. One of those allowed Stephens to sharply boost his rates to AP and L for the gas used in power generation. The power company objected, to no avail. During the same eighteen months, AP and L applied to the PSC for two increases of its own. It was turned down each time. When the power company persisted and applied a third time, the commission finally allowed it a fraction of its requested increase—just enough, it turned out, to pay for the rise in its gas bill. Witt Stephens made no secret of his satisfaction at lining his pockets with money from his adversaries at AP and L.

It can be argued that Faubus, with Stephens providing the goad, broke the generations-long dominance of AP and L over the state of Arkansas. Once the men in charge there understood their new situation, they lined up behind the hillbilly governor. Years later, Faubus could speak of the men at AP and L with friendly warmth. They became good corporate citizens, he said, with no discernible trace of triumph in his face.

There were many others from the moneyed establishment whom he came to count as supporters and in some cases social friends. They included builders, developers, insurance and real estate executives, bond dealers, road builders, heavy machinery sellers, printing company owners, newspaper publishers, and high-powered lawyers. They also included a disproportionate share of the wealthy landowners of the plantation country. These last helped to push the Socialist-reared, egalitarian man from the hills in an unexpected direction on the most explosive domestic issue of the mid-twentieth century.

Race had been the defining quality in southern politics from the beginning. A dominant consideration of the white leaders of the Deep South had been to assure the subordination of the black population. The issue might lie dormant for long years, then erupt when something threatened the racial equilibrium. Much of the Middle and Upper South was not dominated directly by the race issue, but such was the political strength and determination of the low-country black belt—"a skeleton holding together the South," V. O. Key called it—that all of the region was in its grip.[11]

The populist revolt divided the hills from the black belt. The latter allied itself with the conservative business forces in the cities and towns to beat down the radicals flourishing in the hills. That schism continued into the twentieth century. Rebellion simmered in the uplands, but the lowlands seldom lost control of the state governments. Alabama might throw up a Hugo Black or a Jim Folsom, but the "big mules" of the cities and the planters of the black belt finally dominated. The same was true in Arkansas. The hills produced political figures of prominence—J. W. Fulbright, Brooks Hays, J. W. Trimble, Clyde Ellis, Sid McMath—but none of them succeeded without the support of the powerful forces of the delta and their business allies. Any who resisted those forces were punished.

Faubus was the latest in a line of hill-country progressives. The delta landowners were suspicious of him. In the early 1950s, few questioned their ability to punish their opponents at the state capital. And yet there were signs that Arkansas was beginning to turn away from the delta domination and toward a more racially neutral politics. Key, writing in the late 1940s, thought that Arkansas, along with Texas and Florida, seemed destined to develop a non-southern sort of politics, one no longer ruled by the negative influence of race.[12] On the other hand, there was no doubt that race still had the power to inflame large numbers of white voters, and not just in the lowlands. In Arkansas, Jim Johnson demonstrated as late as the gubernatorial campaign of 1956 that white feelings were still intense, especially in the wake of the 1954 Supreme Court decision requiring school desegregation. Indeed, it was

Johnson's strong showing against him in 1956 that persuaded Faubus to pay more attention to the voice from the delta.

But if anyone had been listening for nuance and not simply volume in that voice, he might have detected a note of weakness and even desperation. From the beginning, it had been the white fear of being overrun by blacks that had inspired the success of the delta's political oppression. The term "black belt" referred to a swath of southern counties where African Americans had a majority of the population. Arkansas, admittedly one of the least "threatened" states, had fifteen counties with black majorities in 1900. That number declined steadily as the century wore on: eleven in 1920, then nine in 1940.[13] By 1950, the state had only six counties where blacks predominated.[14] Yet those six counties, relying on the racism of varying virulence to be found in Little Rock and elsewhere, effectively imposed their politics of race on the other sixty-nine counties. Looking back across these forty years, racial fear seems to have been given more authority than it deserved. Alongside the numerical decline in the black "threat," the state was becoming increasingly urban and presumably more politically sophisticated. It was also poised to industrialize and prosper. Altogether, Arkansas was just at the take-off stage in both politics and economics and might have been expected finally to cast off the burden of racial politics. Thanks to a convergence of currents, national and local, it did not.

What happened is well-known. The Little Rock School District was ready to desegregate its first public school in the fall of 1957. A few other Arkansas districts, bowing to the Supreme Court's *Brown* decision of 1954, had already taken that step, and Faubus had accepted their decisions. He balked at Little Rock. Saying he had reason to fear violence if the plan went forward, he ordered out the National Guard to block the nine black pupils assigned to Central High. President Dwight D. Eisenhower sent army troops to suppress segregationist mobs, protect the black youngsters, and enforce the authority of the federal courts that had ordered desegregation. The event dominated headlines for months, not only in Arkansas but around the world. Faubus, by creating a precedent in Little Rock for more forceful federal intervention in the South, probably hastened the end of the southern resistance to black civil rights. His action also ensured him six two-year terms as governor and earned him a reputation, fairly or not, as a sellout to the politics of fear that had been exploited long and effectively by the delta planters.

It might be argued that Orval Faubus captured the delta as certainly as the delta captured him; that the influence of the lowlands was on the wane, and that this canny hill man stepped in at the historically propitious moment and took over the whole state, the delta included. Not much stretch of his sympathies was required. He had always felt warmly toward the poor people of his own section. It was easy to include the poor white people of the delta, along with their betters, in his affections. That his sympathies were not expansive enough to include a public declaration of friendship for the poor black people of the delta might have seemed to him a small price to pay. In any event, a kind of regional harmony ensued that Arkansas had not seen since the swamps were slashed and burned and turned into plantations, to be worked and in a perverse way dominated by slaves and the fear they engendered. For the first time, lowlanders and hill people were not competing for control of the capital. They shared control of the governor's office and, through the harmony Faubus imposed, the legislature, as well.

The race issue, after its last sensational eruption in 1957, finally lost its grip on the Arkansas mind. With the election of Winthrop Rockefeller, the aberrant moderate Republican who succeeded Faubus, the black population pretty well ceased to exercise the power of fear that it had had on the state's politics throughout its history. Black voters achieved this paradoxical loss of control through the happy circumstance of becoming important in the state's electoral system. They had voted in some numbers for several years, but those in the delta had had no real choice on election day. Rockefeller brought blacks into the system in large numbers, voting more or less freely and in any case jubilantly, although there were those who claimed that the millionaire New Yorker voted his blacks as surely as any delta planter ever had. The difference was this: Rockefeller made it worthwhile financially, in some cases, to vote right; the old planter voting his field hands had made voting right a condition of employment.

Before Rockefeller, no statewide candidate who was perceived as soft on the Negro question could attain and hold office if any creditable opponent insisted on exploiting that softness. Since Rockefeller, no candidate has achieved any lasting success without the approval of black voters. Interestingly enough, that change began during the last years of Faubus's administration. He quietly achieved a rapprochement with many black leaders, including L. C. Bates, the husband of his old nemesis, Daisy Bates, who led the Arkansas branch of the NAACP. L. C. Bates frequently offered advice to Faubus during the mid-1960s and on at least one occasion, according to Faubus, urged him to run for reelection.[15] The Faubus administration also supported a reform of the voter registration laws that paved the way for relieving delta planters of the burden of buying thousands of poll taxes and trucking all those black workers to the polls every election day.

Faubus accommodated to the prevailing political realities, as he saw them. He continued into old age to insist that he was a true liberal, meaning a New Dealer. But he kept up a running flirtation with Republicans and conservatives during the decades following his tenure in office. He offered advice to such Republicans as John Connally of Texas and Representative John Paul Hammerschmidt of Arkansas.[16] He had friendly contacts with the Nixon White House and expressed his gratification that Nixon had carried Arkansas in

1972.[17] He was friendly with the conservative administration of Harding College, a Searcy, Arkansas, institution connected to the Church of Christ.[18] He was active in the presidential campaign of George C. Wallace in 1968.

Did Faubus betray his father's idealism when he abandoned the left wing and opted for the more conservative mainstream? This is a more difficult question than it appears to be at a glance. Answering it requires going beyond historical evidence and making a speculative leap of judgment. The heart of the question is this: What kind of Socialist was Sam Faubus? Was he a revolutionary Marxist who would have been at home in Eastern Europe? Or was his socialism more American, that is, more diluted? Even some of America's Socialists were fairly dedicated Marxists; was Sam one of those? If Sam Faubus wanted to overthrow the American capitalist system and install a government-controlled economy, then how could he bear to see his famous son become an established part of the system he hated? But if Sam was actually a populist who liked to call himself a Socialist, then his son's success would have pleased him.

While the more determined Socialists worked for a fundamental change in the economic system, many populists merely raged against its inequities. Remove whatever was causing them momentary discontent—unfair banking practices, railroad domination, trusts—and large numbers of the populist farmers would subside and let capitalism go on its way.[19]

It is hard to know what to make of Sam's beliefs. They probably fell somewhere between populist and socialist. On the one hand, he could write with apparent earnestness, after Franklin D. Roosevelt became president, "This country is owned and controlled by a few bankers and other capitalists and the quicker Mr. Roosevelt takes over all industry the better it will be for the country."[20] During the same season, his friend and fellow Socialist Arch Cornett was denouncing private ownership by "the few" of mines, mills, shops, storehouses, transportation lines, steamship lines, and electric light and water systems.[21] Whether these Madison County Socialists seriously advocated government ownership of those enterprises is not clear, but it seems fair to infer that they did.

On the other hand, southwestern Socialists like these, while generally more emotionally volatile than their comrades in other regions, tended to be less intellectually doctrinaire.[22] At times, it appeared that they would have been satisfied with a thoroughgoing reform, rather than a radical rebuilding, of the economic and political system. They were a little like their hero Eugene V. Debs. He embraced socialism gradually, like a swimmer entering a spring-fed pool. Debs had begun as a Democrat and a craft unionist. Then he supported the Populist Party in 1896 before joining Victor L. Berger to organize the Social Democratic Party. That was the forerunner of the Socialist Party, on whose platform he ran four times for president. The Socialists of Arkansas, Texas, Oklahoma, and Missouri idolized the fiery but undoctrinaire Debs.[23]

The platform of Arkansas's own Socialist Party contained the usual railings against an unjust economic system, but it also carried a number of reform ideas that in time would be considered middle-of-the-road. Socialists in Arkansas opposed the death penalty and corruption in elections. They favored the initiative and referendum, women's suffrage, and the graduated income tax.[24] Sam Faubus worked hard for those reforms. How hard he would have fought in an armed revolution to overthrow the government is anybody's guess. I think he would have stopped far short of that. He was willing to go to prison for his beliefs when he agitated against World War I—and almost did—but I have trouble seeing him at the barricades trying to bring down the government of Calvin Coolidge. Once Roosevelt launched the New Deal, which ameliorated some of the discontents that Sam had suffered, he became a New Dealer. By the time of John F. Kennedy's presidency, he was an enthusiastic Democrat.

Orval became as devoted a New Dealer as his father. The New Deal may seem quaint to today's young liberals, but in its time it stirred fierce emotions. Those emotions had not subsided entirely by the time Orval Faubus became governor. He spent substantially of his political capital to move Arkansas along in its own version of the New Deal, a movement that had been pursued fitfully in the state during the previous twenty years. Faubus most notably stood up to powerful forces—including those of the delta—and pushed through the legislature a 50 percent increase in the sales tax to finance improved education and other state services. He brought more compassion to the state welfare system. He was generally friendly to labor. He spent state funds generously to improve the lot of the mentally ill and retarded. These and other accomplishments are what he had in mind when he described himself as a true liberal, as opposed to the present-day liberal who is concerned—unduly, Faubus believed—with the rights of various cultural, racial, ethnic, and sexual minorities.

One final question remains: If Orval Faubus did not betray his father and the father's idealism, did he then betray his own class? Probably not. The populist, hill-country class that he came from is always ready to forgive the person who escapes it. Far from seeing escape as betrayal of one's fellows, as it was and to some extent remains in the more class-encrusted nations of Europe, rising from one's class is seen with approval in America. David Shannon put it this way: "Americans have generally believed it easier and more desirable to rise *from* their class rather than *with* their class."[25] Orval Faubus escaped into the world he had dreamed of as a boy, a world of fame, power, and material comfort. He never came close to entering the traditional establishment, but there is no doubt that he learned to traffic with the capitalists and power brokers that his father had hated. It could be argued that far from betraying his class, he fulfilled its secret yearnings.

DIVERSITY WITHIN A RACIAL GROUP

White People in Little Rock, 1957–1959

David L. Chappell

Diversity has become a buzzword. It conveys a desire to open institutions of power to previously excluded groups. This is a worthy goal. But in today's discussions, diversity carries a meaning so restricted as to undermine this goal. In the national media, the word now refers almost exclusively to racial and ethnic diversity, implying that a skin-deep racial and ethnic diversity will guarantee diversity of cultural and philosophical perspectives. Stephen Carter, an African American law professor and author, complained recently: "In the new rhetoric of affirmative action, it seems, the reason to seek out and hire or admit people of color is that one can have faith that their opinions, their perspective, will be different from the opinion and perspectives of people who are white—who evidently have a distinctive set of views of their own."[1]

The assumption that black people automatically think differently from white people and that white people think more or less alike—that any given collection of white people lacks diversity—pervades discussions of diversity. This is not necessarily a mark of racial prejudice on the part of those who advocate diversity. One may assume, without prejudice, that American culture is still strictly segregated. But the assumption of intraracial homogeneity may still be incorrect. The best way to test that assumption is to look at a situation in the past that appears to be extremely polarized between black and white, as in the American South during the first two decades after World War II, when intellectuals and other commentators in the national media portrayed white southerners as uniformly provincial and close-minded.[2]

This essay first appeared in the winter 1995 issue of the *Arkansas Historical Quarterly*.

55

Little Rock was the scene of the most dramatic confrontation between black and white in the South before the mid-1960s. So polarized and dangerous did the issue become there that federal troops were sent to maintain order. But even in this most dramatic struggle, there was actually great diversity within the white racial group. Although the extreme segregationists in Little Rock insisted that all white people had a common interest, white people never actually coalesced. Their diversity explains why the outcome of the crisis was different from what the segregationists planned. Ironically, northern liberals shared the segregationist assumption, at least insofar as it applied to *southern* white people. The racial mythology of southern segregationists and northern liberals (still alive in discussions of diversity today) blinded them to the divisions among white people. As things worked out in Little Rock, those divisions made the segregationist consensus impossible to sustain in the face of an integrationist attack, even though the attack in this case came from a small group of integrationists with no mass support.

White diversity in Little Rock revealed itself in several ways, the most obvious of which was ideological. Though the majority of white people in Little Rock, like white southerners elsewhere, favored segregation, they differed so much in the degree of importance they assigned to segregation that they ended up fighting each other as much as they fought the NAACP.[3] There were three basic divisions. The first group was the extreme segregationists, who circulated lurid propaganda about the secret "race-mixing" desires of integrationists and denounced moderates for cooperating with the Supreme Court. They asserted that the *Brown* decision was unconstitutional and called on the state legislature to nullify it. They attacked moderates for their corruption by Yankee dollars. Their propaganda was often anti-Semitic and anti-Catholic as well as anti-Yankee and anti-elite.[4]

The second group was the moderate segregationists, who granted the basic legality of the *Brown* decision. They sometimes expressed the hope that the Supreme Court would change its mind, but they would have no part of the call to flout federal court orders. Moderates called on the pragmatism of the people, asking them to accept the inevitable: economic development required federal contracts and other subsidies, which in turn required compliance with desegregation orders. Moderates avoided racial slurs and refrained from attributing sexual motives to their opponents. They refused to blame Yankees, recognizing that the industrial development of the state depended on northern capital. Most moderates, including both newspapers, initially supported school superintendent Virgil Blossom's plan for gradual token desegregation. Deep down, some of these moderates may have favored greater desegregation, or they may have feared it as much as the extremists, but their inner motives are not under scrutiny here. What made them moderates was the public stance they took—that defying the law was futile and dangerous and that the Blossom Plan was the least painful way to comply with the law. As the *Arkansas Gazette* put it: "Few of us are entirely happy over the necessary developments in the wake of changes in the law. But certainly we must recognize that the School Board is simply carrying out its clear duty—and is doing so in the ultimate best interests of all the school children of Little Rock, white and colored alike."[5]

The third group was the small but crucial number of white people in Little Rock who openly identified themselves with the cause of desegregation. One local white minister, Dunbar Ogden, accompanied the black students to school on their first day and faced the wrath of the segregationist mob. The same day, Grace Lorch protected one of the black students from the mob, nearly provoking an attack upon herself as a "nigger lover." The Reverend Colbert Cartwright published articles supporting integration in national magazines and blamed moderates for temporizing with segregationists. Cartwright, aided by a few less prominent ministers and some members of the Arkansas Council on Human Relations, also met privately with church groups and civic leaders to encourage desegregation.[6]

These divisions created difficult political choices for state politicians. Governor Orval Faubus, the central character in the drama at Little Rock, became a national symbol of southern white intransigence in the fall of 1957. But Faubus began as a moderate, denouncing an extreme segregationist, Jim Johnson, in the 1956 election campaign and defeating him. Extremist publications, in turn, denounced "Awful Faubus" for cooperating with integration. One such publication went so far as to say that Faubus was a "shrewd politician, well-schooled in the tactics of the communist-fronter."[7] But in August 1957, the extremists recognized that their divisive tactics marginalized them, and they courted Faubus, hoping to legitimize their cause. Upon learning that Faubus had ordered the Arkansas National Guard to surround Central High, Roy Harris, a White Citizens' Council leader, recalled, "I sat there . . . just scratching my head and wondering if he called 'em out *for* us, or *agin'* us."[8] As the guard's segregationist mission became clear, "Awful Faubus" became "Orval Fabulous," a segregationist hero. The extremist whom Faubus had defeated in 1956 said, "He used my nickel and hit the jackpot."[9]

Religious diversity compounded the ideological diversity. The Catholic Church had its own school system, a hierarchy that was invulnerable to local public opinion, and a history of its own victimization by bigotry. These facts may explain the steps beyond moderation taken by Catholics. Many Catholic churches and schools in the South were already integrated. At least two schools in Arkansas—in Fort Smith and Paris—admitted black students in 1954. The Catholic bishop of Little Rock, Albert Fletcher, made a forthright statement shortly after the *Brown* decision saying that the Court had cleared "the way legally for the church to act more freely in giving to all races the

same benefits." Fletcher said, "It is especially urgent that Catholic Negro children be admitted to any Catholic school available in places where there is no
Catholic school especially for them," and reminded his listeners "that persons
of every race, creed and nation should be made to feel at home in every
Catholic church."[10] On Columbus Day 1957, shortly after the crisis broke out,
nearly one-third of the Catholic population of Little Rock and North Little
Rock turned out for prayer meetings organized to express disagreement with
segregation. A Catholic spokesman said that the reason for the strong turnout
was not Catholics' sympathy for integration but their "respect for authority."[11]

The national and regional Protestant organizations also made statements
supporting desegregation, and initially their affiliated churches in Arkansas
showed signs of following suit. The state Disciples of Christ, for example,
resolved in April 1956 to "exert efforts toward orderly compliance" with desegregation and called upon political candidates to refrain from race-baiting in the
upcoming election campaign. Little Rock's white ministerial alliance (sixty
ministers) integrated itself with the black ministerial alliance (thirty ministers) in April 1956.[12] But Ernest Campbell and Thomas Pettigrew note in their
study of the Little Rock ministry that most of the local Protestant ministers
did not forthrightly lead their congregations in support of desegregation—
even though many believed that segregation was morally wrong. In other
words, they remained moderates. They opposed lawlessness and violence but
feared reaction from their parishioners if they took controversial positions on
principle. Colbert Cartwright lost 10 percent of his church members; preachers
in less liberal churches feared a greater reaction.[13]

There is evidence that at least some church women did not feel so constrained, adding another dimension of diversity along gender lines. The
Council of Church Women of Little Rock and North Little Rock issued a statement expressing "our Christian conviction that enforced segregation of any
group of persons because of race, creed, or color is a violation of Christian
principle. The national and state bodies of the denominations which we represent are all on record with statements saying that the Supreme Court rulings are in keeping with Christian principles." The church women were
"shocked and dismayed that the governor of our state has placed military
troops within our community to defy the order of the federal court."[14]
Women were also disproportionately present at the Columbus Day prayer
meetings.[15] Groups of church women had a degree of freedom that ministers,
constrained by their direct financial dependence on their congregations,
lacked.

Generational differences may have been as important as gender differences. Campbell and Pettigrew's figures indicate that young ministers were
most likely to oppose segregation, sometimes even challenging their congregations. The most effective resistance to pastors who hinted at integrationist

views came from older, more established church members. The young ministers had little influence but voiced sentiments that senior clergymen dared not express.[16]

Setting aside the gender and generational divisions, there was some correlation of denomination with ideology. Vigorous opposition to integration came from independent sects and small Baptist churches affiliated with the American Baptist Association and the Missionary Baptists of Arkansas, rather than with the Southern Baptist Convention (SBC). In a resolution that was adopted by the American Baptist Association, the pastor of Little Rock's Antioch Baptist Church condemned integration as not only ungodly but unlawful.[17] On the other hand, virtually all the Catholic and Episcopal churches, most of the Presbyterian and Methodist churches, and the larger, SBC-affiliated Baptist churches took the moderate position of opposing resistance to the Blossom Plan without explicitly endorsing integration.[18] Sixteen prominent ministers stretched the moderate position by signing a statement strongly protesting Governor Faubus's use of National Guard troops to prevent integration; most of the signers were pastors of Episcopal, Presbyterian, Methodist, and larger SBC-affiliated Baptist churches.[19]

The ideological and denominational divisions derived in large part from a class division. From the start, there was strong opposition to Blossom's desegregation plan among the lower classes. In a March 1957 school board election, opposition to the Blossom Plan came from a minority (about one-third of all voters) concentrated in the working-class wards of the city.[20] The reason was easy to see: the Blossom Plan called for integration of Central High, a predominantly working-class and lower-middle-class school, while leaving the white upper-class high school, Hall High, untouched. The smaller churches opposing integration were generally working-class churches, and they made a point of attacking the hypocrisy of the upper-class church leaders who supported integration of Central and sent their children to Hall.[21]

Generational differences may be important here as well. Prominent students at Central expressed moderation, and students generally seemed much less opposed to integration than their parents—who were publicly represented by a militantly segregationist group, the Mothers' League of Central High. Shortly after classes opened in the fall of 1957, the student body president at Central, Ralph Brodie, was quoted in the news as saying he did not object to sitting next to black students in class. Asked whether he personally thought black students should be admitted immediately, he replied, "Sir, it's the law. We are going to have to face it some time. . . . If it's a court order, we have to follow it and abide by the law."[22] Earlier that year, Brodie had participated in a goodwill effort to help black students to prepare for their entry into the school.[23] Craig Rains, a white senior and student council member, recalled seeing the first black student being harassed by the mob. "I was just dumbfounded," he said. He could not believe "people would actually be this way to other people. I began to change from somebody who was moderate, who if I had my way, would have said, 'Let's don't integrate, because it's the state's right to decide,' to someone who felt a real sense of compassion for these students. I also developed a real dislike for the people that were out there that were causing problems. It was very unsettling to me."[24] Marcia Webb Lecky, a white girl who was secretary of the senior class, later recalled thinking that the federal troops came "because Faubus was causing problems." She said that most of the students at Central "were glad when the resolution came with President Eisenhower taking charge."[25] In December 1957, Daisy Bates, head of the state NAACP and organizer of the integration effort, stated that inside Central High, the nine black students now faced only "scattered" insults and were "comparatively happy." She said that in a school of nineteen hundred students, there were only fifty to one hundred "agitators" who bothered the black students.[26] One white girl told reporters that there was "very little trouble at all" inside the school and that the majority of her classmates were "disgusted" with the white students who protested desegregation by leaving class. Superintendent Blossom remarked that "the majority of students acted with dignity and tact," and one white school administrator at Central said that many white students "spoke words of encouragement to the Negro children and urged them to 'stay and fight it out.'"[27]

When Governor Faubus chose to identify himself with the extreme segregationists, upper-class business leaders were more open to desegregation than the population as a whole. This was partly opportunism. Winthrop Rockefeller, whom Faubus had appointed to the Arkansas Industrial Development Commission, told the Little Rock Women's Republican Club in 1956 that "big industry is shying away from Southern states" because those states were defying the federal government on segregation.[28] As Elizabeth Jacoway shows in her study of Little Rock business leaders, however, most businessmen were slow to follow this logic to its conclusion and, before extreme segregationists insisted on closing the schools in the fall of 1958, contented themselves with quiet statements of respect for the law.[29]

Responding above all to a breakdown of public authority, business leaders did begin to turn against the extreme segregationists. Faubus's decision to block the desegregation plan with armed force, whatever else it did, challenged the authority of the mayor, police chief, and school superintendent of Little Rock. Faubus testified that increased sales of knives and revolvers among Central students justified his interference. Mayor Woodrow Wilson Mann, however, testified that there was no indication there would be violence. Asked about Faubus's testimony, Police Chief Marvin Potts said, "Let's just say I haven't heard what Gov. Faubus says he has heard." Superintendent Blossom said there was no evidence of increased knife and revolver sales in the police information available to him.[30] When Faubus, under pressure from Washington and the federal courts, withdrew the National Guard and violence did break out, Mayor Mann sent a telegram to Washington saying, "The immediate need for federal troops is urgent. . . . Situation is out of control and police cannot disperse the mob."[31] Only after this breakdown of local authority did President Eisenhower send in the federal troops.

With the city occupied, the division between moderate segregationists and extreme segregationists grew. Realizing that desegregation was the only way to restore order, moderates saw that they could put responsibility for desegregation on an authority distant from themselves. Faubus chose to court lower-class voters in Little Rock, who resented this imposition of outside authority on them. This probably helped him in the state as a whole, but in Little Rock it drove the wedge deeper between the governor and rival claimants of public authority in the city.

From that point on, gender differences are crucial to understanding the position of the white upper class. A group called the Women's Emergency Committee to Open Our Schools formed in July 1958 in anticipation of Faubus's order to close the schools. These were mostly college-educated women married to business managers.[32] Like the churchwomen (with whom their membership overlapped), they were not as vulnerable to economic retaliation as their male counterparts.[33] They could afford to take a controversial position that their husbands and ministers could not take. They may also have had unique resources with which to persuade their husbands. Irving Spitzberg suggested a Lysistrata effect when he quoted a news reporter as asking a member of the Women's Emergency Committee, "Irene, did you instruct your girls to withhold sex if their husbands didn't behave?" She answered, "Damn straight," though she later indicated that she was only joking.[34]

Developments in the public eye gave business leaders reason to redefine moderation as active defense of desegregated schools. In September 1958, sixty-three prominent lawyers declared in a paid advertisement their view that Faubus's effort to operate the schools as private institutions was illegal. They defined the issue as either "a limited integrated school system" or "no public school system."[35] Disorder and school closings hurt business. Investment in new and expanded plants in Arkansas dropped from $130 million in 1956, to $50 million in 1957, to $25 million in 1958.[36]

Segregationism, meanwhile, became associated not only with lower-class resentments but with disorder and violence—all bad for business. The extreme segregationists drove moderates into de facto support of desegregation. Business leaders—often led by their wives—rallied to the cause of keeping the schools open. A new group, Stop This Outrageous Purge (STOP), which was formed at a meeting of some two hundred businessmen, protested the mass firing of forty-four teachers and administrators who had supported the Blossom Plan.[37] The initiative behind STOP came from a Parent-Teacher Association chapter in Pulaski Heights. Two prominent upper-class women were the main organizers. Soon prominent upper-class men joined in, with the industrial director of the Little Rock Chamber of Commerce campaigning for reopened schools and making mildly explicit statements in favor of deseg-regation.[38] The Chamber of Commerce polled its membership and found that 819 favored, while only 245 opposed, "reopening the Little Rock public high schools on a controlled minimum plan of integration acceptable to the federal courts" (83 did not vote). In March 1959, the Chamber of Commerce issued a statement:

> The decision of the Supreme Court of the United States, however much we dislike it, is the declared law and is binding on us. We think that the decision was erroneous and that it was a reversal of established law upon an unprecedented base of psychology and sociology. But we must in honesty recognize that, because the Supreme Court is the court of last resort in this country, what it has said must stand until there is a correcting constitutional amendment or until the Court corrects its own error. We must live and act now under the decision of the Court.[39]

By May 1959, the leader of STOP said that the fear that had kept business and professional men like himself from taking a public stance, because a stance would hurt business, had vanished.[40] A coalition of black and upper-class white voters drove the extreme segregationists off the school board in a recall election that month.

When schools reopened in the fall of 1959, local authority reasserted itself. Little Rock police made twenty-four arrests and used billy clubs and fire hoses to disperse the mob that gathered to resist the reentry of black students. The extreme segregationists retaliated by bombing the fire chief's car and the offices of the mayor and the school superintendent.[41] Terrorism, predictably, thinned the support for defiance of desegregation even further.

The bombings were the most extreme example of the segregationists' divisive tactics. These tactics exacerbated the divisions among the white people of Little Rock, but they did not create those divisions. The Blossom Plan, by aiming at a lower-class school, drove the first wedge between social classes in the city. The moderates' hesitation and lack of conviction probably encouraged Faubus to move boldly against the plan's implementation. But in doing so, he became associated with extreme tactics. The extremists alienated large numbers of moderates, who wanted segregation but did not want disorder. The extremists gained the governor as a de facto ally and helped his political career, but they also drove Little Rock's economic and political leaders into a de facto alliance with the NAACP. They put the NAACP in the position of standing for the most conservative goals, including law and order and a good investment climate. Even the governor could not completely associate himself with the extremists but clung to his position as a protector. The school closings, the purge, and the bombings, though worth the trouble to those who held segregation to be a sacred principle, were too much for those who held segregation as just one priority among many.

White diversity was especially important in Little Rock because there was less black solidarity there than in any other major civil rights battle in the 1950s and early 1960s. The movement in Little Rock was a top-down effort coordinated by the local NAACP leader Daisy Bates, rather than a church-based mass movement. Bates indicated that she was isolated. She said that her friends stopped coming to see her during the crisis, because they were afraid.[42] Although Kenneth Clark reported an increased unity and resolve in the black community because of the crisis, Bates knew the unity was fragile.[43] "If one black child had died," she said years later, "the black community would have chased me out of town." Her position was precarious because local black people saw her as an "outsider," who was "stirring up trouble."[44]

Against that background, had there been greater white solidarity, the segregationists' position would have been secure. Instead, there was enough diversity among the white people for the civil rights forces to gain a limited victory. The most important aspect of that victory was not the token desegregation of Central High School but the decision of the federal government to intervene. Without the conflict and resulting breakdown of local authority, the extremely cautious President Eisenhower would not have taken the risk. Eisenhower's move set a precedent, pitting the executive branch of the federal government against the states' righters. The popularity the defiant governor gained among resentful lower-class voters also set a precedent, one that encouraged other governors to provoke federal intervention in other states.

POWER FROM THE PEDESTAL

*The Women's Emergency Committee
and the Little Rock School Crisis*

Lorraine Gates

In the spring of 1957, Little Rock was, by most accounts, a thriving and progressive southern city. In the postwar decade, the city's leaders vigorously pursued a plan of economic development, and race relations were considered good and improving.[1] In voluntary compliance with the Supreme Court's 1954 *Brown* decision, Little Rock School District officials developed a desegregation plan, and an NAACP representative referred to Little Rock as "the bright spot of the South" in terms of school desegregation.[2] Thus, as the first day of school approached in 1957, no one anticipated that Little Rock would become an international symbol of racism and massive resistance.

On September 2, 1957, just hours before the start of the new school year, Arkansas governor Orval Faubus ordered the National Guard to surround Central High School to prevent integration. For three weeks, Faubus defied a federal court order to proceed with integration, and President Eisenhower ultimately had to send troops from the 101st Airborne Division to Little Rock to ensure that nine black students would be allowed to attend school. The paratroopers occupied the high school for several months, and federalized National Guardsmen remained in the halls of Central High School for the entire school year.

The end of the school year, however, provided little relief for the city. While school officials worked to delay integration, Faubus traveled the state,

---

This article first appeared in the spring 1996 issue of the *Arkansas Historical Quarterly*.

campaigning for reelection as an ardent segregationist. Emboldened by his Democratic primary victory in late July, Faubus called a special session of the legislature, which granted him the power to close schools that fall to prevent integration.

On Friday, September 12, 1958, the U.S. Supreme Court ordered the Little Rock School District to proceed with integration. In response, Governor Faubus immediately closed all of the city's public high schools. As the governor signed this school-closing legislation, three white women gathered in an antebellum mansion just a few blocks from the state capitol. There, beneath the portrait of her father in Confederate uniform, Adolphine Terry sat with Vivion Brewer and Velma Powell, laying the groundwork for the first effective opposition to the city's segregationists. Four days later, they founded the Women's Emergency Committee to Open Our Schools (WEC). In the ensuing months, the women of the WEC publicly challenged the segregationists at every turn, and their actions were instrumental in the defeat of the extremists and the reopening of the city schools.

Although the WEC was the first organized white opposition to the city's segregationists and was central to the resolution of the school crisis, no study of the organization exists. Few accounts have even mentioned the WEC, in part because much of the secondary material on the Little Rock experience is contained in larger works on school desegregation or civil rights.[3] Within such broad surveys, Little Rock is treated as merely one episode in a continuing saga of resistance. Moreover, even in the literature devoted specifically to Little Rock, most studies focus on the first year of the crisis (1957–58), when federal troops occupied Central High and the dramatic conflict between Governor Faubus and President Eisenhower tested the power of the federal government to enforce the Supreme Court's decision.[4] Only a few authors have studied the second year of the crisis, when the power struggles were local and the WEC occupied center stage.

In *The Little Rock Recall Election*, Henry Alexander examines the climactic event in the city's school crisis and makes the first scholarly reference to the WEC in his discussion of the organization's role in the 1959 recall campaign.[5] However, his study gives little information about the membership of the WEC or its development prior to the election. In "Taken by Surprise," Elizabeth Jacoway provides an important introduction to the social origins of the WEC, but her focus is on the failure of Little Rock's civic leadership during the crisis, and she therefore does not provide a full discussion of the WEC's activities.[6] The only work that addresses the development of the WEC and its relationship with other groups in the community is Irving Spitzberg's *Racial Politics in Little Rock*.[7] Nevertheless, Spitzberg did not intend to study the WEC itself, and thus he did not answer several principal questions: Who were these women? What motivated them to form the WEC? What did they accomplish, and how did prevailing notions about appropriate gender roles affect their organization?

In the early days of the crisis, some of Little Rock's leaders attempted to challenge the governor and his segregationist supporters. Mayor Woodrow Wilson Mann condemned Faubus's use of National Guardsmen, as did fifteen ministers from local white churches.[8] Congressman Brooks Hays arranged negotiations between Governor Faubus and President Eisenhower in an attempt to resolve the crisis and repeatedly called for a return to "the rule of law."[9] Just days after the crisis began, the editor of the *Arkansas Gazette* lamented:

> Until last Thursday the matter of gradual, limited integration in the Little Rock schools was a local problem which had been well and wisely handled by responsible local officials who have had—and we believe still have—the support of a majority of people of this city. On that day Mr. Faubus appeared in Chancery Court on behalf of a small but militant minority and chose to make it a state problem. On Monday night he called out the National Guard and made it a national problem. It is one he must now live with, and the rest of us must suffer under.[10]

In the ensuing weeks, the *Arkansas Gazette* made almost daily appeals for a return to law and order. Meanwhile, Little Rock School District superintendent Virgil Blossom continued to urge compliance with court orders to desegregate. Yet Little Rock's business leaders remained noticeably silent.

In his study of the actions of these men during the crisis, Spitzberg has persuasively argued that Little Rock's business leaders "had traditionally exercised a great deal of influence over public policy. . . . These 'civic' leaders had established a long tradition of activism in Little Rock and [when they felt secure in their actions] demonstrated the ability to use economic, social and political power effectively. . . . These men 'could make decisions' because of their economic and social position in the community."[11] As one local minister put it, "These men are the core of the power structure. If they decide to do anything, they can do it."[12] Yet with the exception of a single feeble attempt, when faced with the school crisis, these men made the decision to remain silent.[13]

At the outset of the crisis, segregationists embarked on an intimidation campaign to silence the opposition. Threatening phone calls and hate mail barraged Mayor Mann and Superintendent Blossom. The segregationist Capital Citizens' Council circulated a petition to recall Mayor Mann and police officials who had assisted in the integration of Central High.[14] Outspoken ministers risked "decreased contributions, lowered attendance and even removal."[15] Central High School officials received harassing phone calls, and white students who showed kindness to the black students were often ostracized and threatened.[16]

The most important weapons in the segregationists' arsenal, however, were economic. They waged a boycott against the *Arkansas Gazette* that cost the paper both a million dollars and its comfortable lead over the rival *Arkansas Democrat*. Any business that advertised with the *Gazette* was explicitly threatened with reprisals, and segregationists even warned mothers of *Gazette* paperboys that some harm might come to their sons if they continued delivering the paper.[17] Businessmen feared segregationist-led boycotts and, more important, reprisals from the powerful economic interests surrounding the governor.[18] As editor Harry Ashmore put it, the boycott against the *Gazette* "provided an object lesson for any who doubted the governor's willingness to use his office to support the Citizens' Councils."[19]

Although the moderate business leaders who had helped Little Rock earn its reputation for racial tolerance remained in positions of authority, a McCarthyite atmosphere pervaded the city. Few men had the courage to oppose the well-organized, vocal segregationists, who attacked a desegregationist stance, even a public stand for law and order, as unpatriotic and communistic. "Integrationist" was an epithet applied to anyone advocating desegregation, and integrationists risked their reputations, their livelihoods, and even their physical safety.

It was in the context of this repression that Adolphine Terry invited Vivion Brewer and Velma Powell to her home to discuss the worsening school crisis. In 1958, Mrs. Terry was seventy-six years old. The daughter of a slaveholder and Confederate officer, she was the wife of a New Deal congressman and a member of Little Rock's most prominent family. She was by far the most influential woman in the community. Born and raised in Arkansas, Terry attended Vassar College and lived for several years in Washington. Though she worked for various national causes, including the women's suffrage movement, she had a particular commitment to improving her home state of Arkansas. Her devotion to the state was so strong that she was said to have described it as "holy ground."[20]

In Little Rock, she was a leader in the founding of the symphony orchestra, public libraries, and the juvenile court system. She was also one of the few white women willing to serve as an advisor to the local black chapter of the Young Women's Christian Association (YWCA) and was active in many interracial organizations designed to promote tolerance. One close friend recalled that Terry "felt community issues more strongly than most," which led her to assume a leading role in the resolution of the school crisis.[21]

Throughout the first year of the crisis, she had worked behind the scenes, meeting with school officials, business leaders, and the governor's wife to promote a peaceful resolution of the conflict. By September 1958, however, she had wearied of the "prolonged silence of the city fathers."[22] Using the Association of Southern Women for the Prevention of Lynching as a model, Terry recruited Brewer and Powell to form an interracial organization to educate the community in racial tolerance.[23]

In calling for the creation of such an organization, Terry became the segregationists' primary target. They had succeeded in silencing the city's traditional civic leadership and intended to use a campaign of intimidation to prevent the organization of a moderate opposition. Terry's unique status in the community, however, made her virtually immune to such tactics. In fact, her unrivaled influence was essential in the success of the opposition. As one WEC member put it, "Mrs. Terry had money, family, power and guts, and it took somebody in that position to get the WEC going."[24] Terry was independently wealthy and so prominent that few believed the segregationists' attacks against her.[25] One local attorney noted, "Even though people didn't agree with what she was doing, they didn't want to come out against her because she'd done so much good in the community."[26] There was perhaps no other person in Little Rock who could have organized the first stand against the segregationists and made such opposition legitimate.

On September 16, 1958, over fifty women gathered at the Terry mansion for the first meeting of what was to become the WEC.[27] Through determined effort, the membership of the WEC grew from an initial fifty-eight to nearly fourteen hundred by May 1959.[28] In early 1960, the WEC conducted a survey of its members, most of whom had joined the organization during the first few months of its existence. More than half of the members responded to this anonymous survey, and the leaders' diligence in their efforts to ensure accuracy yielded a very useful profile of the general membership.[29] According to this survey, the vast majority of WEC members were under fifty years of age, married, had children, and had lived in Arkansas or the South for over twenty years. Most WEC families had annual incomes of over eighty-five hundred dollars and owned their own homes. Twenty percent reported incomes of over fifteen thousand dollars. More than a third were country club members, and nearly all were active in civic or religious organizations. An amazing 82 percent of the members had attended at least one year of college, and 20 percent had done some postgraduate work. Interestingly, the majority of those members who had attended college had done so outside the state, as had their husbands. The vast majority of members had also held jobs outside the home before they were married, although fewer than one quarter of the members were employed at the time of the survey.[30]

These statistics stand in sharp contrast to the census figures for Arkansas.[31] In 1959, the average Arkansas family earned $3,184, less than half of the average WEC family earnings. Even when compared with the average family income for white Americans during this period, WEC family incomes were nearly 33 percent higher. Furthermore, the median years of school completed for white females in 1959 was eleven, whereas more than 80 percent of WEC members had attended college. Given that Arkansas traditionally ranks well below the national average in measures of education, the educational attainment of the WEC members was probably even more unusual than these figures suggest.

The survey also indicated that WEC members differed from the rest of the community in their religious affiliations. The most striking revelation is that only 9 percent of the members were Baptist, although nearly half of all the white congregants in Little Rock belonged to a Baptist church. The majority of WEC members were Methodist or Presbyterian. While Methodists joined the WEC in proportion to their numbers in the community, Presbyterians, who represented just 7 percent of the city's white churchgoers, constituted nearly a third of the membership. Little Rock's tiny Jewish and Episcopalian communities were also overrepresented in the WEC.

WEC leaders conducted this membership survey to counter accusations that the organization was composed of outsiders who had no children in the schools and no legitimate interest in the school crisis. Finding that the vast majority were mothers and longtime residents, WEC leaders felt they had "justif[ied] the Committee position in community disagreements on school affairs."[32] However, the survey also confirmed critics' assertions that the WEC represented a small minority of the entire community. As noted above, WEC members were better educated and wealthier than the vast majority of Arkansans. Critics accurately charged that most lived in the exclusive Heights section of Little Rock, an area they referred to as the "silk stocking district."[33] Alluding to their wealth and status, Faubus and other segregationist leaders described the WEC members as the "charge of the Cadillac Brigade."[34] Women's Emergency Committee leaders responded, "If it is to be argued that we are only a small group in the community, it can also be argued that we are a group whose opinion should have considerable weight."[35] That may have been true, but the WEC undeniably represented a small minority of the city's women.

As native southerners, however, they shared widely held expectations about the proper role and duties of a southern white woman. As Sara Evans noted in *Personal Politics*, "The bonds of white womanhood had stretched enough [by the 1930s] to allow a growing level of public activity and social concern, but they were far from broken."[36] Interviews with Little Rock women indicate that most of these white women were raised with the belief that their primary roles in life would be wife and mother.[37] Several remarked that college was just a way to spend time before marriage, and all stressed the importance of community good works.[38] Irene Samuel, an officer in the WEC, remembered that she and her sister were such good students that her father used to say, "It's a shame you were born girls."[39] Kathryn Lambright, a WEC volunteer, described the expectations of a southern woman: "I was never encouraged to pursue anything other than [to] be a wife, mother, have lovely manners. . . . Training in all the social amenities but nothing on training your mind for skills in other areas. . . . A Southern lady is . . . submissive, always gentle spoken, well groomed, versed in social amenities . . . [and] Southern ladies should be conformists."[40] Given these societal expectations, it at first seems surprising that a group like the WEC would form with a membership of upper-class southern white women. However, the membership and work of the WEC conform to a pattern of reform movements throughout American history that have been dominated by white women of the leisure class.[41]

At first glance, it seems incongruous that elite women have dominated social-reform movements, as their class status ensured that they had more to lose by challenging the status quo. However, as Evans and other scholars have noted, working-class women were struggling with issues of basic subsistence and often lacked the luxury to devote time and attention to changing their society.[42] It was not simply an increase in leisure time that led elite women to work for social reform, however. An emphasis on women as moral guardians led many to social action as an outgrowth of the church, and increasing opportunities for education led women to work for social reform as an intellectual outlet.[43] For southern reformers, education played a particularly important role, as it afforded women the opportunity to experience life outside the rigid confines of the segregated South.

Though denied access to traditional means of political action and limited by contemporary sex-role proscriptions, these women used race, class status, education, and an expanded notion of women's role as moral guardians to justify their participation in social reform. Like women reformers of the past, members of the WEC were well educated, upper-class white women with strong connections to Protestant churches. Conforming to traditional patterns of women's reform movements, the intersection of race, class, and gender placed the women of the WEC in a uniquely powerful position in the fall of 1958.

Faced with harassment, threats, social ostracism, and severe economic reprisals, Little Rock's traditional male leadership had been intimidated into silence. Reverend Dunbar Ogden had lost his pulpit as a result of his outspokenness, and the segregationist-led boycott of the *Arkansas Gazette* had served as a strict warning to others. As one WEC member recalled: "For a man to endanger his business and jeopardize his family to all of the threats and things that went on . . . they would have been thought to be foolish to put their family at such risks, and irresponsible."[44] Upper-class white women, however, had little to fear from such economic reprisals. They were not employed outside the home and were not responsible for the economic well-being of their families. Though their husbands were occasionally told, "shut your wife up," most employers accepted that husbands did not have complete control over their wives.[45]

In addition to this protection from economic reprisals, class status provided the women of the WEC with tools for organization. As with earlier women reformers, it provided them leisure time to devote to the organization. Their wealth also ensured the financial stability of the group. Not only could WEC members personally contribute more to the organization, but they could raise money more easily because they knew wealthy people. This issue of access is perhaps the most important benefit of class. As wives of the civic elite, they could make personal appeals to community leaders for funding and eventually for a public stand against the segregationists.

Their wealth could not protect them, however, from threats, harassment, and social ostracism. As soon as the WEC was formed, its leaders began to receive harassing phone calls. Irene Samuel was on the Wednesday- and Saturday-night hate list, and on those nights she received threatening phone calls every fifteen minutes.[46] The women were accused of being "nigger lovers," "race mixers," and "communists." The hate mail poured in, and one woman even threatened to burn down Terry's home.[47] Brewer was a favorite target of the segregationists, not only because she was president of the WEC but also because she lived in a rural area outside of Little Rock and had no children, her only child having died very young. Perceived by segregationists as an outsider, she received numerous death threats, which were all the more troubling because she lived in an isolated area.

Though the hate mail, death threats, and harassing phone calls were directed primarily against the WEC leaders, most of the women who joined faced social ostracism. Given the importance of hospitality and social networking among elite white women in the South, this was not an insignificant repercussion. In the membership survey, fully one-third of the women responded that relations with their neighbors had been changed by the crisis, suggesting that few or none of their neighbors shared their views on the school crisis.[48] Every member interviewed recalled losing longtime friends over this issue, as well as being subjected to a "great coolness" in social settings.[49] Many women who were sympathetic with the cause refused to join or gave only anonymous cash donations for fear of community reprisals. The membership files indicate the degree of intimidation women faced, as members were divided into categories of regular members, members who did not want anything mailed to their homes, and anonymous members whose affiliation with the WEC was not even known to other members.[50]

Many of the women in these anonymous membership categories were hiding their affiliation not only from their neighbors but also from their husbands. Though WEC members were largely exempt from economic and physical reprisals, they were subject to a unique form of pressure from their husbands. Only 6 percent of members surveyed stated that their husbands disagreed with them about the school crisis, but many husbands feared that they would be targeted for their wives' outspokenness.[51] As one WEC officer recalled, "A lot of wives could not use their names because of their husbands."[52] In a very real sense, these women could not use their names because they were not their names. This was perhaps most clearly evidenced in the organization's membership lists, in which each married member was listed by her husband's full name—Mrs. David Terry, Mrs. Joe Brewer.[53] Thus, anonymous membership categories offered women an opportunity to participate in the WEC without their husbands' knowledge. As one member put it, "A lot of women were folding pamphlets and licking envelopes in their homes, and nobody knew they were doing it."[54] For a few women, participation in the WEC against their husband's wishes resulted in divorce.[55]

Pressure from husbands prevented other women from joining at all. One of Terry's closest friends, an educator in complete sympathy with the cause, refused to join the WEC, "because my husband asked me not to" for fear it would ruin his business.[56] In her efforts to recruit new members, Jane Mendel encountered numerous women in similar circumstances. Many were solidly in favor of the committee's work but could not join the WEC because their husbands had told them to "hold off."[57] Yet, despite pressure from their husbands and the community at large, a surprising number of women found the courage to oppose Faubus.

When asked why they joined the WEC, every member interviewed cited frustration with the inaction of the city's male leadership. As Irene Samuel put it, "The men were afraid. . . . There were no leaders. They all chickened out. . . . They were afraid of losing money."[58] Another WEC leader recalled simply, "We felt frustrated. . . . The situation began to get more and more out of hand."[59] This frustration with a lack of male leadership was closely tied to an understanding of the broader effects of the crisis on the city.

In accordance with their commitment to community service, more than 70 percent of the WEC members were active in civic organizations, and Little Rock's reputation was a matter of serious concern to them. In a typical response, Sara Murphy said that she joined the WEC because "I felt like the community was going in the wrong direction. . . . This [integration] is where the country is going and we want to go with it. We want to be in the twentieth century."[60] Adolphine Terry echoed this sense of community humiliation: "We had been disgraced by a group of poor whites and a portion of the lunatic fringe that every town possesses. I wondered where the better class had been while this was being concocted."[61] One local attorney put it more simply: "We were getting no new industry. We were the laughingstock . . . of the universe."[62] Raised in a tradition of civic volunteerism, the women recognized the devastating effect of the crisis on the community and wanted to restore Little Rock's good name and return the city to a path of prosperity.

Self-interest was also an important motivation. The future of the community was of great concern to women raising a family. The vast majority of members had school-age children, and closed schools drastically affected the lives of women, who were their primary caretakers. Fully one-fifth of those members who responded to the survey reported having children who would have attended the closed high schools.[63] As one woman put it, "The schools were closed and their kids were out of school. . . . They were scared to death that [Faubus] might close all of the schools."[64] Thus, in some ways, these women were propelled to take a controversial stand by very traditional definitions of a woman's proper role.

Significantly, none of the members cited social justice as a primary reason for joining the WEC. Though membership itself indicated at least a tolerance of integration, there is little evidence to suggest that members viewed the issue as a moral imperative. Some have argued that the leaders of the organization were more liberal than the general membership; however, few if any of the women involved with the WEC could be considered racial liberals.[65] The membership survey indicates a wide variety of opinions on issues of race relations, but none of the results suggest the presence of a strong liberal contingent within the organization. When asked how they would react if public eating places were opened to black customers, only 37 percent said they would approve. Fifteen percent believed that desegregation would permanently harm public education and that the school board ought to reject "all but a handful of Negro applicants." One-quarter believed that the school district ought to "discourage Negroes from requesting transfers to desegregated schools." When asked how they felt about school integration, sample responses included:

> Believe integration can't work
> Believe school integration will have to be slower
> Prefer segregation but feel law must be obeyed
> Prefer segregation but not to closed schools[66]

This final comment perhaps best describes the WEC members and southern moderates in general. The women of the WEC and the men who would follow them opposed the segregationists because of what their actions were doing to the community's economy and reputation, not because of any commitment to racial equality. This support for desegregation as a civic issue rather than a moral issue was evident at the WEC's first public meeting.

When Terry, Brewer, and Powell met to organize an opposition to Faubus, he had not yet closed the schools. They envisioned an interracial organization with the goal of educating for racial tolerance. However, by the time the first public meeting was held, Faubus had closed the schools, changing the nature of the school crisis. At that first meeting, as Brewer began to outline plans for studies of local race relations and the formation of an interracial committee, a slow but steady trickle of women out of the meeting forced Brewer to "throw away all . . . notes and start over."[67] The women who attended that first meeting were frustrated by the school closing and were insistent that the primary goal of any new organization should be to address this emergency. Interracial organizations had never been popular, and the repressive atmosphere in Little Rock only exacerbated this tendency. Fearing that the WEC might be an integrationist organization, three women who attended that first meeting later asked that their names be stricken from the list.[68] As one historian has described it, "Conceived originally as an organization to work for racial justice, the Women's Emergency Committee quickly scaled down its objectives when the leaders realized the timidity of the ladies and the possibility of using the schools issue to build a broad base of support for a more enlightened position on the race question."[69]

Central to the construction of this broad base of support was the WEC policy to maintain a segregated organization. Political effectiveness dictated that the organization avoid overt challenges to the racial status quo. As Vivion Brewer later recalled, "We could afford no hint of being an integration group if we were going to win any election in the hysterical atmosphere which our governor knew so well how to foment."[70] Thus, Velma Powell was forced to resign her new post as secretary because of her affiliation with the interracial Arkansas Council on Human Relations. Brewer appointed Dottie Morris as the new secretary, and the next day the WEC released a statement outlining its position: "We stand neither for integration nor against integration. We are not now concerned with this. . . . Our sole aim is to get our four high schools open and our students back in their classes."[71] Again borrowing a strategy from the antilynching campaigns, WEC members hoped to use their position as "impeccably respectable Southern white women" to persuade voters that education and the future of the community were at stake, while avoiding the emotionally charged issue of race relations.[72] Although monthly meetings typically included guest speakers and a general discussion of racial issues, the organization that Terry ultimately founded bore little resemblance to the interracial educational panel she had envisioned.[73] In accordance with the wishes of most of its members, the Women's Emergency Committee to Open Our Schools was formed as an exclusively white organization with the immediate goal of restoring Little Rock's public high schools.[74]

The group's first project was to campaign against the segregationists in the school-closing vote. Governor Faubus had scheduled a special election for September 27, 1958, in which the citizens of Little Rock would vote for or against "integration of all schools within the Little Rock School District."[75] Of course, the issue was not integration versus segregation, but rather open schools with token desegregation versus closed schools. However, the women of the WEC faced a tremendous challenge in encouraging people to vote "for integration." With only two weeks to organize and the deck heavily stacked against them, it is not surprising that the women of the WEC lost this first battle by a large margin. However, during this campaign, the WEC adopted the goals and strategies that would guide it throughout the school crisis.

During the first days of the group's existence, the WEC had begun devising an effective election strategy. They rented office space downtown and relentlessly pursued publicity. Media exposure was essential to refute the false charges of the Citizens' Council and to explain to voters that a vote for integration was really just a vote for open schools with token desegregation. They prepared leaflets for distribution door-to-door and planned informational parties at which local attorneys would explain the effects of a vote against integration. Four days before the election, the WEC held its second meeting with more than 150 women in attendance. At that meeting, the women divided up the poll-tax books in an attempt to contact every registered voter by phone. Aware of the need to get every supporter to the polls, they also organized an elaborate carpool system.[76]

In the days before the election, the women of the WEC were the only members of the white community to organize in opposition to Faubus.[77] At the urging of the WEC, several local attorneys bought advertisements in the local papers that criticized Faubus's actions as unconstitutional and called for a return to law and order. Yet in the repressive local atmosphere, organizers had difficulty mustering support for even this measured statement. One attorney who signed the ad and spoke at a few of the WEC's informational parties lost twelve major clients as a result.[78]

After a televised speech by the governor, the WEC sought equal time but was refused by two of the three local networks. The third agreed to sell the WEC a half-hour segment, but given the atmosphere in the community, the women faced great difficulty finding community leaders who were willing to make public statements. Two local attorneys, a minister, the president of the Central High PTA, and a member of the governor's Committee on Education finally agreed to speak. This first televised appearance went so well that the WEC purchased additional time on the night before the election. However, this election-eve program was not as successful as the first, primarily because of greater difficulties in finding willing panelists.[79]

Under these circumstances, the lopsided results of the school-closing election came as no surprise. Nevertheless, the efforts of the WEC in this election laid the groundwork for the segregationists' defeat a few months later. Moreover, the events of the school-closing campaign suggest some of the ways in which gender dynamics dictated the goals and strategy of the organ-ization. Though they were the first group to organize in opposition to the seg-regationists, and their actions were instrumental in the eventual moderate victory, the women of the WEC could not replace the silent leadership of the men. Southern white women were responsible for the home. They were expected to care for their husbands and children and participate in church and worthy civic organizations. Politics was not their domain. In fact, WEC leaders were distressed to find that a large number of their female supporters could not even vote in the first school-closing election because their hus-bands had not paid their poll taxes.[80]

Although their gender helped protect them from the economic and phys-ical threats that had silenced their husbands, the WEC members were forced to design their strategies in accordance with a male-dominated society. One example of this occurred shortly after the WEC was founded, when, as Brewer recalled, "Husbands vetoed night and Sunday work at the office."[81] On another occasion, Marguerite Henry had to obtain "permission from her husband to make a public statement" about the crisis during the WEC's televised special.[82]

In such a male-dominated society, many of the WEC efforts were neces-sarily designed to encourage the men of the community to declare their opposition. As one outspoken liberal recalled years later, "If the damned men didn't have guts enough to do it [oppose the segregationists] then they were going to make them do it."[83] In the aftermath of the school-closing election, the women began with a letter-writing campaign, commending those men who had taken a public stand in favor of law and order and encouraging pub-lic officials to open the schools.[84] Volunteers met with business leaders to dis-cuss the crisis, and although these men refused to take a public stand, many supported the WEC with anonymous cash donations. Jane Mendel, who was an active fundraiser for the WEC, remarked that of all the donations she solicited, "only two gave me personal checks, and one was my husband." Though she admitted that money from any source was essential, "what we really needed were their names."[85]

One of the WEC's major projects was the research and publication of the *Little Rock Report*, an analysis of the effects of the school crisis on the eco-nomic health of the city. This project was undertaken specifically to persuade the city's businessmen to oppose the segregationists. Aware of its own limita-tions as an all-female organization, the WEC hoped to persuade Little Rock's male leadership to take a stand against the city's segregationists. Knowing that appeals to social justice would fail, and not motivated by a commitment to racial equality themselves, they sought to convince the men that their eco-nomic well-being was at stake.

Raised in a society in which women were subordinate to men, the WEC members also employed time-honored traditions of manipulation to achieve their goals. In a discussion of Terry's unique effectiveness as leader, Pat House focused particularly on her ability to manipulate traditional male responses in order to get what she wanted for her organization. According to House, when the WEC needed the cooperation of the men for one of its early projects, Terry insisted that they have the men over for dinner, arguing that "southern gentlemen have been taught to be courteous to their hostess, so when you give men food to eat they cannot be impolite to you and they must do a favor in return."[86] Working within the reality of female subordination, the WEC used similar tactics in selecting its researchers for the *Little Rock Report*. In order to elicit maximum cooperation from city businessmen, "we were very careful to select Southern girls, and girls who didn't have their hair dyed blond, and dressed very modestly, and [who were] not pushy."[87]

But in an interesting subversion of gender dynamics, the WEC also organized a SEX Committee "composed of beautiful young women who 'knew how to act dumb and at the same time get the answers that they want'" to encourage businessmen to oppose the segregationists.[88] Similarly, during the first days of the WEC, the leaders "hastily found eight young women who were willing to be publicized as our steering committee," because Brewer and others believed that younger, more attractive spokeswomen would make their publicity more effective.[89]

Finally, since many of the WEC members were married to prominent businessmen, Irene Samuel encouraged wives to withhold sex from their husbands unless they agreed to take a public stand.[90] Although Samuel made sure that the record showed she was kidding in this statement, Jane Mendel recently said of the WEC's use of this method of persuasion, "I don't know how widely used it was, but it was mentioned at meetings, and everyone laughed, but they were more than a little serious."[91]

From October 1958 to April 1959, as the WEC grew in strength, events in Little Rock continued to worsen. The public high schools remained closed, and the private Raney High School opened its doors to displaced white students in late October. The Arkansas Education Association pledged in early November to preserve the Arkansas public school systems, and in retaliation the Arkansas legislature delayed consideration of the Department of Education budget and ordered all teachers polled as to their opinions on the AEA statement.

That same month, just one week before election day, segregationist school board member Dale Alford announced that he would oppose incumbent congressman Brooks Hays in the general election. Hays had urged moderation throughout the school crisis and had served as an intermediary between Faubus and Eisenhower immediately following Faubus's mobilization of the National Guard. Alford ran a vicious campaign, accusing Hays of being an integrationist with communist leanings, and, as such, unresponsive to the wishes of his constituents.[92] Neither the minutes of the WEC meetings nor the memoir of WEC president Vivion Brewer details the extent of WEC activities during this weeklong campaign. Nevertheless, the WEC clearly gained further political experience by supporting Hays in this election, although it was again on the losing side. Despite the fact that he was a write-in candidate and campaigned for only a week, Alford defeated Hays in the general election.

Two weeks after Hays's defeat, the five moderate school board members bought out Superintendent Blossom's contract and then resigned out of frustration. Fifteen candidates ran for the six vacant school board positions. A group of segregationists endorsed by the Capital Citizens' Council was the first to file for candidacy. Several younger business leaders worked behind the scenes to encourage the presidents of six banks to run on a single slate for the six school board positions. Acknowledging the local atmosphere, these businessmen believed that if all of the bankers ran as moderates, then they would not risk reprisals, because the segregationists could not boycott all of the banks. However, farmers in the eastern part of the state threatened to remove their deposits from Little Rock and place them in Memphis if any of the bankers deviated from the racial status quo. Thus, the slate of bank presidents fell apart. The traditional civic leadership had failed yet again to oppose the segregationists. Grainger Williams, vice president of the Chamber of Commerce and husband of an active WEC member, reported the failure to a meeting of the group's officers. With only twenty-four hours left to organize an opposition slate, Adolphine Terry set to work.

This incident shows once again the limitations that gender placed on the effectiveness of the WEC. Instead of simply running for office themselves, the WEC leaders were forced to convince reluctant men to take a stand. Ted Lamb, owner of a local advertising agency and a liberal, had already agreed to run, but the moderates needed five more brave candidates for their slate. Armed with a list of potential candidates given to her by Williams, Terry began calling Little Rock's silent civic elite. By the time she reached the last name on the list, she had a total of only four committed candidates. Though Russell Matson was in Fayetteville for a football game, Terry tracked him down there and lobbied him to join the "businessmen's slate." He agreed, and, while WEC volunteers worked furiously to obtain enough signatures for the candidates to file, Terry forged Matson's name on a courthouse document in order to hold his candidacy until he returned from Fayetteville. Thus, with the help of the WEC and with one WEC member as a candidate, the city's business leaders finally offered some opposition to the extremists.[93]

During this campaign, Billy Rector, a powerful local businessman, quickly became the leading spokesman for the businessmen's slate. Immediately, he requested that the alliance between the candidates and the WEC be kept secret. The segregationists had successfully labeled the WEC an integrationist organization, and Rector feared that public support of the WEC would only help the Citizens' Council. The WEC agreed. Brewer privately endorsed the businessmen's slate at the December meeting and asked members to volunteer for the campaigns.[94] Although they were careful to minimize the WEC connection, the women employed the same type of ward organization on behalf of the businessmen's slate that they had used in the school-closing election. Meanwhile, Faubus and the segregationist leaders continued their intimidation campaign, charging that the businessmen's slate was composed of "integrationists."[95] As Vivion Brewer put it, "Billy Rector's attempt to counteract this by an announcement that he had given $100 to the Capital Citizens' Council in 1957 . . . did not cheer us."[96] On December 6, Little Rock voters elected three members of the businessmen's slate (Lamb, Matson, and Everett Tucker) and three segregationists to the school board, setting up a stalemate that would climax in a recall election just five months later.

In late November, the state Democratic Party sent letters to every principal and superintendent asking them to solicit five-dollar donations from their teachers. The letter also requested that the principals keep "a complete record of these contributions so that a letter of appreciation can be written to each individual donor."[97] This list of contributors also conveniently allowed Faubus to identify possible opposition from those who refused to contribute. The *Arkansas Gazette* and the WEC denounced these pressure tactics, but, as usual, they were lone voices. The state legislature passed a bill prohibiting members of the NAACP from public employment and authorized local school districts to abolish public schools to avoid integration. Furthermore, Governor Faubus vetoed a bill that would have required the automatic reopening of Little Rock schools in September.

Early in 1959, though, there was reason for renewed hope regarding the school crisis. On January 15, Grainger Williams, whose wife was an officer in the WEC, took office as the president of the Little Rock Chamber of Commerce. Frustrated by the ongoing school crisis and encouraged by his wife to take a public stand, Williams spoke to the cause of public education:

> It is my feeling that the time has come for us to evaluate the cost of public education, and the cost of the lack of public education. I would urge that no matter what our personal feelings might be, each of us encourage the reestablishment of all areas of communication so that we may be able to discuss our principles, our feelings, our differences, our problems, without anger or hatred, without fear of reprisal, but with understanding, tolerance, intelligence and respect for others.[98]

Will Mitchell, a respected local attorney and a moderate, recalled, "There was a gasp of surprise that Williams would dare even mention the topic, but then there was a burst of applause in respect for his courage and position."[99] That an audience of businessmen would gasp in response to such an innocuous statement is testament to the success of the extremists in intimidating the community into silence. Nevertheless, Williams's statement marked the beginning of the end of segregationist control in Little Rock. Though the *Gazette* and a few prominent men had opposed the segregationists for months, for the first time the businessmen of the community were becoming involved in the resolution of the crisis.

In the weeks following Williams's speech, the Chamber polled its members, and 71 percent favored the "reopening of the Little Rock public schools on a controlled, minimal plan of integration."[100] With the support of its membership, the Chamber of Commerce for the first time began to work publicly for a solution to the school crisis. Yet according to Williams, "Even as mild as our statements were in the Chamber, we lost a third of our membership."[101]

By early March, the segregationists were beginning to fear a growing moderate coalition. Thus, they tried to intimidate the most outspoken moderate organization, the WEC. The city board of directors demanded that the WEC submit a list of its members in accordance with state law. The Bennett Ordinance, as it was commonly known, had been passed in February 1957 as part of a series of anti-integration measures designed to intimidate the opposition. After Brewer denied keeping such records, city officials sent two police officers to secretary Dottie Morris's house to demand the list.[102] Having promised to protect the names of their members, however, the WEC officers refused to submit a membership list. They did, however, submit financial statements, a policy statement, a list of executive committee members, and a profile of the organization.[103] The city board of directors, citing newspaper ads and leaflets in which the organization requested a one-dollar membership fee, found this inadequate and threatened to send the officers to jail if they did not comply.[104] However, as John Pagan has argued, "The prospect of dragging a dozen Southern white ladies to jail in the middle of the night was a bit much for even the most ardent extremists, so the WEC leaders were never prosecuted."[105] In this case, the gender and social prominence of the WEC's membership clearly protected the members and the organization.

In the end, though, it was perhaps in victory that the limitations of gender were most obvious. On May 5, 1959, the ongoing school crisis climaxed in a purge of forty-four city teachers and administrators. At a regular meeting of the school board on that day, the annual renewal of teacher contracts was on the agenda. After several hours of stalemate, the three moderate members walked out of the meeting to deny the school board a quorum. The remaining segregationist members continued the meeting and proceeded to fire employees of the public schools systems who were known to have been sympathetic to integration. After nearly a year without public high schools and almost two years of school crisis, it was the firing of forty-four teachers and administrators that finally rallied Little Rock's civic elite and led to the defeat of the extremists.

The WEC was, as usual, the first organization in the city to denounce publicly the actions of the school board. The *Arkansas Gazette* followed with an editorial that read in part: "Those who have complacently said that things had to get worse in the Little Rock school crisis before they could get better now have another grim occasion on which to ponder whether things are finally bad enough."[106] In contrast to the events of the preceding two years, however, the WEC and the *Gazette* were not the only voices denouncing the segregationists. That night, at an emergency meeting of the PTA at Forest Park School, four hundred parents demanded the recall of the segregationist school board members. The next day, the local chapter of the American Association of University Women called the teacher purge "un-American," and the executive committee of the Little Rock PTA Council condemned the school board members for "attempting summary dismissal of school personnel without cause."[107] The local chapter of the League of Women Voters and the Little Rock Ministerial Alliance also criticized the firings, as did the Chamber of Commerce. The most important protest, however, began with three young husbands of WEC members and a *Gazette* reporter over coffee.

On May 6, 1959, the day after the teacher purge, Edward Lester, Maurice Mitchell, and Robert Shults met with Gene Fritz of the *Arkansas Gazette* at Brier's Restaurant. There the four resolved that this latest action by the segregationists should not go unanswered. They were buoyed by the numerous public statements that had already been made in favor of the teachers, especially the statement by the Chamber of Commerce. They each contacted several important local businessmen, and two days later they formed the Committee to Stop This Outrageous Purge (STOP) to recall the segregationist school board members.

It is important to note that not only were three of the four founding members of STOP (Lester, Mitchell, and Shults) married to WEC members, but so were the majority of STOP's general members.[108] Throughout the three-week campaign, the relationship between STOP and the WEC was close, if complicated, and most participants credit the WEC with STOP's success.[109] According to Ed Lester, "STOP could never have been successful if the Women's Emergency Committee had not been organized and ready to work."[110] Another STOP member put it simply, "We could never have done it without them."[111] The men of STOP directed the recall campaign from above, but it was the women of the WEC who did the work, and it was the WEC's ward organization that ultimately made the difference on election day.

In the week following the teacher purges, WEC members solicited over nine thousand signatures in support of recalling the segregationist school board members. Meanwhile, the White Citizens' Council and the Mothers'

League of Central High School organized an opposition group to recall the moderate school board members. They called their organization the Committee to Retain Our Segregated Schools (CROSS). The names of the two campaigns reveal much about their respective strategies. CROSS supporters argued that the election was not simply about the teachers, but that the maintenance of segregated schools was at issue. STOP organizers, by contrast, argued that the teacher purge was the only issue. Of course, STOP organizers realized that school desegregation was at issue, but they also knew that they would lose if voters believed that the election was a referendum on school integration.

The climate of intimidation fostered by the segregationists throughout the school crisis had not diminished by 1959. Immediately following the formation of STOP, the Capital Citizens' Council issued a boycott list that included the names of all known STOP supporters. Maurice Mitchell, who had just launched his own law practice, lost a number of clients and regularly received harassing phone calls.[112] In such an atmosphere, citizens could not rally in support of integration. Moreover, there is no real evidence to suggest that STOP members favored integration. Like their WEC counterparts, STOP members simply favored reopening the schools, and they were willing to accept token integration to achieve that end. However, the teacher purge allowed STOP to avoid even token integration as an issue. Fairness to the teachers was an issue everyone could fight for. As Grainger Williams later recalled:

> A lot of people would work for STOP who wouldn't work with the WEC because the WEC was associated with getting black children in the schools and the STOP campaign was associated with getting those teachers back their jobs. And the nice thing about the STOP campaign was that it gave some people who couldn't come out and do anything an opportunity to do something . . . because the cause wasn't integration. Of course the teachers were being purged because they were integrationist.[113]

STOP leaders thus appealed to voters' sense of fairness and strenuously avoided the issue of integration.

In keeping with this strategy, STOP publicly avoided any association with the WEC, although they were dependent on WEC volunteers and organization. Vivion Brewer bitterly recalled the treatment she and Irene Samuel received at the first full meeting of STOP at the Union National Bank auditorium:

> Averted glances as we entered the hall made it very clear that we were personae non gratae. A few of the men whom we knew best hastened to turn their backs to avoid speaking. . . . There followed a discussion

of groups they hoped to involve in the campaign. . . . The WEC was
conspicuously absent from the list, and Dr. John Samuel made bold to
rise and add our name. There was an enormous silence which spoke
like thunder.[114]

Pat House and Irene Samuel have since disputed this account of the relationship between STOP and the WEC. Both agree that STOP attempted to distance
itself publicly from the WEC for political reasons, but they believe Brewer
exaggerated the extent of STOP's actions—and its success in disavowing the
WEC.[115]

Although participants dispute the significance of STOP's decision to avoid
public association with the WEC, there is considerable evidence that suggests
the existence of a gendered division of labor. As one WEC member has noted,
the relationship between STOP and the WEC conformed to a societal pattern
of male dominance: "Men wanted work done by the women, but didn't want
them to get any of the credit. . . . We wouldn't put up with that today. We
wouldn't do all that work behind the scenes and then get kicked in the teeth
for it, too."[116] Pat House, a WEC officer who worked closely with the STOP
leaders during the campaign, described this division of labor as simply a matter of practicality, as most of the women were not employed outside the
home and thus had more time to work on the project.[117] Jane Mendel has
suggested, however, that many women simply "didn't recognize this gender
dynamic. We were so used to doing what our husbands wanted us to do."[118]

Regardless of how the participants perceived it, a sexual division of labor
did exist. The women of the WEC did most of the actual work with the direction and financial support of STOP. As a STOP member put it simply, "The
STOP campaign was based on petitions, and the women were the ones who
got out and got those petitions signed."[119] In addition, they made handbills,
ran newspaper ads, and carried out the plans made by male leaders. Vivion
Brewer described the WEC office as "the center for hurried, excited men offering advice, directing plans [and] supplying badly needed equipment. . . .
Reporters and photographers filed in and out, assuming this to be the STOP
headquarters, ignoring the WEC staff."[120] Yet it was the WEC's ward organization, assembled during the earlier campaigns, that mobilized voters for the
STOP campaign. Working around the clock, WEC members and volunteers
who came to the campaign through STOP typed the name, ward, precinct, telephone number, and address of nearly every registered voter onto an index card.
They then labeled each card "saint," "salvable," or "sinner." STOP and WEC
members, as well as those who signed the STOP petition, were labeled saints.
Citizens' Council members, Mothers' League members, and those who had
signed the CROSS petition were labeled sinners. All of the others were labeled
salvable. The women then began calling all of the salvables and saints.[121]

WEC members set up carpools, as they had during the school-closing election, because in such a close election, getting out the vote would be essential—especially the black vote. They organized a rally in support of the teachers, and STOP staged an expensive media campaign. Earlier work done by the WEC researching the positions of judges and clerks proved invaluable in getting friendly appointments to election commission vacancies. However, the opposition was also well organized, and the margin of victory was slim, with high-income white voters allying with the city's black voters to defeat the segregationists. Yet after months of work and an intense three-week campaign, it was the men of STOP who were publicly credited with the election victory. As Vivion Brewer recalled, "It was STOP's night."[122]

Following STOP's victory, the *Arkansas Gazette* editorialized:

> Perhaps the best description of Monday's election is a phrase borrowed from Winston Churchill: "This could be the end of the beginning." . . . [The election demonstrated] that we will not entrust our fortunes to reckless men who seek to dominate our public affairs by character assassination, economic coercion and even physical intimidation. . . . The air is clearer today and the future brighter.[123]

Indeed, the STOP victory and the subsequent appointment of three more moderates to the school board paved the way for the reopening of city high schools in September. STOP disbanded immediately after the election, but STOP leaders, together with WEC leaders, formed the Committee for the Peaceful Operation of the Public Schools, which worked closely with the WEC and business leaders throughout the summer to ensure a peaceful reopening of the schools. Late in July, the school board adopted a pupil placement plan and devised a plan to open the schools three weeks early, which prevented Faubus from calling a special session of the legislature. The WEC researched the opinions of local police officers so that no segregationist officers would be placed on duty around the schools.

On August 12, 1959, the Little Rock public high schools reopened, with three black students enrolled at each of the white high schools. A segregationist mob rallied on the steps of the state capitol and then marched toward Central High, but the police and fire departments turned them away and made several arrests. As Spitzberg has argued, "The events of August 12 confirmed the moderates in their position of influence in the community and finished completely the political power of segregationists in Little Rock."[124]

For the next five years, the Women's Emergency Committee continued to oppose Faubus and work in support of public education. WEC leaders helped found similar organizations in Atlanta and New Orleans and encouraged city officials to establish a committee to address problems in local race relations. Most of their efforts, however, were directed toward electing moderate candidates and supporting public school legislation. But with the school crisis resolved, the WEC lacked focus, and members who had been drawn together by a common desire to reopen the schools disagreed about the future of the organization. On November 5, 1963, the Women's Emergency Committee voted itself out of existence. Many of the women who had first become involved in politics through the WEC went on to become leaders in all aspects of civic life. In the tumultuous years to come, they founded organizations to promote public education and civil rights. A few even ran for office. Yet an editorial that ran in honor of the WEC reveals much about the place of these women in their community:

> If the men of Arkansas had more self respect, they would bow their heads at the demise of the Women's Emergency Committee of Little Rock. But if the men of Arkansas had more self respect, the Women's Emergency Committee would never have had to come into existence in the first place. It was a desperate organization by a handful of ladies who knew not what they should do about it but who were dead certain that the State of Arkansas should not be turned over to racists and allied wreckers. . . . The ladies now pass the seals of leadership back to their conventional custodians.[125]

Like the author of this editorial, many scholars have attributed the extent of the Little Rock school crisis to the lack of civic leadership.[126] The men who had, in the postwar decade, attracted new industries, an Air Force base, and new prosperity to Little Rock remained silent throughout the crisis. Segregationists filled the power vacuum left by their inaction. Immediately, the extremists had "established a 'right opinion' which could not be violated."[127] There was no middle ground, and those who opposed Faubus were socially ostracized, harassed, threatened, and economically destroyed. In this climate, elite southern white women occupied a uniquely powerful position.

Though apparently models of deferential southern womanhood, these women were the only individuals in the community who were independent enough and prestigious enough to oppose Faubus. As upper-class women who were not employed outside the home, they were hard to intimidate economically. Moreover, their class status guaranteed them access to the civic elite and financial security for their organization. As white women, they were too prominent to harm physically, and, while avoiding any direct challenge to the racial status quo, they had a much more powerful impact on white public opinion than a biracial or black protest movement could have had. Race, class, and gender thus afforded these women a protective status from which to launch the opposition.

Frustrated by the inaction of the men in their community and motivated in part by traditional notions of an upper-class woman's proper role, the women of the WEC took the first organized stand against the extremists. Yet, as elite southern white women, the WEC members faced unique obstacles. Though largely free from the economic reprisals that had silenced the men of their community, they faced enormous pressure from their husbands. Fearful for their reputations and their businesses, many men refused to allow their wives to associate publicly with the WEC.

Not only did these women have little freedom to act against their husbands' wishes, they also were in no position to permanently replace the city's traditional civic leadership. Thus, the WEC's major goal was always to convince the men of the community to take action. Though the organization and efforts of the WEC were central to the defeat of the segregationists, that victory could never have come without the public support of the city's male leadership.

In a time of crisis, the women of the WEC were empowered by the very traits that traditionally isolated them from politics. However, just as race, gender, and class protected these women from the reprisals that had silenced the rest of the community, these factors also dictated the goals and strategy of the Women's Emergency Committee and limited its effectiveness.

THE LITTLE ROCK CRISIS AND POSTWAR BLACK ACTIVISM IN ARKANSAS

John A. Kirk

"History is something that happens when the White Folks show up," writes civil rights scholar Charles M. Payne in a critical assessment of written accounts of the past.[1] Certainly this analysis rings true when one looks at the work on the 1957 Little Rock school crisis over the past forty years. Numerous firsthand accounts have provided us with a variety of white perspectives, including that of President Dwight D. Eisenhower, Congressman Brooks Hays, Governor Orval Faubus, Superintendent of Schools Virgil T. Blossom, Little Rock's mayor Woodrow Mann, *Arkansas Gazette* editor Harry Ashmore, segregationist politician Dale Alford, school administrator Elizabeth Huckaby, and Women's Emergency Committee to Open Our Schools (WEC) member Sara Murphy.[2] Secondary works have focused on Governor Faubus, massive resistance and the White Citizens' Councils, local white clergymen, local white women, the local white business elite, white judges, and the interaction of (largely white-dominated) national and local political and legal issues.[3]

Useful though these memoirs and studies are, by focusing almost exclusively on the events of September 1957 and Little Rock's emergence in the national spotlight, they offer little insight into how the school crisis fit into a much larger struggle over race relations in the city and state. Even more important, these works, mostly written by and about whites, fail to present a thoroughgoing analysis of the black community and its contribution to the story of race relations in Arkansas. For over thirty years, the only black perspective on the school crisis was the memoir of Daisy Bates, head of the Arkansas National Association for the Advancement of Colored People State Conference of Branches (ASC). Significantly, the second work to emerge from the black community, written by Melba Pattillo Beals in 1994, from the perspective of one of the nine students who integrated Central High, adds little to Bates's account. Like the works by whites, Bates's and Beals's books provide only snapshots of events, lacking a broader context to locate the drama of September 1957.[4] For the white people, we do, at least, have a variety of perspectives. For blacks, we simply do not—and no secondary works have focused on the black community to address this gap in the existing literature. The Little Rock school crisis was, after all, about black civil rights—specifically, about the rights of blacks to have the same access to educational opportunities as whites. Yet where is the black population in the historiography of the school crisis? We know little of what the events of 1957 meant to black Arkansans or how they fit into their collective hopes and aspirations for racial change.

The 1957 Little Rock school crisis had its roots in the growing militancy of black activism in Arkansas after World War II. Prior to the 1940s, the guiding philosophy for most black leaders in the state had been Booker T. Washington's stance of "accommodation," which stressed economic advancement within the boundaries of segregation, instead of head-on racial protest to challenge Jim Crow and disfranchisement. Yet, although accommodation remained the mainstay of the black elite in Arkansas, there had been several black activists who looked to extend the scope of black advancement beyond the world of business. In the vanguard of black political and legal struggles from the turn of the century was Scipio Africanus Jones, a lawyer based in Little Rock. In 1928, after a long, bitter, and hard-fought battle against lily-white forces in the Arkansas Republican Party, who attempted to deny black participation in the party, Jones was elected as a state delegate to the Republican National Convention, forcing whites to acknowledge the legitimacy of black participation in the state organization.[5] In the same year, Dr. John Marshall Robinson, a black physician from Little Rock, founded the Arkansas Negro Democratic Association (ANDA) and launched the first legal attack on the Democratic Party of Arkansas's (DPA) exclusive white primary system.[6]

The number of successful black businesses that flourished in Little Rock, coupled with indigenous leaders and organizations working for black advancement, meant that before the 1940s, national civil rights organizations such as the NAACP failed to make significant progress in the state. Despite a successful defense of twelve black prisoners who were sentenced to death for their alleged role in the Elaine race riot in East Arkansas in 1919, which brought one of the national NAACP's greatest early triumphs, there remained an indifference to the organization among influential black leaders in Little Rock.[7]

The Little Rock branch of the NAACP, the oldest in the state, did not make any headway in building support in the city, let alone the surrounding rural areas. Beyond the efforts of a few dedicated black female secretaries, notably Mrs. Carrie Sheppherdson, who won the NAACP's Madam C. J. Walker Gold Medal in 1925 for her outstanding fundraising drive, the black population of Little Rock showed very little interest in NAACP activities.[8] As Mrs. H. L. Porter, the Little Rock branch secretary, put it in 1933, "The lawyers, Doctors, preachers and businessmen . . . are just a bunch of egoistic discussers and not much on actual doings."[9]

The lack of NAACP support in Little Rock led to a mutual antipathy between the New York organization and the city's black leadership. This was vividly demonstrated when Dr. J. M. Robinson appealed for funds to take on the white-dominated DPA primary elections in 1928. To be sure, similar cases, which overlapped with ANDA's efforts, were being argued in Virginia, Florida, and Texas at the time.[10] Yet it was clear that the ratio of money spent on states was carefully weighed against support offered to the NAACP in return. Walter White, the NAACP's executive secretary, felt particularly strongly that "it is not fair to other states who have by their contributions enabled the Association to continue in existence that we should give disproportionate amounts in cases in states where little has been done to help the Association carry out its work." White added, "We know that there are enough colored men of means in Little Rock alone to finance the case."[11] In a memo to Arthur Spingarn, president of the NAACP, White recommended, as a pragmatic matter, that "we send say fifty or one hundred dollars as a contribution towards this case so that in the event that it turns out to be the one on which we get the definitive decision, we will at least have given something."[12]

During the 1930s, the balance between local support and outside help in the struggle for civil rights shifted. At the same time, as many black businesses crumbled due to the Depression, a newly enlivened constituency for mass black activism emerged, inspired by the promise of the New Deal. Although the effect of the New Deal on black lives was ultimately ambiguous, and its positive aspects very often undermined by segregation and discrimination, federal government aid did mean that more black facilities such as hospitals and schools were built in Arkansas than ever before. The New Deal provided more jobs, training, and access to adult education, offering the black population a small glimpse of the potential that the federal government possessed to make a difference in their lives. New Deal agricultural policies pushed black farmers off the land and into the towns and villages of the delta. In these urban areas, where black people were less vulnerable and isolated, there was greater community cohesion. Mobilization of the black population was easier, and intimidation by whites more difficult, than when blacks were isolated and dispersed in rural areas.[13] Subsequent federal investment in army bases and minor wartime industries accelerated the shift in black population and encouraged a more sustained pursuit of civil rights.[14]

But there was still a distinct lack of direction and leadership for such a movement. The NAACP still showed little interest in Arkansas. The young Pine Bluff–based lawyer William Harold Flowers and the group of young black professionals he founded in 1940, the Committee on Negro Organizations (CNO), sought to get a movement going despite these obstacles. Half a generation younger than the existing black middle-class leadership, this group recognized the need for a mass base.[15]

Flowers founded the CNO after the NAACP refused several times to help organize black Arkansans.[16] The central goal of the CNO was to win organizational support from existing centers of black influence across the state and coordinate their activities in a mass black political organization. Flowers believed that this would be an important first step in challenging the political omnipotence of the DPA, the bastion of white supremacy in the state.[17] After a series of speaking engagements with influential black groups from all sections of the state, Flowers initiated the "First Conference on Negro Organization" at Lakeview, in East Arkansas.[18] Subsequently, Flowers organized statewide poll-tax campaigns coordinated by the CNO and assisted by various local NAACP branches, business groups, civic associations, fraternal and Masonic chapters, and religious organizations.[19] When the poll-tax drives produced a record number of black voters in 1941, the *Arkansas State Press,* a black-owned newspaper in Little Rock, printed Flowers's picture with the caption, "He Founded a Movement."[20]

The burst of activity under Flowers's leadership was successful at pushing blacks in Little Rock to take a more forthright stand for their civil rights. The first evidence of this came in 1942, when Sue Morris, a black schoolteacher, filed suit in conjunction with the NAACP on behalf of the Little Rock City Teachers Association (CTA) for the right to be paid the same salary as white teachers. The case proved to be the first successful attempt by black Arkansans to win equal rights through the courts.[21] The NAACP-sponsored victory started a fruitful association between local blacks and the national organization. The teachers' salary case attracted the help of Thurgood Marshall, one of the NAACP's most successful young attorneys, whose presence in Little Rock helped garner a great deal of support in the city. According to reports from Mrs. H. L. Porter, in Little Rock membership dues began to take a dramatic upswing: "He [Marshall] sure did shoot them some straight dope as to their part and membership to be played in the NAACP cause," wrote Porter, referring to a meeting Marshall held with black Arkansans in 1942. "Then and there . . . we collected $68.50 in membership."[22] In 1945, the ASC was established, and W. H. Flowers was appointed as its chief recruitment officer.[23]

Another important development occurred in Little Rock during 1942, following the shooting of black army sergeant Thomas P. Foster by Officer Abner

J. Hay of the Little Rock police department. White authorities dismissed the case as a "justifiable homicide," claiming that Hay had killed Foster in self-defense.[24] Blacks refused to accept this account, since many eyewitnesses had seen Hay kill Foster in cold blood on crowded downtown West Ninth Street. Black anger was inflamed when the recently established *Arkansas State Press* published a full account of events and continued to crusade for a just hearing on the matter.[25] As a result of pressure from the owners of the *Arkansas State Press*, L. C. Bates and Daisy Bates, a Negro Citizens' Committee (NCC) was established to investigate the incident.[26] When the NCC delivered its report at the First Baptist Church in front of a sizeable black crowd drawn from all sections of the state, its members concluded that the shooting was "unjustifiable" because, at the time Hay shot five bullets into Foster's body, the black sergeant lay defenseless on the ground after an attack by white city police officers.[27] However, successive white-dominated juries refused to convict the white police officer, even when the federal government lent its support to the prosecution's case.[28] In spite of the courtroom defeat, the continued agitation by the *Arkansas State Press* did eventually win some concessions from the city government when, with the support of the U.S. Army, it secured the appointment in late summer 1942 of eight black policemen to police black downtown areas.[29]

The war years in Little Rock thus witnessed two developments that would have important ramifications in the Little Rock school crisis over a decade later: the emergence of the NAACP as a force in the state and the rise to prominence of the Bateses. Still, in the late 1940s, the NAACP and the Bateses had competition for community influence as many new organizations emerged. At the forefront of this new activity was Charles Bussey, who in 1946 founded the Veterans Good Government Association (VGGA) in Little Rock. The VGGA's membership consisted largely of black soldiers who had returned to Arkansas from wartime service abroad. These ex-soldiers were responding to the second-class citizenship still enforced upon them at home and the inability of older black leaders to address that problem. Bussey helped form another new group, the East End Civic League (EECL), led by Jeffery Hawkins, to represent the interests of the run-down, predominantly black east end of Little Rock.[30] Also in the capital city, I. S. McClinton emerged to challenge Dr. J. M. Robinson's claim to speak for black Democrats in Arkansas by forming the Young Negro Democrats (YND), which later became the Arkansas Democratic Voters Association (ADVA).[31]

Mostly newcomers to the city from rural parts of Arkansas, these new leaders looked to build upon the constituency for change wrought by the demographic, political, and social upheavals of the New Deal and World War II. Taking advantage of the growing national sympathy for their struggle, with the federal government increasingly willing to declare its opposition to racial discrimination, and using the leverage from greater black voter registration, they pressed for concessions. To a certain degree, these new leaders and organizations succeeded, particularly in Little Rock, where throughout the postwar period there was a subtle and complex rearrangement of segregation in selected areas. In 1948, for example, Little Rock's city library quietly desegregated; blacks began to gain admission to a few of the city's previously segregated public parks; the Little Rock zoo began to admit blacks on certain days; some of the "white" and "colored" signs were removed from downtown drinking fountains; downtown hotels allowed interracial meetings to take place using their facilities and accepted block bookings from visiting black sports teams; and the *Arkansas Gazette* and *Arkansas Democrat* both began to print stories about and photographs of blacks.[32]

This easing of certain racial restrictions was little more than a tokenistic tampering with segregation. All the concessions were essentially designed to preserve the ethos of social separation between the races. The fundamental goal of the changes was to maintain white control over the segregated system and evade more radical change by federal decree. Even so, within such a hitherto rigid structure of Jim Crow, these developments were significant and marked a new era of race relations. On the one hand, blacks pressed for racial progress but remained wary about provoking a wall of resistance by pushing too hard. On the other hand, white Arkansans remained acutely aware that if they wished to maintain control over their system of race relations without any federal intervention, they would have to make at least some concessions to black demands. Under these circumstances, white Arkansans looked to take a line of appeasement, which offered the most acceptable compromise to them but which also invariably involved the least amount of substantial change to the existing racial order.

Not everyone in the black community was satisfied with this arrangement, least of all the Bateses, who remained skeptical about the potential for any meaningful change within the new context of race relations. Through the *Arkansas State Press*, they complained that some black people were posing as leaders and attempting to use the vote to gain concessions, but only to promote their own aggrandizement and prestige. Even those whom the Bateses found sincere were portrayed as misguided because they settled for compromise within the bounds of segregation rather than exerting pressure to bring an end to discrimination altogether. As the militant voice of black community protest, the *Arkansas State Press* echoed the increasingly insistent line of the NAACP that nothing short of the complete end of segregation would suffice. Often, *Arkansas State Press* editorials went so far as to suggest that the new black leaders were retarding progress by settling for second best and that their failure was the main explanation for the absence of black "parks, playgrounds, enough Negro police, employment . . . and other lacks." The Bateses concluded that any advances in black people's status in the community "will have to be gained through the courts or the ballots and not through BEGGING."[33]

True to their word, the Bateses, through the offices of the NAACP, brought about the most enduring victory for the black community in Little Rock in the immediate postwar period. Backed by the NAACP's legal redress committee, headed by L. C. Bates, the Reverend J. H. Gatlin filed as a candidate for Second Ward city alderman in May 1950, asserting his intention to run in the Little Rock Democratic Party primaries for nomination.[34] When Gatlin attempted to pay the filing fee in order to run for office, his application was returned by Pulaski County Democratic Committee secretary June P. Wooten, who declared that black people could not become members of the DPA.[35] L. C. Bates indicated that Gatlin was ready to take the case to the courts.[36] In June 1950, NAACP lawyers filed the case with the U.S. District Court, arguing that Gatlin should not be denied his place in the primary election "on account of race, color, religion, national origin or any other unconstitutional restriction." The court upheld that contention.[37] Although Gatlin lost the ensuing election, the case finally brought to an end the all-white primary system. With black candidates now able to stand under the banner of the DPA, even die-hard Democrats realized that black membership and full voting rights had to be granted. The party passed a resolution granting both of these at its convention in September 1950.[38]

The NAACP also struck a significant blow in the field of higher education at the state level in 1948 when W. H. Flowers, who by then had been elected president of the ASC, helped persuade officials at the University of Arkansas Law School to admit Silas Hunt, the first black student to enroll since Reconstruction. Pressure exerted through Supreme Court rulings at the national level, coupled with persistent black demands at the state level, eventually convinced university authorities to allow blacks to enroll as graduate students. However, some semblance of segregation was still envisioned, as Hunt was expected to study in a separate classroom, use the library only through a white intermediary, and eat alone, since he was not allowed in the university cafeteria.[39] In practice, Hunt's stay at Fayetteville proved far less lonely than expected: some white students chose to attend Hunt's lectures in the basement of the law school building and share lunch and study sessions with him. Unfortunately, Hunt's admission to the university had a tragic ending when medical problems related to his wartime service forced him to withdraw from studies before completing his first semester. Three months later, he died at the Veterans Hospital in Springfield, Missouri.[40]

Despite Hunt's untimely departure, his admission to the university blazed an important trail. The next black student was Jackie Shropshire, who enrolled the following semester. In 1951, he became the first black student to graduate from the law school. Overcrowding meant that more white students studied with Shropshire in the basement classroom. To counteract what might be seen by some as integration, university authorities put up a small wooden railing to fence Shropshire off from the rest of the class. After protests from white students, the railing was removed, and classes were completely desegregated. Other black graduates followed Hunt and Shropshire through the law school over the next few years, including Christopher Mercer, George Haley, Wiley Branton, and George Howard. Each of these new entrants played an important role in the development of black activism in Arkansas, in particular providing the NAACP with able black lawyers at a local level who could pursue the cause of black rights through the courts.[41] The successful desegregation of the law school also led to the enrollment of the first black student, Edith Mae Irby, in the University of Arkansas Medical School at Little Rock in the fall of 1948 and the establishment of a desegregated graduate summer school program in 1949. Again, these developments produced professionally qualified black people in local communities who would play important leadership roles in the future.[42]

These victories came at a tumultuous time of internal wrangling within the ASC. Black conservatives within the organization balked at the election of a young dynamic leader such as Flowers, and allegations of financial misconduct were leveled against him.[43] However, a subsequent investigation from the head office found no cause for concern.[44] Indeed, the NAACP was flourishing under the leadership of Flowers. Membership figures in Pine Bluff alone reached 4,382, constituting almost a fifth of the black population there.[45] At the 1948 ASC annual conference, NAACP regional secretary Donald Jones described spirits within the state organization as "high and militant," adding, "Largely responsible for the fine NAACP consciousness in Pine Bluff and the growing consciousness in the state is Attorney Flowers whose . . . tremendous energy ha[s] made him the state's acknowledged leader."[46]

All the same, relations quickly soured in 1949 when the ASC defaulted on its contribution to the NAACP Southwest Regional Conference Fund, with which it was affiliated. Fearing that this confirmed the accusations of older black leaders, the NAACP's national headquarters immediately demanded the resignation of Flowers.[47] When this move raised a storm of opposition from NAACP members in Arkansas, the New York office was forced to draw upon the calming influences of executive secretary Roy Wilkins and former executive secretary Walter White, who both called for unity in the interests of the organization. The dissent only abated when Flowers resigned voluntarily.[48] Even then dissatisfaction continued to smolder among Arkansas's NAACP members. Many were extremely reluctant to accept Flowers's replacement, Dr. J. A. White, who represented the old guard of black leaders imposed upon them by the head office. Shortly afterward, Lulu B. White, a member of the Texas NAACP State Conference of Branches, observed, "No place in the country is there so much strife and division amongst Negroes as [there] is in Arkansas." White reported that the disillusionment with the national organization was so great that "they say the work of the NAACP is in charge of a few favorites in the state, who are Lackies, what ever that is, for New York, and that New York is not worth a D——to them."[49]

Though the initial storm after Flowers's resignation from office slowly abated, the attitudes of local members made it almost inevitable that a conservative president of the ASC would not be tolerated for long. When J. A. White fell ill and resigned from office in 1951, he was replaced temporarily by W. L. Jarrett, a veteran of early CNO campaigns.[50] The issue of a conservative versus activist leadership at the head of the ASC was finally resolved in the 1952 contest for the presidency, which resulted in the election of Daisy Bates. In a resigned manner, the regional NAACP attorney, U. Simpson Tate, questioned Bates's ability to work with older, more established leaders in the state and warned of her tendency "to go off the deep end at times" in her forceful pursuit of black rights. But, he concluded, "[although] I am not certain that she was the proper person to be elected[,] I permitted it because there was no one else to be elected who offered any promise of doing anything to further the work of the NAACP in Arkansas."[51]

Daisy Bates's election as president of the ASC in 1952 coincided with a national and local intensification of the black struggle for equality in education, focused intently on attacking discrimination in secondary schools. The first suit filed by the NAACP in Arkansas, against the Fort Smith School District in 1948, was a slow-moving affair that finally ground to a halt without any success in late 1949 after pressure from local whites on the black plaintiffs.[52] W. H. Flowers, working independently of the NAACP, proved far more successful in organizing community lawsuits against segregated facilities. In 1949, Flowers organized a Citizens' Committee of black parents at DeWitt to petition the school board for equal facilities for black students there. Although the case was stalled in the courts, it was the first suit of its kind to go to trial in Arkansas. Wiley Branton saw it as the "ice breaking" litigation for further suits attacking discrimination in schools in later years.[53] The DeWitt action was followed by lawsuits in the Fordyce, Gould, and Hughes school districts.[54] Although Flowers's efforts were met with more delaying tactics, events at a national level finally overtook the local challenge to segregation in Arkansas schools. On May 17, 1954, the U.S. Supreme Court handed down its ruling in *Brown v. Board of Education of Topeka,* which declared that segregated schools were "inherently unequal." Following to a logical conclusion its decisions concerning black graduate education throughout the 1940s, the Court maintained that "in the field of public education the doctrine of 'separate but equal' [established by *Plessy v. Ferguson* in 1896] has no place."[55]

The *Brown* decision appeared to herald an end to the ambiguities of race relations in postwar Arkansas. Daisy Bates's sentiments were the same as those of other NAACP members, and she insisted that "the time for delay, evasion, or procrastination was past."[56] For black activists, the Court decision vindicated their rejection of half measures and insistence upon full equality. With the law of the land firmly in their corner, over the next few years, many other black Arkansans steadily became converts to a more direct assertion of full citizenship rights.

The *Brown* decision also precipitated a realignment in Little Rock's black leadership, which would come to a head with the 1957 school crisis. Throughout this period, the older, traditional leadership was pushed firmly into the background. With an increasing polarization in city and state over the school desegregation issue, a breakdown in the channels of communication between the white elite and the older black leaders led to an erosion of the latter's prestige and influence. The more hostile racial climate also paralyzed the new leaders, who used politics rather than petition as their primary vehicle to advance black rights. White leaders refused to deal with black politicians, since doing so might lead to condemnation by militant segregationists for consorting with the "enemy," so the influence of the new leadership also declined.[57]

Beyond the NAACP, only two other organizations openly continued to campaign for civil rights in the city. The first was the ADVA, under the leadership of I. S. McClinton, which attempted to challenge the growing influence of militant segregationists. ADVA was one of the chief signatories of a petition that urged state legislators in the 1955 Arkansas General Assembly not to adopt a pupil assignment bill. Still attempting to exercise black political power, ADVA refused to commit black electoral support to either Jim Johnson or Orval Faubus in the 1956 Democratic Party primaries because both candidates exploited race in the campaign. In another effort to coordinate the potential power of the state's black electorate, ADVA spearheaded opposition to segregationist measures proposed on the November 1956 ballot.[58]

The second group to try to take a bold stand for civil rights was the Arkansas Christian Movement (ACM), an association of black ministers formed specifically to challenge the constitutionality of segregation measures passed by the 1957 Arkansas General Assembly.[59] This rare clerical engagement in the struggle for civil rights in Little Rock was prompted by the arrival of newcomer Reverend Roland Smith. Smith, a founding member of the Southern Christian Leadership Conference (SCLC) and a friend of its leader, Martin Luther King Jr., tried to encourage black activism among the clergy in Arkansas.[60]

The efforts of ADVA and ACM were significant but ultimately only played supporting roles to the NAACP. The NAACP's move from the periphery to the center of black community politics during the years after the *Brown* decision was the most important development in black activism in Arkansas. The NAACP focused on attempts to persuade the Little Rock school board, with the largest school district in the state, to set an example of compliance with court-ordered school desegregation. Recognizing the pivotal importance of Little Rock's response to desegregation, the local branch of the NAACP attempted to begin negotiations with the city's school board prior to the *Brown* decision. Through the offices of an interracial group, the Little Rock Council on Schools (LRCS), NAACP representatives, along with a handful of white sympathizers, petitioned the school board to consider a proposal for limited desegregation. The proposal, which outlined a plan for black students to use the print shop at Little Rock (later Central) High School, since the black Dunbar High did not have one, was considered seriously by several board members. Only the presence of Superintendent Harry A. Little, a committed segregationist, cast a shadow over the proceedings. Nevertheless, the school board agreed to meet further with the LRCS.[61] Before another meeting could be arranged, however, a local NAACP lawyer, Thaddeus Williams, in an effort to enhance his prestige in the black community, leaked news of the meeting with the school board to the press. The move backfired, as it breached the board's insistence on confidentiality. This ruined the prospect of further negotiations.[62]

That the Little Rock school board had been prepared at least to consider proposals for change gave heart to those who believed that the capital city would lead the way for compliance with the *Brown* decision. Certainly this was the view of those in the delegation who gathered to hear what the new superintendent of schools, Virgil T. Blossom, who succeeded Little in the first half of 1953, had to report about the plans of the Little Rock school board four days after the *Brown* decision had been handed down. However, Blossom informed those present that the school board would not take immediate action but would instead await the Supreme Court's implementation order scheduled for a year later, and the mood of the meeting turned from one of "high spirits" to bitter disappointment. Blossom told the delegation that, despite their obvious displeasure at the turn of events, the school board was not proposing to "delay for delay's sake, but to do the job right."[63]

The initial disappointment over the school board's response to the *Brown* decision was quickly followed by the NAACP's attempt to press for a declaration of definite plans for desegregation. At a meeting with Virgil Blossom, NAACP representatives were informed that before any desegregation could take place, the school board planned to build two new schools, Horace Mann High in the predominantly black eastern part of the city and Hall High in the affluent white suburbs of the west. Blossom stressed that although the two new schools were to be located in black and white residential areas, they would have no set racial designation. Rather, Blossom assured NAACP members, the school board planned to desegregate all three of the city's high schools, Horace Mann, Hall, and Central, along the lines of new color-blind "attendance zones" in 1957, with elementary schools to follow some time around 1960.[64]

The Blossom Plan met with a mixed reaction among members of the Little Rock NAACP. Militant members like the Bateses opposed the plan on the grounds that it was "vague, indefinite, slow-moving and indicative of an intent to stall further on public school integration." But a clear majority supported the plan and cautioned against pushing the school board too hard. Most felt that Blossom and the school board should be given a chance to prove their good intentions, that the plan they had drawn up was reasonable, and that, most importantly, the plan would be acceptable to the white community. The local branch therefore decided that it would await further developments before taking any action.[65] When the Supreme Court handed down its implementation order for school desegregation in May 1955, it undermined black hopes for change. The Court ambiguously told school districts to desegregate "with all deliberate speed" and failed to provide specific guidelines. Blossom had made changes in the plans for school desegregation that, it subsequently became clear, betrayed the trust NAACP members had placed in him. The most detrimental was a new transfer system that would allow students to move out of the attendance zone to which they were assigned. Under the original Blossom Plan, school districts had been gerrymandered to ensure a black majority at Horace Mann High and a white majority at Hall High. The subsequent assignment of black students to Horace Mann, even though they lived closer to Central, confirmed the intention of the school board to limit the impact of desegregation as much as possible. Even so, under the original plan, a substantial amount of integration would have occurred. The revised plan, however, allowed white students to "opt out" of attendance at Horace Mann without giving blacks the right to "opt in" to Hall. To encourage the shift of white students from Horace Mann, the school board assigned an all-black teaching staff to it. The school board also declared that it intended to open Horace Mann as a segregated black school in February 1956, a move intended to establish a precedent for all-black attendance the year before the school was to desegregate.[66]

The revised Blossom Plan infuriated many members of the NAACP, even those who had been willing to go along with the original plan. To add insult to injury, Blossom did not even bother to consult NAACP members about the changes. Daisy Bates subsequently told reporters that the Little Rock NAACP was demanding a meeting with the school board and that further action would depend upon the outcome of the meeting. When NAACP representatives met with the school board to request the immediate integration of the city's schools, Dr. William Cooper, president of the school board, told them that they would receive a written reply to their request within a week. Shortly afterward, the school board rejected the NAACP's proposal outright.[67] The evasion and delay in school desegregation in Little Rock set the pattern for other school districts across the state. Ignoring a declaration by the executive committee of the ASC, which stated that any school board not ready to enact a plan for desegregation by September 1955 would be liable to court action, the three other largest school systems in the state, at Fort Smith, North Little Rock, and Hot Springs, drew up plans that delayed any school desegregation until Little Rock made the first move.[68]

Repeated attempts by the local NAACP to find common ground with the school board resulted in failure. Finally, in December 1955, exasperated at having exhausted every other channel of action, the Little Rock NAACP voted to file a lawsuit against the school board. On January 23, 1956, thirty-three black students, who claimed hardship under the revised Blossom Plan (for example, some students who lived much closer to Central were now being forced to attend the segregated Horace Mann), applied for admission to the school of their choice. The principals of the schools refused entry to the students and referred them to Virgil Blossom. Daisy Bates accompanied nine of the students to Blossom's office, where he denied their request to enroll in white schools. Bates told reporters after the meeting, "I think the next step is obvious. We've tried everything short of a court suit." On February 8, 1956, Wiley Branton filed suit against the Little Rock school board on behalf of the thirty-three students under the title *Aaron v. Cooper.*[69]

The team of lawyers the school board hired to argue *Aaron v. Cooper* found little to go on in the preliminary depositions they took on May 4, 1956. When the case came to trial, however, confusion within the ranks of the NAACP handed the school board a relatively easy victory. The local NAACP had carefully constructed its own case, which demanded only that the original Blossom Plan be upheld, based upon selected plaintiffs who would suffer particular hardship under the revised plan. Yet when regional NAACP attorney U. Simpson Tate arrived from Dallas, he proceeded, without consulting local branch members, to argue the national NAACP's line of complete and immediate integration of all schools. This breakdown in communications between the national and local branches of the NAACP, an echo of past experiences in the state, cost local members the legal initiative, since they had quite rightly sensed that the courts would only uphold specific grievances and would not challenge desegregation plans that exploited the ambiguities in *Brown* II. The court rejected Tate's argument, and Wiley Branton's attempts to revive the case on appeal failed.[70]

The potentially damaging defeat for the NAACP was quickly put aside when attempts to desegregate Central High in September 1957 deteriorated into a highly publicized crisis. The military confrontation thrust Daisy Bates and the NAACP into the national spotlight since other local black leaders were unwilling to come forward in a climate of increasing racial tension. This was confirmed in a 1958 study by black sociologists Tilman C. Cothran and William Phillips Jr., from Arkansas AM&N College in Pine Bluff, in which twenty-two of twenty-six black leaders interviewed in Little Rock identified Bates as "the most influential Negro in the community" and twenty-four of the twenty-six described her as "the most influential Negro in determining policy on educational desegregation." One interviewee described Bates as "the only outspoken Negro leader," adding that "the other Negro leaders have remained silent and have allowed her to become spokesman." A parent of one of the black students at Central High agreed that "the NAACP President is the only leader who has stood up for these children. She has been more helpful than anybody." Alluding to the criticisms that many black people leveled at the inactivity of traditional community leaders, this parent added, "We have a shortage of leaders. . . . There are a lot of would-be leaders, but the problem is that when the trouble starts they won't stand up and be counted."[71]

The unprecedented amount of support for Daisy Bates and the NAACP from 1957 to 1959 coincided with a period during which white people in Little Rock were forced to confront the issue of race head-on. Since this period has generally been viewed as the most important phase of race relations in postwar Arkansas, Daisy Bates and the NAACP have been viewed as the representative voice of black activism. Important as Bates and the NAACP were during those years, this is an erroneous assumption. Black activism in Arkansas did not emerge out of nowhere in 1957 and disappear in 1959, as often appears to be the case. Rather, the 1957 Little Rock school crisis was part of a much larger attempt by black Arkansans to assert their civil rights, which involved a number of leaders, organizations, and tactics and unfolded over many years. Black activism in 1957 had numerous precedents. Only after the national spotlight shifted away from Little Rock did the legacies of those years become apparent, as more new organizations and leaders in the black community came forward to address a changed climate of race relations in the city and to provide new direction for the ongoing civil rights struggle there. Only when historians begin to locate the 1957 Little Rock school crisis within this much longer struggle for freedom and equality will the full implications of the dramatic events of 1957 be fully understood.[72]

INTERNATIONAL PRESSURE AND THE U.S. GOVERNMENT'S RESPONSE TO LITTLE ROCK

Azza Salama Layton

Segregation received more international criticism than any other area of U.S. race relations in the post–World War II period. The Truman and Eisenhower administrations' racial reforms were a response not only to an increasingly effective civil rights movement in the U.S. South but also to international politics. Segregation hindered appeals to potential allies in competition with the Soviet bloc. So in its famous 1947 report, President Truman's committee on civil rights concluded:

> Our position in the postwar world is so vital to the future that our smallest actions have far-reaching effects. . . . The treatment which our Negroes receive is taken as a reflection of our attitudes toward all dark-skinned peoples. . . . We cannot escape the fact that our civil rights record has been an issue in world politics. . . . *The United States is not so strong, the final triumph of the democratic ideal is not so inevitable that we can ignore what the world thinks of us or our record.*[1]

Truman's secretary of state, Dean Acheson, cared little about black rights per se, but he was acutely conscious of the same connection. "School segregation

---

This article first appeared in the autumn 1997 issue of the *Arkansas Historical Quarterly*.

has been singled out for hostile foreign comment in the United Nations and elsewhere," he warned the attorney general in 1952.[2] The State Department used particularly strong language in its amicus brief for the *Brown* case, argued in December 1952:

> During the past six years, the damage to our foreign relations attributable to [race discrimination] has become progressively greater. The United States is under constant attack in the foreign press, over the foreign radio, and in such international bodies as the United Nations. . . . The undeniable existence of racial discrimination gives unfriendly governments the most effective kind of ammunition for their propaganda warfare. . . . The view is expressed that the United States is hypocritical in claiming to be the champion of democracy while permitting practices of racial discrimination here in this country. . . . Other peoples cannot understand how [school segregation] can exist in a country which professes to be a staunch supporter of freedom, justice, and democracy. . . . Racial discrimination remains a source of embarrassment to this government in the day-to-day conduct of its foreign relations. . . . It jeopardizes the effective maintenance of our moral leadership of the free and democratic nations of the world.[3]

The president's statements also bear the imprint of international pressure. As historian Richard Dalfiume notes, "Just about every speech . . . [Harry Truman] made on the civil rights issue . . . always brings up this point: The rest of the world is watching us. We must put our own house in order." The Truman administration's efforts to desegregate the armed forces and commit the Democratic Party to black rights in 1948 must in part be understood as serving Cold War motives.[4]

The Eisenhower administration moved reluctantly in its first term. But in its second term, the 1955 murder of fourteen-year-old Emmett Till; widely publicized discriminatory sentences by southern state courts; the 1955–56 Montgomery bus boycott; and, most dramatically, southern defiance of federal school desegregation orders all generated negative international publicity.[5] At the Bandung Conference of 1955, representatives from Africa and Asia denounced Western racism. During the Hungarian crisis of 1956, when the U.S. delegation to the United Nations pushed for sanctions against the Soviet Union, several foreign governments responded that the American government violated the civil and human rights of its own colored citizens.[6] A similar response greeted U.S. efforts during the Berlin crisis of 1948–49. Secretary of State John Foster Dulles even suggested at one point that the U.S. government's refusal to take a firm stand against South Africa's apartheid policy grew out of a fear of being charged with hypocrisy.[7]

While the Supreme Court's 1954 *Brown* decision helped improve America's image abroad, defiance of the decision attracted worldwide attention and resulted in a new round of criticism. State legislatures all over the South, often under pressure from local White Citizens' Councils, passed laws evading or thwarting implementation of the decision. This massive resistance movement culminated in the showdown at Little Rock in 1957–58.

The Little Rock battle attracted more international attention than any previous civil rights battle, and international pressure led the Eisenhower administration, particularly the State Department, to conclude, as the Truman administration had done before, that civil rights at home had crucial international significance for the United States as a world power. Largely for that reason, the Eisenhower administration, aided by the leaders of both parties in Congress, began to take steps toward what would become known as the civil rights revolution of the 1960s.

The Autherine Lucy case of 1956 was an important prelude to Little Rock. Following the *Brown* decision, Lucy had registered to attend the University of Alabama, which provoked violent outbursts and marked the first clash between federal and state law-enforcement agencies over the issue of school segregation. It was also the first school segregation case to become an international event. According to an opinion survey conducted by the United States Information Agency (USIA) in Western Europe, "the Autherine Lucy case qualifies as not less than an international *cause célèbre* with from a quarter to a third in Western Europe alluding more or less specifically to the incident as a basis of recent unfavorable impressions of the treatment of Negroes in the U.S." The USIA report concluded that the positive effect of the *Brown* decision was wearing off, and America's prestige was suffering because of Autherine Lucy and similar incidents. The State Department emphasized that "the opinions of the more influential elite were no less adverse than the opinions of the rest of the population in every country surveyed."[8] A USIA official confirmed that attempts to publicize positive racial stories were being overshadowed by the public exposure of racial discrimination, lamenting, "If it were not for our racial problems, we would be way ahead of the game by now. As it is, it seems we are just able to hold our own."[9]

Following the Autherine Lucy affair, international outrage over school segregation in the United States subsided for a while. But in September 1957, Little Rock brought a full-scale international outburst over racial conditions in the United States.

President Eisenhower was at first reluctant to enforce desegregation. He had opposed desegregation of the armed forces in 1948, made his respect for states' rights clear, and refused to endorse the *Brown* decision.[10] In 1956, he declared that achieving equality should be handled at the local and state levels, because racial issues were "matters of the heart not of legislation." After

Arkansas governor Orval Faubus defied the court desegregation order and sent National Guard troops to bar black students from Central High School, Eisenhower waited twenty days before sending federal troops to enforce the order.[11]

The timing of this federal-state showdown was unfortunate. On August 29, 1957, Congress had passed the first civil rights legislation since Reconstruction.[12] President Eisenhower signed the bill on September 9. But the positive effect of the 1957 Civil Rights Act was lost on international audiences as the world watched mobs defy the federal troops and attack black students.

Most criticism came from Europe and Africa, but Asia, the Middle East, South America, Canada, and Australia contributed their share.[13] Indonesian citizens sent an open letter, published in the newspaper *Suluh Indonesia,* to the American ambassador and American citizens in Indonesia, expressing "disgust" over Little Rock. The letter asked how Americans hoped to convince the Asian people of their belief in democracy "as long as there is still ill-treatment of Negroes such as happened again in Little Rock." It said that photographs of Little Rock spoke louder than the U.S. government's words and suggested that white southerners should go to Asia to learn something about tolerance. The U.S. embassy confirmed to the State Department that the writers of the letter were not communists.[14]

Many Libyans bitterly criticized the United States for calling itself the "mother of liberty and democracy while permitting sixteen million African Americans to be smashed under the soles of the white and live a life of humiliation." A newspaper editorial in Tripoli asked Americans why Libyans should believe U.S. propaganda when they were aware of the "tragedies" that were taking place.[15]

Many Brazilians denounced "so-called" American democracy. The American consul general in São Paolo told the State Department that Little Rock had made the favorable side of Negro progress hard to present and that statements by Louis Armstrong and Eartha Kitt about Negro progress were not helpful.[16] Argentines sent open letters to President Eisenhower and various U.S. student bodies. Some asked Eisenhower how he expected to convince Russia and the rest of the world of the advantages of democracy when he could not persuade his own subordinate, Governor Faubus, to obey the law.[17]

Critics in these and other countries, according to the State Department, included elite groups, university students, labor unions, and professional syndicates, as well as average citizens (whose sentiments were revealed mostly through public-opinion surveys). The volume and intensity of international criticism and the expressed concerns of U.S. officials over the implications of Little Rock were, according to a USIA report, "tremendous."

The Little Rock crisis captured the attention of "the very large majority of the population in major world capitals, invoking worldwide reaction," according to the USIA. Not only was international opinion about the treatment of African Americans in the United States "highly adverse, but more often than not the predominant feeling [was] that Negro-white relations have been worsening rather than improving over the past few years." The strongly prevailing feeling in cities across the world was that the current developments lowered the United States' standing and prestige in the world. The USIA estimated that the "losses" to the U.S. were "of such a magnitude as to outweigh the effects of any recent factors which have contributed to increases in U.S. standing."[18]

The U.S. diplomatic mission in Denmark was "embarrassed over Danish reaction to Little Rock," stating that the Danish people were "appalled" by the violence. The American embassy in Copenhagen asked the State Department for help in responding to the public protest.[19] The Swedish media were filled with derogatory news coverage of Little Rock. The liberal *Svenska Morgonbladet* strongly condemned "the United States, which went to war to fight Nazism and its racial persecutions." The semiofficial *Morgon tidningen* expressed concern over the damage to U.S. prestige abroad.[20]

Swiss editorial and news coverage of Little Rock exceeded any previous publicity given to the United States, the U.S. embassy in Bern reported with alarm, saying the crisis was "inflicting grave damage on the moral position of the western world at a precise time when the U.N. General Assembly [is] debating the Hungarian tragedy." Embassy officials concluded that Little Rock would "adversely affect American position and prestige in the mind of the average Swiss" and that the general reaction was "one of sober dismay over display of such violence." The Swiss believed that Little Rock had resulted in "incalculable harm" to the Western position throughout the non-European world.[21]

According to the American consul general in Amsterdam, even the reserved Dutch, who usually did not publicize their feelings, spoke fervently about a state governor's forcibly denying Negro children the right to a good education. Dutch citizens viewed events in Little Rock "as un[be]coming of a nation which continually affirms to the world its devotion to principles of liberty, equality, and equal opportunity for all citizens." The Dutch also worried "lest what is happening in Arkansas weaken America, in her contest with Soviet communism over the uncommitted areas of Asia, Africa and the Middle East—areas where there is a real sensitivity to color discrimination. They believe that a weakening of America's moral leadership in the world indirectly hurts America's allies." The consul general quoted the Communist organ *De waarheid* as saying, "Washington wishes to impose its will on the World but in Arkansas Eisenhower is powerless."[22] U.S. officials in Amsterdam quoted government officials and members of the press as saying that there was very little difference between "Hitlerian methods and the activities of

American racists," adding that this widespread opinion "hurts America in the eyes of the world."[23]

The *Irish Times* accused the southern states of "put[ting] a new heart into [the] Negro-baiting KKK" and giving communist propagandists "considerable material for innumerable sermons to colored people everywhere."[24]

The news media in Luxembourg suggested that Little Rock had done more harm to "America's moral voice, especially among colored people of the world, than is befitting [of] the leader of the free world" and that Little Rock was "a happy find for the Communists as a means of overshadowing the condemnation of the Hungarian massacre and the new anti-Semitism in the Soviet Union." One Luxembourg paper mocked Governor Faubus for comparing the occupation of Little Rock by federal troops to the German occupation of Paris and the Soviet attack on Budapest.[25] The official organ of the Luxembourg government declared that Little Rock had made a very bad international impression; the United States had been using dollars and weapons to stop the Russian offensive in the Middle East and elsewhere among colored peoples, and "Little Rock was like a cold shower."[26]

In Belgium, events in Little Rock drew greater interest than any other American domestic issue. Newspapers sharply questioned the sincerity of the high moral attitude adopted by the United States in international affairs. According to the American embassy in Brussels, the Belgian media seemed more concerned about the effects of the Arkansas events on American prestige in Asia and Africa than about their effects on Belgium.[27]

The British often expressed cynicism regarding Americans' lecturing them about having "an empire in India" and "a colony in Africa" while they had Little Rock. A British correspondent told American journalist Mike Wallace that "respectable people in Britain are saying they do not want to hear of Rev. Billy Graham coming to preach another crusade. He'd better stay home and Christianize the Americans. We have been preached at enough."[28]

Many Europeans sent letters and petitions directly to U.S. officials. Student bodies in Austria sent open letters to Faubus comparing his actions and attitude with those of "Hitler . . . whose regime persecuted men only because of their race." The letters stated that black soldiers fought against fascism in World War II, yet the governor was denying their rights and that "events in Arkansas have most seriously shaken the belief of the world in the freedom mission of the US."[29] The International Federation of the Union of Education, "in the name of seven and a half million teachers," expressed its indignation to President Eisenhower over the events at Little Rock and demanded "respect for the rights of Negro children and the banning of all educational segregation."[30]

Reaction to Little Rock was restrained in some European countries. In Germany, for example, people's awareness of their own vulnerability on the question of persecuting racial minorities seemed to restrain them, comparatively speaking, from blaming Americans and reporting on Arkansas with indignation. In addition, German political parties were competing for U.S. support, which seemed in those days to increase electoral popularity. Nevertheless, some German editorials stressed that the United States must guard its "world wide reputation as benefactor and guardian of democracy" and avoid providing "grist for Soviet propaganda."[31]

In Africa, the Little Rock crisis provided an avenue for attacking American foreign policy and for criticizing the United States, which was seeking leadership in Africa and the world on behalf of the "liberty of the individual."[32] With the competition between the United States and the Soviet Union for an African sphere of influence at its height, Little Rock provided opportunities for political maneuvering for many African nations.

Political parties in Uganda, seeking to attract voters and to increase political clout, used Little Rock to compete for "the title of sole Uganda champions of American Negro rights."[33] The Uganda National Congress, one of the leading nationalist parties in Africa, sent Eisenhower a letter questioning his sincerity in light of Little Rock: "Before America can tackle any international problem, she should first and foremost show a clean record at home and we believe this is a prerequisite to American success abroad." The Congress warned that American attempts to establish influence in emerging African nations "are incompatible with the present events in your country. . . . [We] will never cooperate with any country whose racial policy is short of equality."[34] The United Congress, the main nationalist competitor of the Uganda National Congress, sent a letter to Eisenhower expressing "great shock" that the Little Rock crisis could take place in a country that Uganda perceived as a leader in human rights. Such "obstruction of justice" was damaging to the prestige of America in Africa.[35]

The Nigerian press attacked Governor Faubus "for giving the U.S. one more black-eye in the eyes of the world." Asian and African U.N. delegates, one editorial observed, would be in jail if they happened to be in Little Rock. The editorial asked, "What moral right have Americans to condemn apartheid in South Africa while still maintaining it by law?" The Nigerian news media concluded that the United States could not be champion "of the colonial peoples while championing inequality in its backyard."[36] U.S. embassy officials in Lagos characterized the Nigerian attack as comparatively tolerant but warned that "this tolerance will [not] continue in the presence of any future racial disturbances" in the United States.[37]

In Mozambique, Little Rock became a symbol of black-white relations in the United States at a time when America was trying "to condemn colonialism or racial segregation elsewhere in the world," the distressed American consul there noted. Embassy personnel in Lourenço Marques warned the State

Department that "there seems to be no question but that our moral standing has been very considerably damaged" and that "any pretension of an American to advise any European government on African affairs at this point would be hypocrisy."[38]

An instructive sidelight to the criticism of American racism in Africa was the reaction of racial minorities in Africa. In Kenya, Little Rock received more attention than developments in Ghana, Malayan independence, or the United Nations debates on Hungary. Leaders of the Asian minority in Kenya expressed sympathy for black Americans, given that they themselves "would perhaps become victims of discrimination at the hands of Africans" when Kenya gained its independence.[39]

The reaction to the Little Rock crisis by other racist regimes exemplifies the complexity of the Cold War pressures the U.S. government faced. Several countries used the event as a bargaining chip. The French in West Africa, for example, used the Little Rock case to show the world that, when it came to race, France did a better job than the United States. According to one U.S. diplomat in Africa, the French regarded Little Rock as a political opportunity to blackmail the United States. They hoped Little Rock "would make the U.S. a little more sympathetic to France's problem in Algeria, especially at the [up]coming U.N. session."[40]

Although news coverage of Little Rock in South Africa was overshadowed by coverage of the Soviet satellite *Sputnik,* U.S. officials there said the episode was "one of the worst [U.S. officials] have had to cope with."[41] Influential Afrikaners used Little Rock as proof that integration would not work and that forces against integration were gaining ground in the United States.[42]

When President Eisenhower, with great reluctance, finally ordered federal troops to Little Rock to protect the nine black students at Central High, he explained his action to Americans by stressing the international ramifications of the crisis: "It would be difficult to exaggerate the harm being done to the prestige and influence, and indeed to the safety, of our nation and the world. Our enemies are gloating over this incident and using it everywhere to misrepresent our whole nation."[43]

Eisenhower's intervention received mostly positive international response, though some accused him of procrastination, which "leaves a bitter aftertaste," as one foreign newspaper put it, and of taking a weak stand on civil rights legislation.[44] The Swedish press reminded Eisenhower that the Western world would be watching with concern and that failure would undermine the position of the United States in the free world.[45] Some foreigners described federal intervention in Little Rock as a continuation of America's international role in protecting human rights, a role it had played during World War II in Europe.[46] Many viewed Eisenhower as merely completing the work begun by Abraham Lincoln.[47] African politicians in French West Africa told

U.S. officials that, until Eisenhower actually sent the troops to Little Rock, African opinion was that the president "would not dare use federal troops to enforce desegregation."[48]

Many diplomats and other figures in foreign countries perceived international pressure as contributing to Eisenhower's decision to intervene. One Costa Rican diplomat said Eisenhower's protection of the Little Rock Nine was "in large part determined by the convenience of international politics. The non-white peoples inhabiting the planet are many and very great. The persecution of Negroes is of no advantage to the international policies of the United States."[49]

Celebrating the U.S. government's action in Little Rock, Brazilian officials praised the freedom of the U.S. press in reporting racial incidents, compared to the "concealment of crimes by Russia."[50] A number of United Nations delegates appealed to their organization for measures that would force Americans to respect the law. An incident such as Little Rock, they said, should not happen again: "Democratic people everywhere are disturbed and ashamed at the continued racist discrimination against and [the] oppression of the Negro people in the United States."[51]

Like the *Brown* decision, Eisenhower's decision to intervene at Little Rock, however belatedly, did improve America's image abroad. Nevertheless, federal action could not stop the long-term negative impact the event had on U.S. prestige, international public opinion, and America's geopolitical objectives. In 1958, USIA surveys revealed that "irritation at the United States is very widespread" and that Little Rock was one of the leading causes of anti-American sentiment. While international opinion of race relations in the United States was already generally negative, "Little Rock confirmed previously held views of racial discrimination." Because of Little Rock, there was a dramatic decline in foreign confidence that "what America says" equaled "what America does."[52]

USIA officials explained away the negative reactions of some countries to the Little Rock crisis by saying, "America's standing in the area of race relations [in those countries] was already in a very depressed state prior to the Arkansas desegregation incidents, and hence not readily susceptible to further decrease."[53] But others found it difficult to dismiss the negative effect of the crisis. The president of the Union of Hebrew Congregations, Maurice Eisendrath, for example, told the *New York Post* after a five-month world tour that America's failure to address racial discrimination, magnified by Little Rock, had alienated millions of Asians and Africans. He said that "the reservoir of goodwill toward America is being dried out" and suggested that Eisenhower should impress on state governors the connection "between America's foreign policy interests, its national security, and race policies at home."[54]

In 1959, the Civil Rights Commission issued a stern warning that "the pace of progress during the 96 years since emancipation has been remarkable. But this is an age of revolutionary change. The colored peoples of Asia and Africa, constituting a majority of the human race, are swiftly coming into their own. . . . The future peace of the world is at stake."[55]

Racial segregation in the United States was a primary target of international criticism and pressure. In addition to the rising power of the black vote and the increased organization and militancy of the civil rights movement, the atmosphere of the Cold War and the rise of new independent nations in Africa and elsewhere pushed the federal government to become an active partner in the struggle against segregation. The success of the civil rights movement in the 1950s and 1960s is partly the result of the way civil rights activists themselves framed America's race problem in an international context. As an observer at a religious student conference a few weeks before the sit-ins of 1960 reported, "hundreds" of southern black students "listened, discussed and evidently thought a great deal as militant African nationalists 'stole the show' with predictions of a 'new order.'" And a journalist visiting black campuses in 1960 noted that "even the most unintellectual black students were envious of the African independence movement and vaguely moved by it."[56] When Martin Luther King Jr. tried to explain the seemingly sudden "Negro revolution" of the 1950s and 1960s, he said:

> The American Negro . . . realized that just thirty years ago there were only three independent nations in the whole of Africa. He knew that by 1963 more than thirty-four African nations had risen from colonial bondage. The Negro saw black statesmen voting on vital issues in the United Nations and knew that in many cities of his own land he was not permitted to take that significant walk to the ballot box. He saw black kings and potentates ruling from palaces—and he knew he had been condemned to move from small ghettos to larger ones.[57]

America's friends and foes around the world used the opportunities that American segregation provided to advance their causes in their own countries and in the international arena.

The United States could not champion human rights and freedom abroad unless it was showing progress and setting an example at home. The timing of successful desegregation efforts is not mere happenstance. These efforts went hand in hand with international events and radical changes in the map of Africa and the rest of what we now call the Third World—changes the United States wished to influence in competition with the Soviet Union. Southern defiance of the global interests of America in the Cold War opened the United States to great international criticism and, consequently, to an increasingly active government.

The practical requirements of America's foreign policy helped focus national attention on racial conditions that the nation had long ignored. Only in these circumstances was the government prepared to accept the obligation to fulfill the promise of freedom and equality embodied in the Fourteenth and Fifteenth Amendments. Domestic pressures alone might have brought the same result, but surely only after greater delay and considerably more bloodshed in American streets than actually took place in the 1950s and 1960s. The height of the Cold War did not simply coincide with the height of the civil rights revolution but had a strong causal relationship to it.

AFTER 1957

Resisting Integration in Little Rock

Ben F. Johnson III

Adolphine Fletcher Terry grew despondent. The resistance by vocal, organized citizens to school integration roiled Little Rock. She regretted that influential and prominent community leaders remained on the sidelines. Characteristically, she did not hold her fire. Her status as a member of one of the city's leading families, as well as her involvement in the twentieth century's signal reform movements, invariably assured her a hearing. After Terry made clear her views on this school crisis, the *Arkansas Gazette* hailed her as "one of Little Rock's most esteemed civic leaders." Nevertheless, she could not shake the dread that her beloved city would meet calls for equality and opportunity with evasion and delay: "I cannot bear to see my town ruined by the stupidity (or is it the cupidity?) and indifference of its citizens."[1]

This cry of anger or despair came not in 1957, amid the agonies of the Central High desegregation crisis, but thirteen years later. And among those Terry blamed for bolstering segregation in 1970 was an erstwhile ally from that earlier conflict. William F. Rector feared that school integration plans that breached the boundaries between black and white neighborhoods threatened the value of his suburban real estate holdings. He fought doggedly against such plans and those who supported them. Although forgotten in the midst of the commemorations of the 1957 crisis, the victories won by Rector and his allies obstructed integration for many years afterward and decisively influenced the subsequent development of the Little Rock schools.

Through the years, memory, public commemorations, and popular accounts of Little Rock school desegregation have shaped a portrait of a singular catastrophe, framed by disruption and reconciliation, separated from historical developments and forces. Yet Adolphine Terry well understood that the reopening of the Little Rock high schools in 1959 had not resolved the crisis nor set in motion the extinction of a dual education system. In the ensuing decade, the school board, first through a pupil assignment plan and then through a "freedom-of-choice" approach, had without apology sustained largely single-race classrooms. The district leaders insisted such policies did not harm basic rights as long as those rare students who wished to apply to a school where they would be in a small minority were permitted to do so. While claiming to safeguard educational quality, school officials routinely rejected student applications that would have led to greater desegregation. In May 1965, Ozell Sutton, a rising African American leader in Little Rock, detailed how the district crafted plans to prevent desegregation. Paul R. Fair, the deputy superintendent, accepted the critique: "[The courts] do not specifically state that it is the responsibility of schools to integrate or desegregate or mix the races in the school."[2]

By 1967, liberal organizations that had sprung from the 1957–59 crisis had backed the election of reformers to the school board, and the new majority accepted the need for authentic integration in light of bolder federal court orders. Fierce, adamant opposition to the new school board proposals erupted from the affluent western neighborhoods that had once been bulwarks in support of the 1959 open-school movement. With Rector at the helm, the latter-day resistance to desegregation of classrooms in the city's most prosperous and whitest ward routed the new initiatives and purged the liberals from the school board. Adolphine Fletcher Terry in 1970 denounced Rector for recruiting and bankrolling an opponent of the last remaining white supporter of districtwide integration on the board. This was Terry's last battle, and she lost. Federal judge Henry Woods later observed in a 1984 ruling that the Little Rock school board in the late 1960s offered desegregation plans "in a good faith effort to provide a solution to continuous litigation" but that they "failed in the hysterical political atmosphere of the period."[3]

Adolphine Terry's conflict with other figures from her city's white elite had its roots in her involvement in an Arkansas reform tradition that had gradually come to encompass civil rights. This tradition for the most part was top-down. Throughout her life, Terry believed that injustice and oppression grew from the failure of a socially responsible elite both to recognize the humanity of African Americans and to check white populist racism. Her convictions were embedded in family history. In 1900, her father, John G. Fletcher, had run as the business-establishment candidate for governor to stave off Attorney General Jeff Davis, whose fortunes crested on rural white anger over the exploitative practices of town merchants and competition from black farmers. Davis humiliated Fletcher on the stump, and the new governor's three terms confirmed white supremacy and disfranchisement as the foundation of the Arkansas Democratic Party. The less fractious Progressive governors who followed Davis advanced a program that accorded with urban goals of modernization and economic development, while leaving in place Davis's racial settlement. The reformers believed that partisan rancor and debates over black rights diverted attention from the good fights for efficient government and expanded public services.[4]

If the color line had hardened in the opening decades of the century, women in Arkansas as elsewhere were transforming domestic obligations into public activism. White women, who had been the foot soldiers in turning out the dry vote in local-option elections around the turn of the century, identi-fied a set of reforms that touched upon home and family. Minnie Rutherford Fuller, president of the state Woman's Christian Temperance Union, was a well-regarded lobbyist who drafted the law that set up the first juvenile court system. Adolphine Terry also pushed to keep minors from being treated the same as adult offenders, as well as promoting school consolidation, setting up libraries, and marching in suffrage parades. But as with the male reformers, this first generation of women social activists formed no alliances with their African American counterparts. Suffrage advocates instead brandished the racist argument that white women should not be denied the voting rights allowed black men. Shortly after World War I, though, Terry was initiated into biracial social uplift when she agreed to serve as one of three white advisors imposed upon the newly formed Phyllis Wheatley Young Women's Christian Association, the first African American "Y" in Little Rock. Terry recounted in her memoir that the YWCA meetings forced her to realize how segregation distorted history and blinkered whites' perspective on contemporary condi-tions: "We, the daughters of Confederate veterans who had heard a great deal about the white side of the war, now learned of the suffering of the black pop-ulation, before, during and after the war, and of the lacks from which they still suffered."[5]

As with most other white liberals before the civil rights era, Terry's per-sonal experience awakened an awareness of "another world" without convert-ing her into an antisegregationist. During the 1930s, Terry enlisted a formidable number of white women's religious and educational organizations in the anti-lynching crusade through appeals based on Christian duty. As social-justice Progressives in the South evolved into New Dealers, they concluded that the traditional campaigns against the region's endemic violence and poverty would fall short if the "lacks" plaguing African Americans were ignored. Terry was better able to tap federal relief agencies on behalf of the Little Rock poor after her husband, David Terry, took his seat in the U.S. House of Representa-tives in 1935. She and other white liberals, including Edwin Dunaway, lob-bied city officials to establish a local housing authority that in turn could secure federal aid to clear blighted neighborhoods and construct public housing blocks. In 1940, the Little Rock board of directors set up the new authority and appointed as its first chair the head of the local realtors association. Little was done until voters in 1950 designated bond money slated for improving the only park for black residents as a match for federal dollars to underwrite urban-renewal projects. Both Terry and Dunaway were directors of the Little Rock chapter of the biracial Urban League that for years had demanded the city develop an African American park with amenities equal to those found in the numerous white recreational facilities. Terry believed neighborhood refurbishment complemented the benefits of play and outdoor activity. Leading up to the May 1950 election, she rallied women's organizations to recognize that razing slums would protect the health and welfare of the poor. The proposal provoked bitter recriminations from white landlords but passed on the strength of votes from African Americans, influential businessmen, and upper-class whites. Nine years later, a similar coalition would oust segregationist school board members and reopen the city's high schools.[6]

The discovery of a housing crisis in Little Rock did not arise from the availability of manna from Washington alone. World War II marked the state's most significant push toward urbanization, and no city in the South grew more crowded than Little Rock. Rural whites flocked to the city for jobs in wartime plants and other booming businesses, but the African American population grew even faster as the federal Fair Employment Practices Committee gradually compelled federal contractors to hire black workers. White migrants from the delta entered a world where familiar conventions and rituals no longer framed their everyday life, including the jagged racial etiquette that was second nature in the countryside. Pockets of black neighborhoods blossomed throughout the eastern and central sections of Little Rock, adjoining white residential blocks. The hub for these dispersed enclaves was the bustling West Ninth Street district, which flourished with new African American businesses and customers. As demonstrated by the votes to secure a black park and provide public housing, a new generation of African American activists capitalized upon a growing constituency not bound to old-line leaders to set forth a more assertive agenda. The efforts of local advocates for equal rights confirmed that congressional civil rights bills and judicial rulings in the postwar era would not remain muffled rumblings of a distant storm. White political and business leaders anticipated the vulnerability of the Jim Crow racial order in the years leading up to *Brown v. Board of Education* and experimented with less constitutionally suspect forms of segregation. In the case of Little Rock, influential figures responded to the social and legal challenges to the status quo by reapportioning the city according to race.[7]

The hopes of Adolphine Terry and African American voters that the 1950 urban-renewal bond issue would provide decent housing for poor families thus faded. The city housing authority seemed most concerned with using those federal dollars to consolidate the black population into the eastern precincts. In 1952, municipal officials razed an African American neighborhood of mixed lower- and middle-income residences near Dunbar High School. Homeowners protested the barrage of heavy-handed intimidation and the threats of evictions that effectively drove out property owners. They emphasized that their homes represented long years of hard work and a dedication to a neighborhood that was thriving and vital. A lawsuit failed to halt the bulldozers. One resident of the Dunbar neighborhood charged in a letter to the *Arkansas Gazette*, "I feel the choicest area of the Negro residential section has been selected for clearance." Some displaced residents were eligible to move into the newly constructed, four-hundred-unit Joseph A. Booker Homes, a public housing project for African Americans located near Granite Mountain on the southeastern margin of the city. Segregated public housing anchored the concentration of black residents, curbing their search for homes closer to the white western sections.[8]

The intent to section off neighborhoods by means of government funds and coercive authority, rather than to let matters take their course, was calculated and apparent. In testimony entered into the record in a later federal desegregation case, B. Finley Vinson, who worked for the housing authority in the 1950s, acknowledged the fundamental purpose behind the placement of the Booker homes: "It should be made very clear that . . . this was a device to maintain segregation of races. . . . There was no bones made about it." Little Rock's most passionate integration advocate recognized the forces behind the new currents of migration. In 1953, L. C. Bates, the editor of the *Arkansas State Press,* upbraided those black leaders who had ignored the clear aims of a housing authority in thrall to real estate interests: "We told you the move was to centralize all Negroes in one area and forget about them while the city progresses in another direction."[9]

The controlled racial segmentation of Little Rock provided Virgil Blossom a propitious template as he drew up high school attendance zones in the wake of the *Brown* decision. The school district unveiled modern Horace Mann High School in line with the older equalization strategy to enhance African American education within a single-race institution. Beginning in 1957, white students in the western enclaves were set to enroll in the newly constructed Hall High School. Blossom proposed to desegregate only Central High School, winnowing a selected number of African American students from a pool of two hundred who resided in the predominantly white working-class zone. Before the start of the 1957 term, audiences at white civic clubs and business groups listened approvingly as the superintendent unveiled plans that dovetailed with managed residential segregation. Influential figures believed Blossom's plan of minimum compliance changed little, while defusing an eruption of open resistance that could damage the city's reputation. In March

1957, Everett Tucker Jr., who recruited industry for Little Rock, thanked Blossom for helping to cajole a manufacturing prospect who feared a disruptive backlash to *Brown* in a southern capital: "You may not realize it but these people were exceedingly apprehensive over the integration problem and the material you gave me on short notice one afternoon several months ago went a long way toward allaying their anxieties on this score."[10]

White residents with modest incomes in the Central High neighborhoods were acquainted with the politics of privilege and assumed that the affluent western Fifth Ward (home to every school board member) was protecting its own from judicial decrees. Class resentments among white families deepened their anger over the dismantling of the racial caste system. Nevertheless, many in the crowds that ringed the school during the crisis came from outside the city and would not have withdrawn if a few African American students had also been assigned to Hall High School. In later years, white resisters to Little Rock desegregation and their family members would parse motives to exclude racism and single out class defiance to explain the September days of rage. Yet the rhetoric and propaganda of those who can be termed militant segregationists (openly defiant of court orders) unequivocally revealed the intensity of their antiblack sentiment. Their torrid jeremiads against even prominent whites revealed a shift in the white consensus at the dawn of the civil rights era. The ardent white supremacists decried the accommodation to *Brown* promoted by Virgil Blossom and the business establishment, though this moderate segregationist alternative offered minimal, incremental compliance as a viable defense of the racial status quo.[11]

White southern-elite preference for order, along with federal scrutiny, constrained the explosions of mass crowd violence that had suppressed African American aspirations throughout the Jim Crow decades. Open, uncompromising resistance in 1957 depended upon the rise of organizations that unfurled the banners of heritage and tradition, while engaging in the up-to-date tactics of popular mobilization, pressure politics, direct action, and manipulation of the media. Emerging out of the delta, an outcropping of the black belt empire, Arkansas's White Citizens' Council movement sought to prop up segregation pure and simple in the state's urban core. The Arkansas leaders of the councils did not share the elite background of their counterparts in Deep South states, indicating that delta political influence was already eroding, even before the Supreme Court's 1962 one-person, one-vote decision effectively dissolved rural hegemony. Although the Arkansas councils were slapdash affairs mired in factional infighting and personal acrimony, a talented statewide figure, James Johnson, and the tireless provocateurs of the Capital Citizens' Council (CCC), Wesley Pruden and Amis Guthridge, transformed the political dialogue to equate acceptance of minimum desegregation with support for full-scale, thorough integration. Proponents of law and order were derided as favoring "race mixing." Revolving around charismatic figures, the CCC and the ancillary Mothers' League had only tenuous links to community institutions but found a ready constituency among those with roots in the delta or who still lived in the rural sections of Pulaski County. The councilors' campaigns of harassment, threats of boycotts, cultivation of friendly reporters, and boisterous demonstrations gave their circumscribed uprising the appearance of a community in revolt. The radical segregationists persuaded Governor Orval Faubus that defying them would spell his political ruin and treated the deployment of troops at Central High as an opportunity to prove desegregation was unworkable without massive intervention. Coordinated disruptions by small groups of white students throughout the 1957–58 school year were highlighted and amplified in news columns to substantiate council assertions that proscribing embedded traditions invited chaos.[12]

Given its creaking underpinnings, the militant segregationist movement in Little Rock would have collapsed if city political and business leaders had exercised their customary authority. The civic elite had nominally assented to Blossom's evasive policy without committing to lend a hand if events spun out of control. They subsequently waited amid the ruins of the superintendent's plan to see if the methods of the councils' cadres would more effectively keep desegregation at bay. Little Rock did not possess strong civic institutions to buttress public order and welfare in times of crisis, depending instead on the personal courage and responsibility of its self-appointed circle of leaders. If the council movement inverted the usual class pyramid in Little Rock, the triumph won by Daisy Bates and L. C. Bates, the nine African American students who attended Central High and their families, and other activists affiliated with the NAACP over the racial radicals was little short of a revolution. Throughout the crisis year, the Bates home was under constant attack, companies bankrupted the *Arkansas State Press* by pulling their advertisements, the city council approved laws that drained the NAACP coffers through lawsuits, and employers summarily fired family members of the Little Rock Nine. But eight of the nine students remained in school, despite the isolation and physical assaults by students backed by the CCC and the Mothers' League. The national NAACP judged that defeat in Little Rock would compromise the promise of the *Brown* decision and steadfastly supplied funds, expertise, and advice to Daisy and L. C. Bates. The aid from external allies contrasted with the absence of federal protection and relief for the embattled students and their supporters. Though this victory came at great cost, the graduation of Ernest Green in May 1958 forced both the white racial radicals and the business establishment to recognize that rank intimidation and sustained violence would not deter the African American community from pursuing civil rights.[13]

On September 12, 1958, a unanimous U.S. Supreme Court refused the request by the Little Rock School District to suspend implementation of its desegregation program. The district argued that the disruptions incited by the council's narrow base of supporters represented communitywide intransigence and imperiled the education of all students. Yet the district's attorneys implicitly acknowledged that the hard tactics of the extreme segregationists or popular defiance posed less of an obstruction than the actions of a single individual. The requested two-and-one-half-year delay would permit the school board to restart desegregation following the end of Governor Faubus's current term. The justices' sharp rebuff to the district's argument that the deeply felt preferences of local whites superseded constitutional protections confirmed that the aims of the Citizens' Council were outside the law. Whatever James Johnson's theories on states' rights, the district and business community leaders knew that they could not legally operate a racially separate school system. Faubus apparently reached the same conclusion. A few hours after the Court's ruling, the governor signed the school-closing law, and the CCC shifted from keeping black students out of white schools to keeping all students out of public high schools. The radicals were now on the inside, and the true insiders, the civic elite, were adrift. As Little Rock citizens ratified Faubus's school-closure decision, the influential movers and shakers advanced no proposals to counter the councilors' assertions that enrollment of even the slightest number of African American students in white schools amounted to the demise of segregation. Months would pass before the civic leaders attached themselves to an open-school movement. This movement proved to be another chapter in the urban-reform program defined and carried out by elite white female activists.[14]

In general accounts, the origin of the Women's Emergency Committee to Open Our Schools (WEC) has been suffused with a mythic quality, the sudden appearance of a deus ex machina. This standard tableau is ideologically innocent: Velma Powell and Vivion Brewer join Adolphine Terry in September 1958 at Terry's family mansion at Seventh and Rock streets and conclude that good women must set about to put things right again. In truth, Terry had been attending interracial gatherings of women at the Dunbar community center throughout the spring of 1958, and, as had been the case at the Phyllis Wheatley YWCA, she had heard views that often did not reach the ears of even like-minded white moderates. If reluctant compliance with desegregation rulings represented the moderate stance, Terry slowly and with ambivalence began to move beyond that, regarding the crisis as a matter of extending justice. In a diary entry, she observed, "Of course no one really wants integration, there are too many problems, but it is here and it[']s right." The three women meeting in the antebellum residence envisioned an organization resembling the earlier association to prevent lynching that would generate a public dialogue on tolerance and respect for the law. Black and white participants in the group would explore common aims and challenge the segregationist assumptions that had stifled debate. The white women invited to the initial organizational meeting, however, quickly replaced the goal of promoting racial understanding with the aim of keeping the high schools operating. To fend off charges that the WEC was an integrationist body, the attendees voted to exclude African Americans from membership. The three founders believed it fruitless to contest this conservative revision of their initial plans for the group.[15]

Terry's prestige anchored the WEC, while her decades of practical experience on behalf of progressive reforms, as well as on her husband's congressional campaigns, shaped the WEC's grassroots electioneering. The chronic corruption plaguing Arkansas balloting had made modern get-out-the-vote campaigns irrelevant. The WEC activists transformed politics by organizing urban precincts based on identifying and maintaining strong contacts with likely supporters. The group gained valuable lessons even as it failed to turn the tide on the school-closing referendum or the defeat of Representative Brooks Hays in November 1958. The WEC's electoral proficiency solidified the group, but not to the point that its members reached agreement on the central question of integration. With no stated position on the extent of desegregation in reopened schools, WEC fortunes waited upon white Little Rock voters to conclude that inconvenience, risks to their children's well-being, and weakening economic growth made holding the line on segregation too dear. As these costs became more obvious, the WEC found sympathizers in influential quarters.

An early, though prickly, collaborator with the WEC from the business community was William F. Rector, the great-grandson of the state's first Confederate governor. Rector had started off in insurance in the 1940s but decided that the wide-open, unregulated sector of real estate better suited his temperament. In her memoirs, Brewer recalled him as "decisively abrupt, almost belligerent." An early supporter of Faubus, Rector broke ranks with the governor after national media coverage of the Central High crisis led an out-of-state investor to break off negotiations on a deal that had promised Rector a lucrative return. Rector had firm segregationist views but believed the school closings shredded the city's appeal to new business prospects. In December 1958, the WEC, working covertly with Chamber of Commerce leaders, hurriedly recruited a slate of candidates (referred to as the businessmen's slate, although it included WEC member Margaret Stephens) to oppose arch-segregationists for school board posts. Rector agreed to stand as one of the business candidates but angered WEC leaders when he buttressed his segregationist credentials by boasting of past financial support for the Citizens' Councils. Still, the business bloc distinguished itself from the militant segregationists by advocating the reopening of the schools, while hedging on the response to court desegregation orders. With WEC precinct captains on the job, three of the businessmen overcame opposition to garner school board seats. Rector fell short in his bid and, in a bitter exchange at the Terry mansion, excoriated the WEC for causing his defeat before he abruptly left the house.[16]

The WEC's hope that the election of three school board members in favor of opening the high schools signaled a shift in the outlook of the business establishment seemed fulfilled in March 1959, when the Little Rock Chamber of Commerce took out newspaper advertisements that declared a majority of its membership favored putting the schools back in business. More importantly, though, chamber leaders for the first time assured white citizens that legal means were in place to keep the newly open schools almost completely segregated. The Arkansas General Assembly, in its just-completed session, had approved as one of a host of segregationist measures a new pupil assignment law modeled after an Alabama statute that had already passed muster with the U.S. Supreme Court. The Chamber of Commerce advertisement clarified that such a law would enable school authorities to satisfy all but die-hard segregationists: "North Carolina's pupil assignment system has worked well in controlling integration. At one time there were 14 Negroes in the white schools of North Carolina while only 11 are enrolled now." The Arkansas measure allowed a school board to use a list of criteria to determine "the transfer and continuance of all pupils among and within the public schools within its jurisdiction." In effect, Little Rock officials could sit in judgment of student applications for enrollment as Virgil Blossom had done in 1957, when he chose students for admission to Central High School. The Arkansas act also held that "no child shall be compelled to attend any school in which the races are commingled when a written objection of the parent or guardian has been filed with the Board of Education."[17]

The new school board had dismissed Blossom in November 1958, but his strategy to control and minimize desegregation was revived to the same broad approval from the white elite that his original plan had once enjoyed. The expulsion of the remaining radical segregationists from the school board in a May 1959 recall election removed the last obstacles to reopening the schools in the fall term. Many factors shaped the outcome of this election, but the dilution of white allegiance to segregated education was not one. Empty high school classrooms exacted a high toll on families, while the business offer of minimal compliance aligned the opening of schools with a return to the status quo. Just as critically, the Citizens' Council cadres were overmatched in this round by the WEC's organizational muscle and retail electioneering. Upper-income white women from the city's western Fifth Ward became a familiar sight as they knocked on doors throughout the city. In the end, though, African American voters provided the victory margin. Harry Ashmore, the *Arkansas Gazette*'s executive editor, later noted that the arch-segregation-ists fell to "a coalition of the country club set and the black community." But given the widely divergent views on what constituted meaningful integration, this coalition would not hold.[18]

In August 1959, Everett Tucker, the new school board member and a close associate of William Rector, explained to the *New York Times*, "I think both the whites and the Negroes would be better off in their own schools." Earlier that summer, the Pulaski County school board had ignored the list of persons recommended by the WEC to replace the three recalled ultra-segregationist Little Rock board members. The appointed newcomers joined with Tucker and the other survivors from the businessmen's slate to wield the pupil place-ment law for its intended purposes. Before the start of the fall term, the school board rejected requests from fifty-nine black students to attend pre-dominantly white Central and Hall high schools. As Little Rock chief of police Eugene Smith dispersed the white crowd of protesters headed toward Central High on opening day, three African American students were on the rolls at Central, while the same number had been admitted to Hall. In the coda to the first school crisis, three fewer black students attended white high schools than had walked up the steps to Central High in the fall of 1957. With the high schools in full swing, the no-compromise stance of the CCC faded into the grumblings of bitter-enders. The white majority in Little Rock embraced a plan touted by the school board as "token integration," a policy that changed little in their lifetimes. The liberal *Arkansas Gazette* editorial page articulated the revived white consensus, praising the pupil assignment law for making possible peaceful, gradual compliance: "The courts have never required inte-gration, unless this is necessary to prevent discrimination in an individual case. . . . No district is required to merge its white and colored schools."[19]

The downfall of the councilors cheered the founders of the WEC, but token integration left the women unsettled. Vivion Brewer recalled in her memoirs: "Our emergency program to open our high schools had been achieved but our long term program to help solve the social problem of inter-racial relations seemed stagnant." In February 1960, Terry invited a group to lunch at the mansion that included a small number of WEC members and white businessmen to discuss the formation of a permanent interracial com-mittee to advance integration through cooperation. Rector and Tucker insisted that the WEC leaders were alarmist and that such initiatives could send events out of control. A month later, Rector confirmed his views in a let-ter to his hostess: "Dear Mrs. Terry: In order that there will be no misunder-standing, I want to state very clearly that I will not participate in any program of gradual desegregation of any facilities in our community."[20]

Rector did not "participate" in the business community's acquiescence to civil rights activists' demands for the desegregation of municipal facilities as

well as downtown stores in 1963, but neither did he obstruct these negotiations with the Council on Community Affairs (founded by black medical professionals in 1961), Philander Smith students, and the Student Nonviolent
Coordinating Committee. Black and white customers side by side at Main
Street lunch counters were of little concern to Rector, whose real estate holdings were centered in the expanding white western neighborhoods. On the
other hand, a districtwide school integration plan that traversed the carefully
drawn lines of residential segregation would directly touch his interests.[21]

Throughout the 1960s, civic leaders pressed forward with the management of Little Rock's racial topography that had begun with the Granite
Mountain housing projects. Officials flattened black neighborhoods through
federally financed urban-renewal projects that ultimately dislocated fifty-five
hundred families. Nearly all African Americans in Little Rock who gained
assistance under a 1968 federal housing act purchased houses once owned by
whites in the central area. Mortgage-loan officers did not approve loans to
applicants who would be a racial minority on their new block, and real estate
agents "steered" buyers into either white or African American areas. In 1971,
a study by the U.S. Commission on Civil Rights cited the effects of "blatantly
discriminatory advertising" on real estate transactions. A local broker explained
to the federal investigators that the use of the phrase "Anyone Can Buy" in
the newspaper classified sections was "a signal to the colored" that the property was not off-limits to African Americans. Court documents submitted in
later school desegregation litigation cited the dismissal of an African American
agent from his firm after he sold a house in a white neighborhood to a black
family. Andrew Jeffries was almost denied his license for violating a regulation of the Arkansas Real Estate Commission that stipulated that "a realtor
should never be instrumental in introducing into a neighborhood a character of property or occupancy, members of any race or nationality, or any individuals whose presence will clearly be detrimental to property values in that
neighborhood." Federal judge Henry Woods drew a stark conclusion in 1984,
after reviewing extensive evidence detailing the actions of public and private
bodies to channel families into prescribed sections of Little Rock: "The goal
of preserving residential segregation has been successful." Notwithstanding
later assumptions about "white flight," separate housing patterns were unmis-
takable prior to the integration of schools in white neighborhoods.[22]

In September 1964, school officials directed an African American family
to place their four children in all-black schools after they attempted to enroll
the children in nearby white ones. Attorneys affiliated with the NAACP Legal
Defense Fund, including local attorney John Walker, filed a suit on behalf of
Sergeant Roosevelt Clark and Delores Clark to challenge the constitutionality of the pupil assignment scheme. The district's attorney, Herschel Friday,
had artfully tinkered with the assignment plans to throw federal judges off

the scent but realized that these serviceable evasions were on their last legs. Even before the federal district court ruled in the Clark case, Friday drew up a "freedom-of-choice" plan based on models tried out in other southern cities. Under such plans, school districts shrugged off responsibility for deseg-regation by insisting that no one was defiantly blocking any schoolhouse door or steering students to certain schools. Little Rock school leaders prom-ised to respect the choice of any student to attend a certain school, unless that school was out of room, in which case preference would be given to those living near the crowded school. In December 1966, the appeals court upheld the district's new approach despite evidence offered by the plaintiffs that in the 1965–66 school year only 621 black students out of 7,341 were attending majority-white schools. The school lawyers assured the judges that the racial-balance figures were improving, but the following year Little Rock still lagged behind the overall rate of desegregation in southern cities. At the beginning of the 1966–67 year, no white students attended Horace Mann High School, and 15 percent of Central High students were African American, while only 7 black students joined 422 whites at perpetually crowded Hall High. In addition to the other obstacles faced by African Americans wanting to go to schools in the western portion of the city, the district did not main-tain a bus fleet for transportation. Interested students from working-class black families would be on their own in finding a way to make the commute to the distant subdivisions.[23]

While upholding the district's freedom-of-choice policy, the federal court had retained jurisdiction to assure "that the goal of a desegregated, non-racially operated school system" was "rapidly and finally achieved." The lack of progress toward that goal under the newly adopted choice plan, coupled with stricter desegregation guidelines from the Department of Health, Edu-cation, and Welfare under the authority of the 1964 Civil Rights Act, left school board members to choose between shifting toward full compliance and devising new strategies of delay. In 1966, signs of a break with reflexive obstructionism included the retirement of Everett Tucker, the conservative school board president who had stanched desegregation since 1959, and the arrival of a new liberal bloc. The new faces on the board owed their election victories to maturing grassroots organizations that represented the advent of urban liberalism in Little Rock. In contrast to the older Progressive model of elites solving social problems through administrative expertise, this urban-reform movement was based upon participatory decision making and broader concepts of social justice. Following the disbanding of the WEC in 1963, younger members committed to integration and equal rights formed and joined interracial organizations bent upon revamping the city's governing institutions. White liberals allied with the black leadership group Council on Community Affairs to develop electoral majorities for reform neighborhood by neighborhood. Although school board members were still elected at large, the customary low turnout in these elections provided an opening for the liberals, who were well tested in get-out-the vote operations.[24]

In August 1966, the school board contracted with education professors at the University of Oregon to investigate conditions and to offer recommendations that would end the dual education system in Little Rock. Submitted in June 1967, the lengthy report observed that the trauma of the original Little Rock crisis had eased objections to integration, even among influential businessmen whose personal preferences ran to perpetuating segregation as long as possible. The authors did briefly note that real estate firms were more likely to be "concerned with the locations of schools" than were downtown business and financial interests. The investigators also explained that since 1960, the "poor whites" who had backed the Citizens' Council's movement to defend pure segregation had become "politically inert" and "politically dispirited." Although enthusiasm for school integration did not extend beyond liberal whites and African Americans, the Oregon researchers believed that their recommendations for consolidating students from throughout the city into certain schools and for building new schools closer to the center of Little Rock would not provoke intense and widespread opposition. They were wrong. Among the recommendations the Oregon researchers viewed as politically viable was the assignment of all students in the eleventh and twelfth grades, regardless of race, to Hall High School, while students in the lower high school grades would be distributed among schools in the central and eastern sections of the city. Within days of the report's release, west-side families organized the Education First Committee to pressure the school board to ignore the researchers' proposals. As opposition flared on the city's affluent flank, Superintendent Floyd Parsons renounced the Oregon report, frustrating those school board members who believed it offered a constructive and fair approach.[25]

The defiance of upscale families to the integration of schools attended by their own children did not foment street demonstrations or storming of police barricades. Their resistance centered on balloting instead. Realtors served as a ready-made interest group to recruit candidates and bankroll campaigns, but they did not need to stoke the ardent reactions of Fifth Ward school patrons. Hailing from the precincts that had once defied the segregationist radicals to open the high schools, the Education First partisans employed the language of neighborhood unity and individual freedom, rather than the Citizens' Council rhetoric of heritage and racial integrity. Believing that neighborhood segregation arose from market forces and personal choice, these affluent homeowners were innocent as to how they had benefited from concerted policies to thwart residential integration. The whiteness of the Fifth Ward was a constructed environment, but those living there believed that school integration advocates were the ones using social engi-neering to artificially turn the community inside out. In their statements and campaign materials, the suburban anti-integrationists charged that "sociolog-ical" aims should not override the imperative to guarantee children a first-rate education.[26] Everett Tucker, who in 1959 had asserted that separate schools were best for black and white students, defended the freedom-of-choice plans in 1968, saying, "I can't think of anything fairer than letting each child go where he wants to"—though his own school board had devised mechanisms to prevent black children from attending the schools of their choice.[27]

Even with the official scrapping of the Oregon plan, the two incumbents up for reelection in the September 1967 school board races faced opponents who promised that no element of the report would ever become district pol-icy on their watch. James (Jimbo) Coates, the school board member whose avid backing of the report had created a rift with Superintendent Parsons, denounced in public appearances the freedom-of-choice approach and pro-posed that the enrollment of African American students in each high school should not exceed their proportion of the student population as a whole. The Fifth Ward voters provided the decisive margins that ousted Coates and the other incumbent, who had kept his distance from the Oregon report, in favor of the challengers, one of whom owned a real estate firm. The turmoil over integration fueled a large turnout for the election, blunting the advantage of liberals, who had previously built their winning margins on the apathy and indifference of likely opposition blocs. Following his defeat, Coates explained the new alignments to journalist John Egerton, who was visiting Little Rock to eye the changes on the tenth anniversary of the school crisis:

> We have perpetuated the dual school system, leaving worn-out schools to Negroes in the center of the city and building nice new ones for whites in the suburbs. I live out there, too, but I know we can't keep on getting away with that. . . . Most of the people who are raising the hell were the so-called liberals of 10 years ago. They want integration for everyone but themselves—and these are my friends and neighbors.[28]

If the Oregon recommendations were not to be resurrected, the school board also understood that it would soon cede decision making to the federal courts if the district continued to maintain racially distinct schools. In the fall of 1967, the board ordered Parsons to set aside Herschel Friday's freedom-of-choice plan and offer proposals to bring about districtwide integration. In December, Parsons surprised many white and African American critics who had disparaged his precipitous abandonment of the Oregon plan by detailing the most thorough integration plan offered by a school administrator since the filing of *Aaron v. Cooper*. The superintendent proposed closing predominantly black Horace Mann High School, while drawing districtwide attendance zones to desegregate the remaining three academic high schools: Central, Parkview, and Hall. The attendance zones would run in an east/west direction and slice across racial and class boundaries.[29]

In March 1968, city voters were in effect called upon to ratify the superintendent's recommendations by increasing the tax millage to pay for construction projects included in the plan. The defenders of the Parsons plan staked out the middle ground by insisting that it would forestall draconian remedies. One pro-Parsons advertisement suggested that failure of the plan would open the door for the federal courts "to decide where our children go to school . . . what they read . . . what they wear . . . what they say." Prominent businessmen such as Wilton (Witt) Stephens, the utility magnate and statewide power broker, reinforced the image of the plan as modest and practical by throwing their support behind the superintendent. But residents in the restive Fifth Ward had little patience for a moderate approach and complained that Parsons had borrowed too liberally from the Oregon report. His proposal to provide transportation to students living over two miles from the high school in their attendance zone incited charges that the district was "busing" students to engineer racial balances. William Rector emerged from the background to openly organize and fund the campaign against the millage increase, as well as to target the two board members running for reelection on their support of the Parsons plan. The feisty real estate magnate single-handedly cowed the Little Rock Chamber of Commerce board of directors into backing off from a near-unanimous endorsement of the Parsons plan. The African American precincts soundly backed the white incumbents but split on the millage issue that would have led to greater desegregation. Most liberal and African American organizations favored Parsons's proposal, but several black leaders objected to shuttering Horace Mann. Distrust of Parsons's motives led the state NAACP to reject the plan, while John Walker, the civil rights attorney, feared its adoption would discourage federal courts from considering more far-reaching and rapid integration. Once again, the western tail wagged the municipal dog. The onslaught of Fifth Ward voters was so great that additional voting machines had to be hauled into polling stations. The millage lost by a nearly two-to-one margin, and the two incumbents were beaten handily. One of the new, anti–Parsons plan board members had earlier removed his daughter from Little Rock public schools when she was assigned to a class taught by an African American teacher. In its editorial postmortem, the *Arkansas Gazette* philosophized on cyclical trends: "For years the forces of reaction were in eclipse in Little Rock, but they are now resurgent and, indeed, have regained control of the school system."[30]

Two months after the election, the U.S. Supreme Court, in the landmark *Green v. County School Board*, shelved the *Brown*-era language of "all deliberate speed" by requiring school boards to eradicate segregation "root and branch." Although the Court did not explicitly exclude freedom-of-choice plans, the majority decision made the districts responsible for integrating schools. School leaders no longer could claim they need do no more than officially prohibit segregation. The judicial handwriting on the wall could be read all the way from Little Rock, but the forces that had rejected the moderate compromise of the Parsons plan were in no mood to relent. The March 1970 school board elections provided the opportunity to continue the purge of integrationist school board members. The rump liberal bloc was represented by Thomas E. Patterson, an African American educator, and Winslow Drummond, a white attorney who had been president of the Little Rock Urban League.[31]

While no opponent was recruited to run against Patterson, Rector and Everett Tucker revived the Education First Committee to fund a challenger to Drummond. This fresh intervention by Rector prompted the launching of a barbed riposte from the columned mansion in the heart of old Little Rock. The eighty-seven-year-old Adolphine Terry had not been engaged in community politics since the WEC disbanded, but she had been paying attention. In her private correspondence, she faulted Rector for using his clout to continue the post–World War II drive to sort different races among the neighborhoods. She perceived the link between Rector's west-side investments and his apprehensions over integration. Still, her shrewd observations on residential patterns and networks of influence remained tinged with her habitual judgments on class and obligation. In the midst of the 1970 Drummond race, she remonstrated with the patrician Tucker: "I can't understand why you follow Billy's lead. You have better brains, more education, you are better looking and have a better personality, and better manners—People instinctively like you, they are not attracted to Billy Rector."[32]

In her open letter requesting friends to back Drummond, Terry identified Rector as a longstanding source of reaction and self-serving cronyism: "W. F. Rector is a fine example of an American family man, but as a civic leader, with the philosophy of the 1880s, he is an agonizing catastrophe. He boasts that he has defeated every progressive program or candidate in our city; and he has announced that he is the man to see if you hope to get anything done." Following the letter's publication, an editorial cartoon by Bill Graham in the *Arkansas Gazette* depicted Rector tying up a horse and buggy on a downtown avenue filled with cars. If not a gifted agitator on the order of James Johnson, Rector lost few fights in Little Rock, even those that required him to step from behind the scenes to arouse voters. And Terry's appeal barely echoed in the Fifth Ward, which had once supplied electoral majorities for the WEC.[33]

Following Drummond's defeat, the school board in July 1970 approved a new desegregation plan that slightly altered school attendance zones. Superintendent Parsons admitted that he could not predict the level of integration arising from changes but was confident that the proposals would result in "a minimum of disruption to our schools." As in the 1957 confrontation, a settlement that satisfied the Little Rock business community unraveled as civil rights attorneys demanded constitutional relief from the courts. In July 1971, federal district judge J. Smith Henley largely overturned the school district plan in response to the petition by the Clark plaintiffs, represented by Walker. In light of the April 1971 U.S. Supreme Court decision in *Swann v. Charlotte-Mecklenburg Board of Education,* which permitted busing as a remedy, Henley determined that the racial balkanization of Little Rock left him no choice but to order the transportation of high school students for the 1971–72 school year to achieve integration.[34]

In 1957, William F. Rector had opposed Orval Faubus's open defiance of federal authority, and in 1971 he did not press the school board to circumvent the courts. Instead, he found a way to escape the reach of the Constitution. Soon after the Supreme Court decision on busing, Rector revealed to a meeting of six hundred cheering whites that he was building a private school near the golf course in his western subdivision development. Echoing the freedom-of-choice justifications, Rector announced that his school, Pulaski Academy, would accept all students regardless of race but left little doubt as to who would be welcomed: "I even hope we'll be allowed to play 'Dixie' if we want to without having a riot about it." By September, five of the seven members of the school board that had been remade by Rector's campaign against integration had placed their children in private schools. Rector did not achieve fully his aim to halt white flight from his western Little Rock subdivisions to surrounding communities, but the city's private academies flourished as white students withdrew from public schools. By 2003, district officials estimated that only half of the white children in school were sitting in public classrooms, pushing Little Rock into the top ten of metropolitan areas with large percentages of white private-school enrollees. In that same year, 1 black student was among the 102 Pulaski Academy graduates, while all but 43 of the 283 graduates of Hall High School were African American. Notwithstanding the importance of the original school crisis in the nation's civil rights history, the conservative takeover of the school board by 1970 and rejection of the Parsons plan more decisively shaped the development of education in Little Rock over the following decades.[35] The landmark rulings in the early 1970s did indeed sweep aside evasions impeding districtwide integration. Nevertheless, the rhetoric of the affluent resistance continued to echo in the claims of white families that the courts had sacrificed educational quality and well-run neighborhood schools in favor of abstract justice. Those fleeing integrated Little Rock public schools asserted rightful prerogative and common sense, rather than racial animus.

Adolphine Fletcher Terry died in 1976. The tributes at the time were preludes to later writings that fixed her on the pedestal as one who turned the tide in 1958 through founding the WEC. Her career was subsumed in the drama of the school crisis. Even the involvement of the iconic Terry could not keep the clashes over segregated schools in the late 1960s from falling into obscurity. This historical elision contributed to the tone of resignation in the postscripts to many narratives of the Central High crisis. Such accounts suggest continuing court oversight of district operations and persistent racial divisions were problems that required changes in the hearts and minds of citizens before programmatic and structural reforms could succeed.[36] Yet the conflicts of the late 1960s defy explanations that ascribe continuing resistance to embedded cultural traditions and unbending federal coercion. Rector's triumph in preserving his interests was not inevitable, nor did it necessarily reflect an entrenched white consensus to preserve discrimination at all costs. Mustering opposition to the real estate mogul was not the equivalent of going against the grain of southern history.

William L. Rector died one year before Adolphine Terry. In 2006, the Walton College of Business at the University of Arkansas installed him in the Arkansas Business Hall of Fame. The biographical profile in the induction-ceremony program celebrated his resolve and audacity: "He was a man who made things happen. Not afraid of controversy, he functioned as a catalyst for the state's economic boom in the mid-century." In the only reference to civil rights and desegregation, the profile revealed that his "concern for the business climate" led Rector to stand up as the "first businessman" to oppose Faubus's use of the National Guard in 1957. And one thing more: "One of Rector's proudest accomplishments was the creation of Pulaski Academy."[37]

On February 23, 2007, U. S. district judge William R. Wilson declared the Little Rock school system unitary and released the district from court oversight and monitoring for the first time since 1957. In his opinion, Judge Wilson observed, "I want to express my heartfelt best wishes as LRSD [the Little Rock School District] begins to operate, as our Founders intended, under control of the citizens of the City of Little Rock." Reminiscent of the 1958 referendum that closed the high schools, Little Rock citizens in successive elections between 1967 and 1970 had placed at risk that authority over their schools rather than support the efforts of local officials to fulfill constitutional obligations. One-time opponents of the Citizens' Council mobilized to forge a formidable popular movement to shield predominantly white schools when integration plans threatened to dissolve the privilege of residential address. The new resistance partisans insisted that reserving for their children safe, nearby schools with modern facilities and solid instruction was a racially neutral right. Such a claim failed to acknowledge the civic policies that had governed school location and constrained opportunities for African American students. Without the open defiance and racial invective that drew national attention in 1957, the official and electoral efforts to reinforce school segregation did not compromise the city's recovered moderate reputation. Little Rock boosters contrasted the turmoil of the Central High desegregation crisis with the seeming peace and order that followed to demonstrate the city's constructive adaptation to a new racial order. When historians begin to fully examine school desegregation after 1957, they may well conclude that this adaptation represented little more than the gentrification of segregation.[38]

Notes

Introduction: The 1957 Little Rock Crisis—A Historiographical Essay

1. This essay includes material produced up until its completion in Dec. 2006 and therefore precludes discussion of a number of important works published in 2007 to coincide with the fiftieth anniversary of the school crisis.

2. Overviews of the crisis include Corinne Silverman, *The Little Rock Story* (University: University of Alabama Press, 1959); Dewey Grantham, *The Regional Imagination: The South and Recent American History* (Nashville: Vanderbilt University Press, 1979), 185–97; Tony Freyer, *The Little Rock Crisis: A Constitutional Interpretation* (Westport, CT: Greenwood Press, 1984); Juan Williams, *Eyes on the Prize: America's Civil Rights Years, 1954–1965* (New York: Viking, 1987), 91–119; and John A. Kirk, *Redefining the Color Line: Black Activism in Little Rock, Arkansas, 1940–1970* (Gainesville: University Press of Florida, 2002), 106–38.

3. Michael J. Dabrishus, "The Documentary Heritage of the Central High Crisis: A Bibliographical Essay," in *Understanding the Little Rock Crisis: An Exercise in Remembrance and Reconciliation,* ed. Elizabeth Jacoway and C. Fred Williams (Fayetteville: University of Arkansas Press, 1999), 153–61. See also "Little Rock School Integration, 1957," Special Collections, University of Arkansas Libraries, Fayetteville, http://libinfo.uark.edu/specialcollections/manuscripts/integration1957.asp.

4. Wilson Record and June Cassels Record, eds., *Little Rock, U.S.A.* (San Francisco: Chandler Publishing, 1960); "Fighting Back (1957–1962)," episode 2 of *Eyes on the Prize,* dir. Henry Hampton (Boston: Blackside, 1987); Clayborne Carson, David J. Garrow, Gerald Gill, Vincent Harding, and Darlene Clark Hine, eds., *The Eyes on the Prize Civil Rights Reader: Documents, Speeches, and Firsthand Accounts from the Black Freedom Struggle, 1954–1990* (New York: Viking Penguin, 1991), 61–106; Henry Hampton and Steve Fayer, eds., *Voices of Freedom: An Oral History of the Civil Rights Movement from the 1950s through the 1980s* (New York: Vintage, 1994), 35–52; "Little Rock, Arkansas," episodes 11–15 of *Will the Circle Be Unbroken? An Audio History of the Civil Rights Movement in Five Southern Communities and the Music of Those Times,* prod. George King (Atlanta: Southern Regional Council, 1997).

5. Karen Anderson, "The Little Rock School Desegregation Crisis: Moderation and Social Conflict," *Journal of Southern History* 70 (Aug. 2004): 603–36; David Chappell, *Inside Agitators: White Southerners in the Civil Rights Movement* (Baltimore: Johns Hopkins University Press, 1994); Chappell, "Diversity within a Racial Group: White People in Little Rock, 1957–1959,"

Arkansas Historical Quarterly (hereafter *AHQ*) 54 (Winter 1995): 444–56; Pete Daniel, *Lost Revolutions: The South in the 1950s* (Chapel Hill: University of North Carolina Press, 2000), 251–83; C. Fred Williams, "Class: The Central Issue in the 1957 Little Rock School Crisis," *AHQ* 56 (Autumn 1997): 341–44.

6. John F. Wells, *Time Bomb (The Faubus Revolt)* (Little Rock: General Publishing, 1962); Robert Sherrill, "Orval Faubus: How to Create a Successful Disaster," in *Gothic Politics in the Deep South: Stars of the New Confederacy* (New York: Grossman, 1968), 74–117; David Edwin Wallace, "The Little Rock Central Desegregation Crisis of 1957" (Ph.D. diss., University of Missouri, Columbia, 1977); Wallace, "Orval Faubus: The Central Figure at Little Rock Central High School," *AHQ* 39 (Winter 1980): 314–29.

7. Thomas F. Pettigrew and Ernest Q. Campbell, "Faubus and Segregation: An Analysis of Arkansas Voting," *Public Opinion Quarterly* 24 (Autumn 1960): 436–47; Roy Reed, "Orval E. Faubus: Out of Socialism into Realism," *AHQ* 54 (Spring 1995): 13–29; Reed, *Faubus: The Life and Times of an American Prodigal* (Fayetteville: University of Arkansas Press, 1997); Reed, "The Contest for the Soul of Orval Faubus," in Jacoway and Williams, *Understanding the Little Rock Crisis*, 99–105.

8. Orval E. Faubus, *In This Faraway Land* (Conway, AR: River Road Press, 1971); Faubus, *Down from the Hills* (Little Rock: Pioneer Press, 1980); Faubus, *Down from the Hills, II* (Little Rock: Democrat Printing and Lithographing Company, 1986); Faubus, *Man's Best Friend: The Little Australian, and Others* (Little Rock: Democrat Printing and Lithographing, 1991); Faubus, *The Faubus Years: January 11, 1955, to January 10, 1967* (N.p.: n.p, 1991); Orval E. Faubus, interview with author, Conway, AR, Dec. 3, 1992, Pryor Center for Oral and Visual History (hereafter Pryor Center), University of Arkansas, Fayetteville.

9. Virgil T. Blossom, *It Has Happened Here* (New York: Harper and Brothers, 1959); Numan V. Bartley, "Looking Back at Little Rock," *AHQ* 25 (Summer 1966): 101–16; Bartley, *The Rise of Massive Resistance: Race and Politics in the South during the 1950's* (Baton Rouge: Louisiana State University Press, 1969), 251–69 (quotation, 252); John A. Kirk, "Massive Resistance and Minimum Compliance: The Origins of the 1957 Little Rock School Crisis and the Failure of School Desegregation in the South," in *Massive Resistance: Southern Opposition to the Second Reconstruction,* ed. Clive Webb (New York: Oxford University Press, 2005), 76–98; Elizabeth Jacoway, "Richard C. Butler and the Little Rock School Board: The Quest to Maintain 'Educational Quality,'" *AHQ* 65 (Spring 2006): 24–38.

10. L. Brooks Hays, *A Southern Moderate Speaks* (Chapel Hill: University of North Carolina Press, 1959), 130–94; Dale Alford and L'Moore Alford, *The Case of the Sleeping People (Finally Awakened by Little Rock School Frustrations)* (Little Rock: Pioneer Press, 1959); Sherman Adams, *Firsthand Report: The Story of the Eisenhower Administration* (New York: Harper, 1961), 253–78; Hays, *Politics Is My Parish: An Autobiography* (Baton Rouge: Louisiana State University Press, 1981), 179–98; D. Nathan Coulter, "A Political Martyr for Racial Progress in the South: Brooks Hays and the Electoral Consequences of the Little Rock Crisis" (B.A. thesis, Harvard University, 1982); John Kyle Day, "The Fall of Southern

Moderation: The Defeat of Brooks Hays in the 1958 Congressional Election for the Fifth District of Arkansas" (M.A. thesis, University of Arkansas, Fayetteville, 1999); Day, "The Fall of a Southern Moderate: Congressman Brooks Hays and the Election of 1958," *AHQ* 59 (Autumn 2000): 241–64; Terry D. Goddard, "Southern Social Justice: Brooks Hays and the Little Rock School Crisis," *Baptist History and Heritage* 38 (Spring 2003): 68–86.

11. Randall Bennett Woods, *Fulbright: A Biography* (Cambridge: Cambridge University Press, 1995); Brent J. Aucoin, "The Southern Manifesto and Southern Opposition to Desegregation," *AHQ* 55 (Summer 1996): 173–93; Tony Badger, "'The Forerunner of Our Opposition': Arkansas and the Southern Manifesto of 1956," *AHQ* 56 (Autumn 1997): 353–60; Badger, "The White Reaction to *Brown:* Arkansas, the Southern Manifesto, and Massive Resistance," in Jacoway and Williams, *Understanding the Little Rock Crisis,* 83–97; John A. Kirk, "Arkansas, the *Brown* Decision, and the 1957 Little Rock School Crisis: A Local Perspective," in Jacoway and Williams, *Understanding the Little Rock Crisis,* 67–82; Badger, "Southerners Who Refused to Sign the Southern Manifesto," *Historical Journal* 42 (June 1999): 517–34.

12. Robert R. Brown, *Bigger than Little Rock* (Greenwich, CT: Seabury Press, 1958); Ernest Q. Campbell and Thomas F. Pettigrew, *Christians in Racial Crisis: A Study of Little Rock's Ministry* (Washington, DC: Public Affairs Press, 1959); Campbell and Pettigrew, "Racial and Moral Crisis: The Role of Little Rock Ministers," *American Journal of Sociology* 64 (Mar. 1959): 509–16; Mark Newman, "The Arkansas Baptist State Convention and Desegregation, 1954–1968," *AHQ* 56 (Autumn 1997): 294–313; Carolyn Gray LeMaster, "Civil and Social Rights Efforts of Arkansas Jewry," in *The Quiet Voices: Southern Rabbis and Black Civil Rights, 1880s-1990s,* ed. Mark Bauman and Berkley Kalin (Tuscaloosa: University of Alabama Press, 1997), 95–120; Clive Webb, *Fight against Fear: Southern Jews and Black Civil Rights* (Athens: University of Georgia Press, 2001); Colbert Cartwright, "Walking My Lonesome Valley," unpublished manuscript, and Dunbar H. Ogden III, "My Father Said 'Yes,'" unpublished manuscript, both in private possession of family members.

13. David Chappell, "Religious Ideas of the Segregationists," *Journal of American Studies* 32 (Aug. 1998): 237–62; Chappell, *A Stone of Hope: Prophetic Religion and the Death of Jim Crow* (Chapel Hill: University of North Carolina Press, 2004); Jane Dailey, "Sex, Segregation, and the Sacred after *Brown,* " *Journal of American History* 91 (June 2004): 119–44; Chappell, "Disunity and Religious Institutions in the White South," in Webb, *Massive Resistance,* 136–50; Dailey, "The Theology of Massive Resistance: Sex, Segregation, and the Sacred after *Brown,*" in Webb, *Massive Resistance,* 151–80.

14. Elizabeth Jacoway, "Taken by Surprise: Little Rock Business Leaders and Desegregation," in *Southern Businessmen and Desegregation,* ed. Elizabeth Jacoway and David R. Colburn (Baton Rouge: Louisiana State University Press, 1982), 12–41; Tony Badger, "Segregation and the Southern Business Elite," *Journal of American Studies* 18, no. 1 (1984): 105–9 (quotation, 108).

15. Harry S. Ashmore, *The Negro and the Schools* (Chapel Hill: University of North Carolina Press, 1954); *The Editorial Position of the* Arkansas Gazette *in the*

Little Rock Crisis (Little Rock: Arkansas Gazette, 1957); Ashmore, *An Epitaph for Dixie* (New York: W. W. Norton, 1958); *Crisis in the South: The Little Rock Story* (Little Rock: Arkansas Gazette, 1959); Ashmore, *Hearts and Minds: The Anatomy of Racism from Roosevelt to Reagan* (New York: McGraw-Hill, 1982); Ashmore, *Civil Rights and Wrongs: A Memoir of Race and Politics, 1944–1994* (New York: Pantheon, 1994); Nathania K. Sawyer, "Harry S. Ashmore: On the Way to Everywhere" (M.A. thesis, University of·Arkansas at Little Rock, 2001); Griffin Smith, ed., *Little Rock, 1957: Pages from History: The Central High Crisis* (Little Rock: WEHCO Publishing, 1997).

16. Karr Shannon, *Integration Decision Is Unconstitutional* (Little Rock: Democrat Print and Lithographing, 1958).

17. Alford and Alford, *Case of the Sleeping People;* Bartley, "Looking Back at Little Rock"; Bartley, *Rise of Massive Resistance;* Neil R. McMillen, "The White Citizens Council and Resistance to School Desegregation in Arkansas," *AHQ* 30 (Summer 1971): 95–122; McMillen, *The Citizens' Council: Organized Resistance to the Second Reconstruction, 1954–1964* (Urbana: University of Illinois Press, 1971); Michal R. Belknap, *Federal Law and Southern Order: Racial Violence and Constitutional Conflict in the Post-Brown South* (Athens: University of Georgia Press, 1987); Graeme Cope, "'A Thorn in the Side'?: The Mothers' League of Central High School and the Little Rock Desegregation Crisis of 1957," *AHQ* 57 (Summer 1998): 160–90; Elizabeth Jacoway, "Jim Johnson of Arkansas: Segregationist Prototype," in *The Role of Ideas in the Civil Rights South: Essays,* ed. Ted Ownby (Jackson: University Press of Mississippi, 2002), 137–55; Cope, "'Honest White People of the Middle and Lower Classes'? A Profile of the Capital Citizens' Council during the Little Rock Crisis of 1957," *AHQ* 61 (Spring 2002): 36–58; Cope, "'Marginal Youngsters' and 'Hoodlums of Both Sexes'?: Student Segregationists during the Little Rock School Crisis," *AHQ* 63 (Winter 2004): 380–403; Frances Lisa Baer, "Race over Rights: The Resistance to Public School Desegregation in Little Rock, Arkansas, and Beyond, 1954–1960" (Ph.D. diss., University of Alabama, 2004); Karen S. Anderson, "Violence and Southern Social Relations: The Little Rock, Arkansas, School Integration Crisis, 1954–1960," in Webb, *Massive Resistance,* 203–15.

18. George Lewis, *The White South and the Red Menace: Segregationists, Anticommunism, and Massive Resistance, 1945–1965* (Gainesville: University Press of Florida, 2004); Jeff Woods, *Black Struggle, Red Scare: Segregation and Anti-Communism in the South, 1948–1968* (Baton Rouge: Louisiana State University Press, 2004); Woods, "'Designed to Harass': The Act 10 Controversy in Arkansas," *AHQ* 56 (Winter 1997): 443–60.

19. Joseph Peter Kamp, *The Lowdown on Little Rock and the Plot to Sovietize the South* (New York: Headlines, 1957); James E. Jackson, *U.S. Negroes in Battle: From Little Rock to Watts: A Diary of Events, 1957–1965* (Moscow: Progress Publishers, 1967).

20. Robert W. Coakley, *Operation Arkansas* (Washington, DC: Histories Division, Office of the Chief of Military History, Department of the Army, 1967); Elizabeth Huckaby, *Crisis at Central High, Little Rock, 1957–58* (Baton Rouge: Louisiana State University Press, 1980); Lamont Johnson, dir., *Crisis at*

Central High (CBS Entertainment Productions, 1981); Phoebe Christina Godfrey, "Sweet Little Girls? Miscegenation, Desegregation and the Defense of Whiteness at Little Rock's Central High, 1957–1959" (Ph.D. diss., State University of New York at Binghamton, 2001); Godfrey, "Bayonets, Brainwashing, and Bathrooms: The Discourse of Race, Gender, and Sexuality in the Desegregation of Little Rock's Central High," *AHQ* 62 (Spring 2003): 42–67.

21. Sondra Hercher Gordy, "Teachers of the Lost Year, 1958–1959: Little Rock School District" (Ed.D. thesis, University of Arkansas at Little Rock, 1996); Gordy, "Empty Classrooms, Empty Hearts: Little Rock Secondary Teachers, 1958–1959," *AHQ* 56 (Winter 1997): 427–42; Beth Roy, *Bitters in the Honey: Tales of Hope and Disappointment across Divides of Race and Time* (Fayetteville: University of Arkansas Press, 1999); "The Lost Year Project," http://www. thelostyear.com/.

22. Gary Fullerton, "New Factories a Thing of Past in Little Rock," *Nashville Tennessean,* May 31, 1959; Michael Joseph Bercik, "The Little Rock School Crisis of 1957 and Its Impact on the Economy of Arkansas" (Ph.D. diss., University of Pittsburgh, 1999); James C. Cobb, "The Lesson of Little Rock: Stability, Growth, and Change in the American South," in Jacoway and Williams, *Understanding the Little Rock Crisis,* 107–22.

23. Michelle Leslie Davidson, "Vivion Brewer and the 1957 Little Rock Central High Crisis" (M.A. thesis, University of Arkansas, Fayetteville, 1994); Lorraine Gates, "Power from the Pedestal: The Women's Emergency Committee and the Little Rock School Crisis," *AHQ* 55 (Spring 1996): 26–57; Elizabeth Jacoway, "Down from the Pedestal: Gender and Regional Culture in a Ladylike Assault on the Southern Way of Life," *AHQ* 56 (Autumn 1997): 345–52; Laura A. Miller, *Fearless: Irene Gaston Samuel and the Life of a Southern Liberal* (Little Rock: Butler Center for Arkansas Studies, 2002); Miller, "Challenging the Segregationist Power Structure in Little Rock: The Women's Emergency Committee to Open Our Schools," in *Throwing Off the Cloak of Privilege: White Southern Women Activists in the Civil Rights Era,* ed. Gail S. Murray (Gainesville: University Press of Florida, 2004), 153–80.

24. Sandra Hubbard, dir., *Women's Emergency Committee to Open Our Schools, 1958–1959* (Morning Star Studio, 1998); Sara Murphy, *Breaking the Silence: Little Rock's Women's Emergency Committee to Open Our Schools, 1958–1963* (Fayetteville: University of Arkansas Press, 1997); Vivion Lenon Brewer, *The Embattled Ladies of Little Rock, 1958–1963: The Struggle to Save Public Education at Central High* (Fort Bragg, CA: Lost Coast Press, 1999); Adolphine Fletcher Terry, "Life Is My Song, Also," unpublished manuscript, box 2, Fletcher-Terry Papers, Special Collections, University of Arkansas at Little Rock Libraries.

25. Irving Spitzberg, *Racial Politics in Little Rock, 1954–1964* (New York: Garland, 1987), 12–30, 110–41; Henry M. Alexander, *The Little Rock Recall Election* (New York: McGraw-Hill, 1960); Jacoway, "Taken by Surprise"; Kimberly M. Bess, "Good Men Doing Nothing: Desegregation in Little Rock Public Schools" (M.A. thesis, University of Arkansas, Fayetteville, 2005).

26. Woodrow Wilson Mann, "The Truth about Little Rock," *New York Herald Tribune,* Jan. 19–31, 1958; George G. Iggers, "An Arkansas Professor: The NAACP

and the Grass Roots," in Record and Record, *Little Rock, U.S.A.*, 283–91 (note that the editors misspell Iggers's first name and give the wrong middle initial); Tony Freyer, "Objectivity and Involvement: Georg C. Iggers and Writing the History of the Little Rock Crisis," in *Crossing Boundaries: The Exclusion and Inclusion of Minorities in Germany and the United States,* ed. Larry Eugene Jones (New York: Berghahn Books, 2001), 172–92; Freyer, "Crossing Borders in American Civil Rights Historiography," in Jones, *Crossing Boundaries,* 213–32; Nat Griswold, "The Second Reconstruction in Little Rock," unpublished manuscript, ser. 2, subject files, box 11, folder 8, Sara Alderman Murphy Papers, Special Collections, University of Arkansas Libraries, Fayetteville.

27. Osro Cobb and Carol Griffee, *Osro Cobb of Arkansas: Memoirs of Historical Significance* (Little Rock: Rose Publishing, 1989); Thomas R. Wagy, "Governor LeRoy Collins of Florida and the Little Rock Crisis of 1957," *AHQ* 38 (Summer 1979): 99–115; Wagy, *Governor LeRoy Collins of Florida: Spokesman of the New South* (University: University of Alabama Press, 1985), 84–103.

28. Daisy Bates, *The Long Shadow of Little Rock: A Memoir* (New York: David McKay, 1962; reprint, Fayetteville: University of Arkansas Press, 1987); Jacqueline Trescott, "Daisy Bates: Before and after Little Rock," *Crisis,* June 1981, 232–35; Anne Standley, "The Role of Black Women in the Civil Rights Movement," in *Women in the Civil Rights Movement: Trailblazers and Torchbearers,* ed. Vicki L. Crawford, Jacqueline Anne Rouse, and Barbara Woods (Brooklyn: Carlson Publishing, 1990), 183–202; Carolyn Calloway-Thomas and Thurmon Garner, "Daisy Bates and the Little Rock School Crisis: Forging the Way," *Journal of Black Studies* 26 (May 1996): 616–28; John A. Kirk, "Daisy Bates, the National Association for the Advancement of Colored People, and the 1957 Little Rock School Crisis: A Gendered Perspective," in *Gender in the Civil Rights Movement,* ed. Peter J. Ling and Sharon Monteith (New York: Garland Publishing, 1999), 17–40; Linda Reed, "The Legacy of Daisy Bates," *AHQ* 59 (Spring 2000): 76–83; Amy Polakow, *Daisy Bates: Civil Rights Crusader* (North Haven, CT: Linnet Books, 2003); John Adams, "'Arkansas Needs Leadership': Daisy Bates, Black Arkansas, and the NAACP" (M.A. thesis, University of Wisconsin, 2003); Grif Stockley, *Daisy Bates: Civil Rights Crusader from Arkansas* (Jackson: University Press of Mississippi, 2005); Brynda Pappas, "L. C. Bates: A Champion of Freedom," *Arkansas Gazette,* Oct. 19, 1980; C. Calvin Smith, "From 'Separate but Equal' to Desegregation: The Changing Philosophy of L. C. Bates," *AHQ* 42 (Autumn 1983): 254–70; Irene Wassell, "L. C. Bates, Editor of the Arkansas State Press" (M.A. thesis, University of Arkansas, Little Rock, 1983).

29. Ted Poston, "Nine Kids Who Dared," *New York Post,* Oct. 23–31, 1957; Clarence Laws, "Nine Courageous Students," *Crisis,* May 1958, 267–318; Moses J. Newson, "The Little Rock Nine," *Crisis,* Nov. 1987, 40–44; Elizabeth Eckford, "The First Day," *Southern Exposure* 21 (Spring–Summer 1993): 67–68; Eric Laneuville, dir., *The Ernest Green Story* (Buena Vista Video, 1993); Melba Pattillo Beals, *Warriors Don't Cry: A Searing Memoir of the Battle to Integrate Little Rock's Central High* (New York: Pocket Books, 1994); Beals, *White Is a State of Mind: A Memoir* (New York: G. P. Putnam's Sons, 1999); Rob Thompson, dir., *Journey to Little Rock: The Untold Story of Minnijean Brown Trickey* (North East Productions,

2001); Elizabeth Jacoway, "Not Anger but Sorrow: Minnijean Brown Trickey Remembers the Little Rock Crisis," *AHQ* 64 (Spring 2005): 1–26; Janelle Collins, "'It Was a Form of Creativity, Our Going to Central': An Interview with Minnijean Brown Trickey," *Arkansas Review: A Journal of Delta Studies* 36 (Aug. 2005): 90–98.

30. Iggers, "Arkansas Professor"; Tilman Cothran and William Phillips Jr., "Negro Leadership in a Crisis Situation," *Phylon* 22 (Summer 1961): 107–18; Wiley A. Branton, "Little Rock Revisited: Desegregation to Resegregation," *Journal of Negro Education* 52 (Summer 1983): 250–69; Brian James Daugherity, "'With All Deliberate Speed': The NAACP and the Implementation of *Brown v. Board of Education* at a Local Level, Little Rock, Arkansas" (M.A. thesis, University of Montana, 1997); Kirk, *Redefining the Color Line;* Judith Kilpatrick, "Wiley Austin Branton and *Cooper v. Aaron:* America Fulfils Its Promise," *AHQ* 65 (Spring 2006): 7–21.

31. Tony A. Freyer, "Politics and Law in the Little Rock Crisis, 1954–1957," *AHQ* 40 (Autumn 1981): 195–219; Daniel A. Farber, "The Supreme Court and the Rule of Law: *Cooper v. Aaron* Revisited," *University of Illinois Law Review,* no. 2 (1982): 387–412; Freyer, *Little Rock Crisis;* Jack Greenberg, *Crusaders in the Courts: How a Dedicated Band of Lawyers Fought for the Civil Rights Revolution* (New York: Basic Books, 1994), 225–43; Freyer, "The Little Rock Crisis Reconsidered," *AHQ* 56 (Autumn 1997): 361–70; David Kirp, "Retreat into Legalism: The Little Rock School Desegregation Case in Historic Perspective," *PS: Political Science and Politics* 30 (Sept. 1997): 443–47; Kermit L. Hall, "The Constitutional Lessons of the Little Rock Crisis," in Jacoway and Williams, *Understanding the Little Rock Crisis,* 123–40; Freyer, "The Past as Future: The Little Rock Crisis and the Constitution," in Jacoway and Williams, *Understanding the Little Rock Crisis,* 141–51; Freyer, "*Cooper v. Aaron:* Incident and Consequence," *AHQ* 65 (Spring 2006): 1–6; Jacoway, "Richard C. Butler"; Freyer, *Little Rock on Trial.*

32. Jack W. Peltason, *Fifty-Eight Lonely Men: Southern Federal Judges and School Desegregation* (Urbana: University of Illinois Press, 1971); J. Harvie Wilkinson III, *From Brown to Bakke: The Supreme Court and School Integration: 1954–1978* (New York: Oxford University Press, 1979); Jack Bass, *Unlikely Heroes: The Dramatic Story of the Southern Judges of the Fifth Circuit Who Translated the Supreme Court's Brown Decision into a Revolution for Equality* (New York: Simon and Schuster, 1981); Michael J. Klarman, *From Jim Crow to Civil Rights: The Supreme Court and the Struggle for Racial Equality* (New York: Oxford University Press, 2004).

33. Adam Fairclough, "The Little Rock Crisis: Success or Failure for the NAACP?" *AHQ* 56 (Autumn 1997): 371–75.

34. Michael J. Klarman, "How *Brown* Changed Race Relations: The Backlash Thesis," *Journal of American History* 81 (June 1994): 81–118; Klarman, *From Jim Crow to Civil Rights,* 344–442.

35. Dwight D. Eisenhower, *The White House Years: Waging Peace, 1956–1961* (Garden City, NY: Doubleday, 1965); Philip Norton, *Eisenhower and Little Rock: A Case Study in Presidential Decision Making* (Hull: University of Hull, 1979); Ouseph Varkey, "Crisis Situations and Federal Systems: A Comparative Study of

America and India," *Indian Journal of American Studies* 9, no. 1 (1979): 65–79; James C. Durham, *A Moderate amongst Extremists: Dwight D. Eisenhower and the School Desegregation Crisis* (Chicago: Nelson-Hall, 1981); Robert F. Burk, *The Eisenhower Administration and Black Civil Rights* (Knoxville: University of Tennessee Press, 1984); Michael S. Mayer, "With Much Deliberation and Some Speed: Eisenhower and the *Brown* Decision," *Journal of Southern History* 52 (Feb. 1986): 43–76; Mark Stern, "Eisenhower and Kennedy: A Comparison of Confrontations at Little Rock and Ole Miss," *Policy Studies Journal* 21 (Autumn 1993): 575–88; Steven R. Goldwitz and George Dionisopoulos, "Crisis at Little Rock: Eisenhower, History and Mediated Political Realities," in *Eisenhower's War of Words: Rhetoric and Leadership,* ed. Martin J. Medhurst (East Lansing: Michigan State University Press, 1994), 189–221; Paul Greenberg, "Eisenhower Draws the Racial Battle Lines with Orval Faubus," *Journal of Blacks in Higher Education* 18 (Winter 1997–98): 120–21.

36. John W. Anderson, *Eisenhower, Brownell, and the Congress: The Tangled Origins of the Civil Rights Bill of 1956–1957* (University: University of Alabama Press, 1964); Arthur Brann Caldwell, *Justice Department Civil Rights Policies Prior to 1960: Crucial Documents from the Files of Arthur Brann Caldwell* (New York: Garland, 1991); Herbert Brownell, "Eisenhower's Civil Rights Program: A Personal Assessment," *Presidential Studies Quarterly* 21 (Spring 1991): 235–42; Brownell, with John P. Burke, *Advising Ike: The Memoirs of Attorney General Herbert Brownell* (Lawrence: University Press of Kansas, 1993).

37. Hoyt H. Purvis, "Little Rock and the Press" (M.A. thesis, University of Texas, 1963); Allison Graham, "Remapping Dogpatch: The Northern Media on the Southern Circuit," *AHQ* 56 (Autumn 1997): 334–40; I. Wilmer Counts, *A Life Is More than a Moment: The Desegregation of Little Rock's Central High* (Bloomington: Indiana University Press, 1999).

38. Hannah Arendt, "Reflections on Little Rock," *Dissent* 6 (Winter 1959): 45–56; Gwendolyn Brooks, "The *Chicago Defender* Sends a Man to Little Rock," in *The Bean Eaters* (New York: Harper and Bros., 1960), 132–34; Sue S. Park, "A Study in Tension: Gwendolyn Brooks's 'The *Chicago Defender* Sends a Man to Little Rock,'" *Black American Literature Forum* 11 (Spring 1977): 32–34; Richard H. King, "American Dilemmas, European Experiences," *AHQ* 56 (Autumn 1997): 314–33; Hank Kilbanoff, "L. Alex Wilson," *Media Studies Journal* 14 (Summer 2000): 60–68; King, *Race, Culture and the Intellectuals, 1940–1970* (Baltimore: Johns Hopkins University Press, 2004), 96–119; Vicky Lebeau, "The Unwelcome Child: Elizabeth Eckford and Hannah Arendt," *Journal of Visual Culture* 3, no. 1 (2004): 52–62.

39. *Mingus Ah Um* (Columbia, 1959); *Charles Mingus Presents Charles Mingus* (Candid, 1960); Brian Priestley, *Mingus: A Critical Biography* (London: Quartet Books, 1982); Normand Guilbeault Ensemble, *Mingus Erectus* (Ambiances Magnetiques, 2005).

40. Penny M. Von Eschen, *Race against Empire: Black Americans and Anti-Colonialism, 1937–1957* (Ithaca: Cornell University Press, 1997), 179–80.

41. Harold R. Isaacs, "World Affairs and U.S. Race Relations: A Note on Little Rock," *Public Opinion Quarterly* 22 (Autumn 1958): 364–70; Mary L. Dudziak, "The

Little Rock Crisis and Foreign Affairs: Race, Resistance, and the Image
of American Democracy," *Southern California Law Review* 71 (Sept. 1997):
1641–1716; Azza Salama Layton, "International Pressure and the U.S. Government's Response to Little Rock," *AHQ* 56 (Autumn 1997): 257–72; Melinda M.
Schwenk, "Reforming the Negative through History: The U S. Information Agency
and the 1957 Little Rock Integration Crisis," *Journal of Communication Inquiry* 23,
no. 3 (1999): 288–306; Dudziak, *Cold War Civil Rights: Race and the Image of
American Democracy* (Princeton: Princeton University Press, 2000), 115–51;
Layton, *International Politics and Civil Rights Policies in the United States, 1941–1960*
(Cambridge: Cambridge University Press, 2000), 107–39; Cary Fraser, "Crossing
the Color Line in Little Rock: The Eisenhower Administration and the Dilemma
of Race for U.S. Foreign Policy," *Diplomatic History* 24 (Spring 2000): 233–64.

42. "The Revolution since Little Rock," *Life*, Sept. 29, 1967, 92–112; Paul
Fair, "Little Rock: Then and Now," *Theory into Practice* 17 (Feb. 1978): 39–42;
Sybil Stevenson, "Reflections on Little Rock," *Theory into Practice* 17 (Apr. 1978):
179–82; Branton, "Little Rock Revisited"; Henry Woods and Beth Deere,
"Reflections on the Little Rock School Case," *Arkansas Law Review* 44, no. 4
(1991): 972–1006; Mary Caroline Proctor, "A History and Analysis of Federal
Court Decisions in School Desegregation Cases: Implications for Arkansas"
(Ph.D. diss., University of Mississippi, 1992); Robert L. Brown, *The Second Crisis
of Little Rock: A Report on Desegregation within the Little Rock Public Schools* (Little
Rock: Winthrop Rockefeller Foundation, 1998); Brown, "The Third Little Rock
Crisis," *AHQ* 65 (Spring 2006): 39–44.

43. John A. Kirk, "'A Study in Second Class Citizenship': Race, Urban
Development and Little Rock's Gillam Park, 1934–2004," *AHQ* 64 (Autumn
2005): 262–86.

44. In addition to works cited above, see James W. Vander Zanden, "The
Impact of Little Rock," *Journal of Educational Sociology* 35 (Apr. 1962): 381–84;
David Terrell, "Little Rock Story," *American Preservation* 1 (Oct.–Nov. 1977):
62–72; Chris Mayfield, "Little Rock, 1957–1960: 'The Middle Ground Turns to
Quicksand,'" *Southern Exposure* 7 (Summer 1979): 40–44; John Egerton, "Little
Rock, 1976: 'Going Back Would Be Unthinkable,'" *Southern Exposure* 7 (Summer
1979): 45–46; Mike Masterson, "Little Rock, 1979: 'There Have Been Changes,'"
Southern Exposure 7 (Summer 1979): 46–47; Harry S. Ashmore, "The Lesson of
Little Rock," *Media Studies Journal* 11 (Spring 1997): 6–15.

45. D. LaRouth S. Perry, "The 1957 Desegregation Crisis of Little Rock,
Arkansas: A Meeting of Histories" (Ph.D. diss., Bowling Green State University,
1998); Damon W. Freeman, "Reexamining Central High: American Memory and
Social Reality," *Organization of American Historians Newsletter* 28 (Feb. 2000): 1, 3,
6; Cathy J. Collins, "Forgetting and Remembering: The Desegregation of Central
High School in Little Rock, Arkansas: Race, Community Struggle, and Collective
Memory" (Ph.D. diss., Fielding Graduate Institute, California, 2004).

46. Townsend Davis, *Weary Feet, Rested Souls: A Guided History of the Civil
Rights Movement* (New York: W. W. Norton, 1998), 133–38; Johanna Miller
Lewis, "'Build a Museum and They Will Come': The Creation of the Central
High Museum and Visitor Center," *Public Historian* 22 (Fall 2000): 29–45.

Looking Back at Little Rock

1. *Brown v. Board of Education of Topeka,* 347 U. S. 483 (1954).
2. *Southern School News,* Jan. 1958.
3. Silverman, *Little Rock Story,* 36.
4. Silverman, *Little Rock Story,* 36; *Arkansas Gazette,* Mar. 10, 17, 1957.
5. For evaluations of the broad significance of Little Rock, see Samuel Lubell, *White and Black: Test of a Nation* (New York: Harper & Row, 1964); Alexander M. Bickel, *The Least Dangerous Branch: The Supreme Court at the Bar of Politics* (Indianapolis: Bobbs-Merrill, 1962).
6. Oscar Handlin, *Fire-Bell in the Night; The Crisis in Civil Rights* (Boston: Little, Brown, 1964), 44–45; Bickel, *Least Dangerous Branch,* 266. The latter interpretation is well developed in Peltason, *Fifty-Eight Lonely Men,* 155–65.
7. Blossom, *It Has Happened Here,* 10.
8. *Race Relations Law Reporter* 1 (Oct. 1956): 853.
9. *Race Relations Law Reporter* 1 (Oct. 1956): 854–55.
10. Blossom, *It Has Happened Here,* chap. 2, defends the plan; Iggers, "Arkansas Professor," offers sharp criticism.
11. The tendency for Little Rock citizens to divide along class as well as racial lines on racial questions is amply demonstrated by voting statistics. See the tables in Silverman, *Little Rock Story,* 36–38.
12. Colbert S. Cartwright, "Lesson from Little Rock," *Christian Century,* Oct. 9, 1957, 1194.
13. Comments by William T. Shelton, city editor, *Arkansas Gazette,* letter to the author, Oct. 5, 1965.
14. Bates, *Long Shadow of Little Rock,* 51–52.
15. Blossom, *It Has Happened Here,* 14.
16. Cartwright, "Lesson from Little Rock," 1194. A Little Rock minister at the time of the crisis, Cartwright offers perceptive observations. See also Cartwright, "The Improbable Demagogue of Little Rock, Ark.," *Reporter* 17 (Oct. 17, 1957): 23–25; and Robert R. Brown, *Bigger than Little Rock.*
17. Silverman, *Little Rock Story,* 6.
18. Woodrow Wilson Mann, *New York Herald-Tribune,* Jan. 29, 1958. Mann's account of the crisis was serialized in the *Herald-Tribune,* Jan. 19–31, 1958.
19. Hays, *Southern Moderate Speaks,* 166, 170.
20. Mann, *New York Herald-Tribune,* Jan. 27, 1958.
21. Campbell and Pettigrew, *Christians in Racial Crisis,* chap. 3, provides an able analysis of the segregationist activity of "sect" ministers.
22. Silverman, *Little Rock Story,* 36–38.
23. *Arkansas Gazette,* May 1, July 9, 17, 21, 1957; *Southern School News,* Aug. 1957, Sept. 1957; Blossom, *It Has Happened Here,* 35–47; Campbell and Pettigrew, *Christians in Racial Crisis,* 45; Robert R. Brown, *Bigger than Little Rock,* 16–17.
24. *Arkansas Gazette,* Aug. 23, 1957.
25. Qtd. in *New York Times,* Sept. 9, 1957. "Georgia: Rallying Point of Defiance," *Look,* Nov. 12, 1957, 34, provides accounts of the visit by both

Griffin and Harris. "Text of TV Interview with Governor Faubus," *Memphis Commercial Appeal,* Sept. 9, 1957, gives Faubus's account. All are in agreement.

26. Qtd. in "Georgia: Rallying Point of Defiance," 34.

27. Fletcher Knebel, "The Real Little Rock Story," *Look,* Nov. 12, 1957, 32.

28. Qtd. in *Southern School News,* Sept. 1957.

29. Blossom, *It Has Happened Here,* 48.

30. "Statement Made by Blossom to FBI," Sept. 7, 1957, reprinted in *Arkansas Gazette,* June 18, 1958; Peltason, *Fifty-Eight Lonely Men,* 162; *Arkansas Gazette,* Aug. 30, 1957.

31. Blossom, *It Has Happened Here,* 49.

32. Blossom, *It Has Happened Here,* 50. The district court upheld the Phase Program in *Aaron v. Cooper, Race Relations Law Reporter* 1 (Oct. 1956): 851–60.

33. "Statement Made by Blossom to FBI," Sept. 7, 1957. Blossom more fully comments on the discussions in *It Has Happened Here,* 40–75. Other accounts shedding light on these conferences include "School Board Statement," *Arkansas Gazette,* June 18, 1958; Alford and Alford, *Case of the Sleeping People,* 8; Wayne Upton, *New Orleans Times-Picayune,* Jan. 29, 1959; Mann, *New York Herald-Tribune,* Jan. 21, 22, 1958; "The Story of Little Rock—As Governor Faubus Tells It," *U.S. News and World Report,* June 20, 1958, 101–6.

34. Blossom, *It Has Happened Here,* 58.

35. Boyce Alexander Drummond Jr., "Arkansas Politics: A Study of a One-Party System" (Ph.D. diss., University of Chicago, 1957), 91; *Southern School News,* Oct. 1955.

36. "Report of the Bird Committee," *Race Relations Law Reporter* 1 (Aug. 1956): 717–28. The two bills are reprinted in *Race Relations Law Reporter* 1 (June 1956): 579–81, 591–92. *Southern School News,* Dec. 1956, gives election results.

37. Drummond, "Arkansas Politics," covers Arkansas politics through 1956. Otherwise, these observations are based on contemporary newspaper accounts. The four acts of the 1957 legislature are printed in *Race Relations Law Reporter* 2 (Apr. 1957): 453, 456, 491–94, 495–96.

38. Qtd. in *New York Times,* Mar. 25, 1956.

39. Qtd. in *Arkansas Gazette,* July 10, 1956.

40. Qtd. in *New York Times,* July 18, 1957.

41. *Southern School News,* Sept. 1957.

42. *Southern School News,* Sept. 1957.

43. Warren Olney III, "A Government Lawyer Looks at Little Rock," *Congressional Record,* 85 Cong., 2 sess., 5090–92; *New York Times,* Aug. 31, 1957.

44. E. Frederic Morrow, *Black Man in the White House: A Diary of the Eisenhower Years by the Administrative Officer for Special Projects, the White House, 1955–1961* (New York: Coward-McCann, 1963), 91–92. Other helpful accounts of the Eisenhower administration include Sherman Adams, *Firsthand Report;* Emmet John Hughes, *The Ordeal of Power: A Political Memoir of the Eisenhower Years* (New York: Atheneum, 1963); and John W. Anderson, *Eisenhower, Brownell, and the Congress.* The first three are memoirs by members of the White House staff; the latter is an able study of the administration's dealings with Congress on civil rights.

45. Qtd. in *New York Times,* Sept. 4, 1957.

46. *New York Times,* Sept. 6, 1957.

47. Hays, *Southern Moderate Speaks,* 165–71; Blossom, *It Has Happened Here,* 101.

48. *Southern School News,* Sept. 1957; *Arkansas Gazette,* Aug. 30, 1957; *New York Times,* Aug. 30, 1957; *Race Relations Law Reporter* 2 (Oct. 1957): 931–34.

49. *Memphis Commercial Appeal,* Sept. 2, 1957; Knebel, "Real Little Rock Story," 31–32.

50. Blossom, *It Has Happened Here,* 66.

51. Blossom, *It Has Happened Here,* 66.

52. *Race Relations Law Reporter* 2 (Oct. 1957): 960.

53. Qtd. in *Arkansas Gazette,* Sept. 3, 1957.

54. Qtd. in *Arkansas Gazette,* Sept. 27, 1957.

The White Citizens' Council and Resistance to School Desegregation in Arkansas

1. Guerdon D. Nichols, "Breaking the Color Barrier at the University of Arkansas," *Arkansas Historical Quarterly* 27 (Spring 1968): 3–21; *Southern School News,* Sept. 1954, 2, Oct. 1954, 3.

2. Qtd. in *Southern School News,* Sept. 1954, 2.

3. *Southern School News,* Apr. 1955, 3.

4. Qtd. in "Has Arkansas Gone Liberal," *Chicago Defender,* May 7, 1955. The tone of this article in a Negro daily reflects the general optimism expressed by many on the course of desegregation in Arkansas. See also "Integration Is Right in Arkansas," *Charleston News and Courier,* June 2, 1955; "Integration Working in Arkansas School," *Birmingham News,* June 17, 1955.

5. In Sept. 1954, there were two school districts operating on a desegregated basis in the state. Both were to be found in western Arkansas. See *Southern School News,* Oct. 1954, 2. See also a convenient summary of Arkansas school statistics in the same publication, Feb. 1955, 2.

6. *Southern School News,* Mar. 1955, 2, July 1955, 3, Sept. 1955, 10.

7. For thorough coverage of the early stages of the Hoxie story, see "Hoxie Schools Desegregate in Arkansas without Incident," *Southern School News,* Aug. 1955, 15; Cabell Phillips, "Integration: Battle of Hoxie, Arkansas," *New York Times Magazine,* Sept. 25, 1955, 12, 68–76. Compare an account by the White Citizens' Council of Arkansas, "The Hoxie Story," *Arkansas Faith,* Nov. 1955, 9–10.

8. See "A 'Morally Right' Decision," *Life,* July 25, 1955, 29–31. The significance of the *Life* article as a catalyst for prosegregation activity has been recognized by Phillips, "Integration," 68.

9. Phillips, "Integration"; *Southern School News,* Sept. 1955, 10; Dan Wakefield, "Respectable Racism: Dixie's Citizens' Councils," *Nation,* Oct. 22, 1955, 340; *Arkansas Gazette,* Sept. 10, 1955.

10. *Arkansas Gazette,* Aug. 21, 1955; Phillips, "Integration," 68 ff.; "Protests Lead to Closing of School 2 Weeks Early at Hoxie, Arkansas," *Southern School News,* Sept. 1955, 10.

11. The White Citizens' Council of Arkansas newspaper, *Arkansas Faith,* reported that the recording was played to crowds in Dermott, DeWitt, England, Forrest City, Hamburg, Lake Village, and Sheridan, all in the southeastern half of Arkansas (Nov. 1955, 19). See also *Southern School News,* Oct. 1955, 9.

12. *Southern School News,* Dec. 1958, 8–9; Robert Leflar, "'Law of the Land': The Courts and the Schools," in *With All Deliberate Speed; Segregation-Desegregation in Southern Schools,* ed. Don Shoemaker (New York: Harper, 1957), 9.

13. *Arkansas Gazette,* Oct. 14, 1955; *Arkansas Democrat,* Oct. 17, 1955.

14. Eventually, Robert Ewing Brown was retained as executive secretary. See *Southern School News,* Nov. 1956, 12; *Arkansas Gazette,* Sept. 2, 1956.

15. See *Southern School News,* Apr. 7, 1955, 3, Nov. 1958, 8, Sept. 1959, 1–2, 15; *Arkansas Gazette,* June 29, 1957; *Memphis Commercial Appeal,* June 29, 1957; *Pine Bluff Commercial,* Jan. 31, Feb. 1, 1962.

16. See *Memphis Commercial Appeal,* Sept. 1, 1957.

17. See Southern Regional Council, *Special Report: Pro-Segregation Groups in the South* (Atlanta, 1956), and rev. ed. of May 23, 1957.

18. Southern Regional Council, *Special Report,* rev. ed.

19. Forced to make public its records in Nov. 1957, under the city's so-called Bennett ordinances, the CCC revealed that of its 510 members, 295 lived in Little Rock, 86 in North Little Rock, 121 elsewhere in the state, and 8 outside the state. Proposed by state attorney general Bruce Bennett as a weapon to be used against the NAACP, the Bennett ordinances were adopted by Little Rock, North Little Rock, and Crossett. They required the records of "extremist groups" to be made public. See *Arkansas Gazette,* Oct. 27, 31, Nov. 1, 1957; *Southern School News,* Nov. 1957, 7.

20. All but two of the States' Rights Council's twelve incorporators were former members of the CCC (*Arkansas Gazette,* Sept. 5, 18, 1958).

21. Alexander, *Little Rock Recall Election,* 4.

22. For details of that plan, see *Southern School News,* May 1957, 2–3.

23. Bates, *Long Shadow of Little Rock,* 51–52. See also Cartwright, "Lesson from Little Rock," 1193–94. According to Cartwright, pastor of Little Rock's Pulaski Heights Christian Church, "the Little Rock school board and Superintendent Virgil Blossom must share responsibility for the Little Rock debacle."

24. For a scholarly treatment of the crisis, see Bartley, *Rise of Massive Resistance,* 251–69. An early study of the problems of federalism engendered by the crisis is Silverman, *Little Rock Story.* Benjamin Muse's *Ten Years of Prelude: The Story of Integration since the Supreme Court's 1954 Decision* (New York: Viking Press, 1964), 122–45, is also useful. Firsthand accounts, in addition to Bates's, include Blossom, *It Has Happened Here;* Robert R. Brown, *Bigger than Little Rock;* Gloster B. Current, "Crisis in Little Rock," *Crisis,* Nov. 1957, 525–35; Hays, *Southern Moderate Speaks.*

25. Qtd. in *Southern School News,* June 1957, 9.

26. Blossom, *It Has Happened Here,* 34.

27. Qtd. in Blossom, *It Has Happened Here,* 36.

28. *Southern School News,* Aug. 1957, 7.

29. Qtd. in *Birmingham News,* July 19, 1957.

30. Qtd. in *Arkansas Gazette,* July 17, 1957. It should be noted that the NAACP was sharply critical of the Little Rock Phase Program.

31. *Southern School News,* July 1957, 10.

32. *Southern School News,* Aug. 1957, 7.

33. *Southern School News,* Sept. 1957, 6–7; Hays, *Southern Moderate Speaks,* 131–32; Knebel, "Real Little Rock Story," 32–33; George B. Leonard Jr., "Georgia: Rallying Point of Defiance," *Look,* Nov. 12, 1957, 32–34; *Arkansas Gazette,* Aug. 22, 23, 1957.

34. Qtd. in *Southern School News,* Sept. 1957, 7.

35. In his testimony before a federal court, Blossom declared that Griffin's appearance in Little Rock "had more to do with strengthening opposition than anything that happened" (qtd. in *Atlanta Journal,* June 5, 1958).

36. *Southern School News,* Sept. 1957, 6–7.

37. Qtd. in Silverman, *Little Rock Story.* For Faubus's proclamation to the National Guard, Sept. 2, 1957, see *Race Relations Law Reporter* 2 (Oct. 1957): 937.

38. Cartwright, "Improbable Demagogue"; Bartley, "Looking Back at Little Rock," 110–11; Silverman, *Little Rock Story,* 10.

39. *Arkansas Faith,* Nov. 1955, Mar. 1956. See also Carl Rowan, *Go South to Sorrow* (New York: Random House, 1957), 156–57; *Arkansas Gazette,* Oct. 4, 1957.

40. Knebel, "Real Little Rock Story," 32–33; Hays, *Southern Moderate Speaks,* 131–32.

41. Little Rock congressman Brooks Hays, a participant in these maneuverings, wrote "The Inside Story of Little Rock," *U.S. News and World Report,* Mar. 23, 1959, 118–35.

42. Blossom, *It Has Happened Here,* 103–9.

43. Major General Edwin A. Walker, commander of the Arkansas Military District, directed the federal military operation at Little Rock. Although he carried out his assignment with efficiency and even lectured white students on proper deportment before Negroes arrived at Central High, Walker, who became a South-wide Council hero, would later declare that he had fought on the "wrong side" in 1957. On the tenth anniversary of the *Brown* decision, he returned to the Arkansas capital city as a guest of the CCC to deliver an address entitled "The Road from Little Rock: The Unprecedented Exposé of an American Soldier's Battle with the World Police State." School officials refused to let him speak from the steps of Central High (*Memphis Commercial Appeal,* May 18, 1964).

44. *Arkansas Gazette,* May 27, 1958.

45. Qtd. in *Southern School News,* Feb. 1958, 12. See also *Arkansas Gazette,* Jan. 15, 16, 18, 1958.

46. *Columbia State,* Sept. 3, 1957.

47. *Birmingham News,* Nov. 20, 1957; *Charlotte News,* Nov. 20, 1957; *Charleston News and Courier,* Nov. 20, 1957; *Columbia State,* Nov. 22, 1957; *Southern School News,* Nov. 1957, 11.

48. See CCC editorial, *Monroe Morning World,* Jan. 22, 1958; *Southern School News,* Feb. 1958, 12; Blossom, *It Has Happened Here,* 150–51.

49. Broadside, "'Mrs.' Daisy Bates," miscellaneous files, Southern Education Reporting Service (hereafter SERS), Nashville, TN. The NAACP state president informed the press that her 1946 contempt charge was dismissed on appeal and that the 1952 gaming charge stemmed from a police raid on a private home where Mrs. Bates, her husband, and another couple were playing "penny ante" poker (*Memphis Commercial Appeal,* Dec. 18, 1957).

50. Qtd. in *Arkansas Gazette,* Mar. 21, 1958.

51. *Southern School News,* Dec. 1957, 2–3.

52. See Gertrude Samuels, "Little Rock: More Tension than Ever," *New York Times Magazine,* Mar. 23, 1958, 23, 88–90; *Race Relations Law Reporter* 3 (Aug. 1958): 630–41, 644–48; *Southern School News,* Oct. 1958, 5, 7.

53. *Southern School News,* Oct. 1958, 5, 7.

54. *Southern School News,* Nov. 1958, 8–9.

55. *Citizens' Council,* Oct. 1958, 1; *New Orleans Times-Picayune,* Nov. 10, 1958.

56. *Citizens' Council,* Nov. 1958, 1, Dec. 1958, 2; *Southern School News,* Nov. 1958, 5, Dec. 1958, 12; *Montgomery Advertiser,* Oct. 3, 1958; Muse, *Ten Years of Prelude,* 155.

57. *Southern School News,* Dec. 1958, 12–13; Jan. 1959, 14. For Alford's views on race, see a book much vaunted in segregationist circles: Alford and Alford, *Case of the Sleeping People.*

58. House Bill 546, as the board-packing measure was known, was introduced on Feb. 26, upon the request of Faubus and Edward I. McKinley Jr., one of the Council-endorsed school board members. According to its legislative sponsor, the bill was "a little on the dictatorship side but we have no choice. The people voted the man [Faubus] back to do whatever he can to preserve their way of life" (qtd. in *Southern School News,* Mar. 1959, 2).

59. *Arkansas Gazette,* May 6, 1959; *Southern School News,* June 1959, 2.

60. CROSS also invited Dr. Wesley A. Swift to address a rally. Given advance billing as "State Director, Anti-Communist League of California and pastor of a well-known Los Angeles Church," Reverend Swift arrived in Little Rock but did not appear at the segregationists' rally. When the *Arkansas Gazette* revealed that he had been a Klansman and bodyguard for Gerald L. K. Smith, CROSS canceled his scheduled address and used local talent. See editorial, "The Contrast between CROSS and STOP," *Arkansas Gazette,* May 19, 1959; Alexander, *Little Rock Recall Election,* 28.

61. The most balanced and comprehensive analysis of this entire episode is Alexander, *Little Rock Recall Election.* See also "STOP AND CROSS: School Board Election," *Time,* June 8, 1959, 20–21; Jerry Neal, "The Education of Governor Faubus," *Nation,* June 6, 1959, 507–9; "How They Beat Faubus in Little Rock," *New Republic,* June 8, 1959, 7–8; Silverman, *Little Rock Story,* 30–31.

62. *Southern School News,* June 1959, 2; editorial, *Arkansas Gazette,* May 27, 1959. The significance of the purge and the recall election has been ably treated by Colbert S. Cartwright, "HOPE Comes to Little Rock," *Progressive,* Aug. 1959, 7–9.

63. *Southern School News,* July 1959, 8, Aug. 1959, 6, Sept. 1959, 1–2.

64. *Southern School News,* Sept. 1959, 1–3. See also Malcolm G. Taylor to Mayor Werner C. Knoop, Little Rock, Feb. 25, 1960, miscellaneous files, SERS.

65. *Arkansas Gazette,* Sept. 10, 11, 1959, Sept. 15, 1961; *Southern School News,* Oct. 1959, 2, Dec. 1959, 3–4, Mar. 1961, 15.

66. *Southern School News,* Aug. 1960, 5, Sept. 1960, 10. Miller later became identified with the militantly anti-Semite and anti-Negro National States Rights Party. He was listed in the party's publication, *Thunderbolt,* May 1962, as an officer of both the Little Rock and the West Memphis units.

67. *Southern School News,* Nov. 1960, 13, Dec. 1960, 11.

68. See *Arkansas Gazette,* Aug. 15, 21, 1959, Sept. 7, 1960; *Nashville Tennessean,* Aug. 21, 22, 1959, Sept. 7, 1960; *Southern School News,* Sept. 1959, 1–2, 15, Oct. 1960, 11.

69. *Arkansas Gazette,* July 11, 12, 31, 1962; *Southern School News,* Aug. 1962, 6, Jan. 1963, 11. Particularly galling to Councilors was Faubus's announcement early in the campaign that an open break with the segregation group would be of little consequence for his political future. The Citizens' Council, he said, was all but defunct in Arkansas.

Politics and Law in the Little Rock Crisis, 1954–1957

1. For the development and long-range significance of the Little Rock crisis, see Grantham, *Regional Imagination,* 185–98; Lubell, *White and Black;* Bickel, *Least Dangerous Branch;* Paul L. Murphy, *The Constitution in Crisis Times, 1918–1969* (New York: Harper and Row, 1972), 341–44; Peltason, *Fifty-Eight Lonely Men.* The author thanks Project '87 and the Arkansas Endowment for the Humanities for support that made possible research for this study and thanks participants on a panel at the 1980 meeting of the Southern Historical Association where an earlier version of this work was presented. He is indebted, also, to Elizabeth Jacoway for sharing her interest in the Little Rock crisis.

2. Blossom, *It Has Happened Here;* Bates, *Long Shadow of Little Rock;* Handlin, *Fire-Bell in the Night,* 44–45; Peltason, *Fifty-Eight Lonely Men,* 155–65; Bickel, *Least Dangerous Branch,* 266; Olney, "Government Lawyer Looks at Little Rock"; *Crisis in the South.*

3. Faubus, *Down from the Hills;* Alford and Alford, *Case of the Sleeping People.*

4. Bartley, "Looking Back at Little Rock"; Cartwright, "Lesson from Little Rock," 1193–94; Cartwright, "Improbable Demagogue." See also Robert R. Brown, *Bigger than Little Rock;* Campbell and Pettigrew, *Christians in Racial Crisis.*

5. Sources cited above deal in varying degrees with law as an independently definable factor in the crisis. The present study attempts to show, however, that the influence of law as both a political and a symbolic force has been underestimated, at least insofar as developments on the local level are concerned. For this study, law is defined as those rules of conduct or action established and enforced by any governing authority. For law conceived of as both a formal rule and a social institution having ambiguous symbolic content as a value in and of itself (known as "the rule of law"), see Roberto Mangabeira

Unger, *Law in Modern Society: Toward a Criticism of Social Theory* (New York: Free Press, 1976), 5–21, 49–50, 79–92, 245–48. Note that this study treats its theme in terms of developments in Little Rock and Arkansas. No attempt is made to consider the important dimensions of the story involving the Eisenhower administration and national politics.

6. *Brown v. Board of Education of Topeka,* 347 U.S. 483 (1954), and *Brown v. Board of Education of Topeka,* 349 U.S. 294 (1955), are the full citations for *Brown* and *Brown* II. Richard Kluger, *Simple Justice: The History of* Brown v. Board of Education *and Black America's Struggle for Equality* (New York: Knopf, 1976), is a comprehensive study of these two decisions from the point of view of the NAACP. Stephen L. Wasby, Anthony A. D'Amato, and Rosemary Metrailer, *Desegregation from* Brown *to* Alexander: *An Exploration of Supreme Court Strategies* (Carbondale: Southern Illinois University Press, 1977), considers the subject in terms of the dynamics of the judicial decision making of the U.S. Supreme Court. Dennis J. Hutchinson, "Unanimity and Desegregation: Decisionmaking in the Supreme Court, 1948–1958," *Georgetown Law Journal* 67 (Oct. 1979): 1–96, gives the most thorough analysis to date of the Court's decisional process in both *Brown* and *Brown* II and other integration decisions. All of these studies emphasize the ambiguity of the Court's decisions—especially *Brown* II, "deliberate speed," and the extent to which this made delay and gradualism probably inevitable. See also Bickel, *Least Dangerous Branch;* Paul L. Murphy, *Constitution in Crisis Times;* Peltason, *Fifty-Eight Lonely Men.*

7. *Southern School News,* Nov. 1954, 2, May 1955, 2, June 1955, 2. A fuller view of the influence of East Arkansas interests and McCulloch comes through in an unpublished Interim Report of the Special Committee on Interposition and Public Schools, made to Governor Faubus on Feb. 24, 1956. A copy of this report was found in a case file of attorney Leon Catlett, to whom the author is indebted for its use. See also Faubus, *Down from the Hills,* 117, 122, and interviews with J. L. (Bex) Shaver and Faubus. For the influence of sectionalism in Arkansas politics, see Drummond, "Arkansas Politics," esp. 169–86.

8. The McCulloch quotation is from R. B. McCulloch to Harry J. Lemley, Sept. 5, 1958, A-10, box 2, file 4, Federal District Judge Harry J. Lemley Papers, University of Arkansas at Little Rock Library. See also "Statement of Bex Shaver, former President of the Arkansas Bar Association, and former Lieutenant Governor of Arkansas," in "Miscellaneous Bills Regarding . . . Civil Rights," *Hearings Before Subcommittee No. 5 of the Committee on the Judiciary, House of Representatives,* 85 Cong., 1 sess., 1180–89. The author is grateful to Mr. Shaver for this citation. For discussion of pupil assignment laws, see Frank T. Read and Lucy S. McGough, *Let Them Be Judged: The Judicial Integration of the Deep South* (Metuchen, NJ: Scarecrow Press, 1978), 438; Wasby, D'Amato, and Metrailer, *Desegregation from* Brown *to* Alexander, 376–425.

9. The evolution of the Blossom Plan is discussed in Blossom, *It Has Happened Here,* chap. 2. Blossom does not go into detail about the plan that conferred substantial integration, but the degree of change is discussed and criticized in Iggers, "Arkansas Professor." Professor Iggers elaborated upon this theme in an interview with me and in a seven-page single-spaced letter dated

Sept. 17, 1980. The memorandum "A. F. House to Attorney Group," located in the case file of *Cooper v. Aaron,* belonging to Richard C. Butler, contains more on the substantive changes made in the Blossom Plan by May 1955. The author thanks Mr. Butler for the use of this file.

10. The weaknesses in the plan and Blossom's popularization of it are discussed in Bartley, "Looking Back at Little Rock," 104–10; Iggers, "Arkansas Professor"; Iggers to author, Sept. 17, 1980; Hays, *Southern Moderate Speaks,* 184; Robert R. Brown, *Bigger than Little Rock,* 46–65; Campbell and Pettigrew, *Christians in Racial Crisis,* esp. 12–14, 40, 60, 107–8, 172–73; Faubus, *Down from the Hills,* 200.

11. For the view of Faubus as a moderate, see Jim Lester, *A Man for Arkansas: Sid McMath and the Southern Reform Tradition* (Little Rock: Rose Publishing, 1976), 44, 48–49, 83, 90–91, 134; Faubus, *Down from the Hills,* 1–92. For Faubus, the issue of funding for public education, and the prosegregation measures, see *Southern School News,* Feb. 1955, 2, Mar. 1955, 2, Apr. 1955, 3; July 1955, 3. On the defeat of the prosegregation measures, see also the *Americana Annual* (1956), 48. The author is indebted to Marcus Halbrook, director of the Arkansas Legislative Council, who wrote this report for the *Annual* and who discussed the legislation in an interview. For the voting pattern of wards in Little Rock, the author is indebted to Irving J. Spitzberg Jr. for reference to his unpublished manuscript "Racial Politics in Little Rock, 1954–1964," 14. The general character of voter participation is discussed in Drummond, "Arkansas Politics," esp.

12. The fragmentation of the segregationists is reported in the *Southern School News* issues of Mar., Apr., and July cited above; see also McMillen, *The Citizens' Council,* 95.

12. The NAACP case was styled *Aaron v. Cooper,* 143 F. Supp. 855 (E.D. Ark. 1956). The summary of the argument is based upon case files located at the offices of the NAACP Legal Defense and Education Fund, New York City. The record of progress toward the decision by the Little Rock NAACP that a suit was necessary is based on Iggers, "Arkansas Professor"; Iggers to author, Sept. 17, 1980; and Lee Lorch to U. Simpson Tate, Dec. 7, 1955, col. B-1, file 34, Georg G. Iggers Papers, University of Arkansas at Little Rock Library. Interviews with Branton and Iggers contributed further to an understanding of the origins of the suit. See also Bates, *Long Shadow of Little Rock,* 51–53.

13. Information on the attorney group has been obtained from the following sources: interviews with A. F. House (Little Rock, June 16, 1980), Richard C. Butler (Little Rock, Feb. 5, 1980), Leon B. Catlett (Little Rock, July 1, 1980), and Henry E. Spitzberg (Little Rock, Sept. 25, 1980); the private case files of Butler and Catlett (which are used with their kind permission); and Spitzberg, "Racial Politics," 35–36. The summary of the argument is based upon records contained in the Butler and Catlett files.

14. Miller's decision is given in *Aaron v. Cooper,* 143 F. Supp. 855 (E.D. Ark. 1956). The misunderstanding between the NAACP attorneys is mentioned in Iggers, "Arkansas Professor," 290–91, and elaborated upon in Iggers to author, Sept. 17, 1980. See also *Southern School News,* Sept. 1956, 15. The NAACP's appeal was styled *Aaron v. Cooper,* 243 F. 2d. 361 (C.A. 8, 1957).

15. *Arkansas Democrat,* Aug. 29, 1956, 10; *Arkansas Gazette,* Aug. 29, 1956, 4. See also *Southern School News,* Sept. 1956, 15.

16. For the evolution of the segregationists into a united front and the relationship of this to the Hoxie controversy, see *Southern School News,* Aug. 1955, 15; Sept. 1955, 10; Oct. 1955, 10; Jan. 1956, 9; Feb. 1956, 11; see also McMillen, *Citizens' Council,* 95. The litigation concerning Hoxie was styled *Hoxie School District No. 46 of Lawrence Co., Ark. v. Brewer,* 137 F. Supp. 364 (E.D. Ark., 1955); and *Brewer v. Hoxie School District No. 46,* 238 F. 2d 91 (C.A. 8, 1956). Insight into the segregationists' concern about Hoxie as a possible model for integration of East Arkansas schools and the role of the Federal Bureau of Investigation (FBI) was gained in an interview with Arkansas Citizens' Council leader and activist James Johnson (Little Rock, Sept. 4, 1980).

17. The connection between interposition and gubernatorial campaign politics was established in interviews with former lieutenant governor Shaver (Wynne, AR, Aug. 15, 1980), former governor Faubus (Little Rock, July 15, 1980), and former justice of the Arkansas Supreme Court James Johnson (Little Rock, Sept. 4, 1980). Bartley, *Rise of Massive Resistance,* 126–49, is a good discussion of interposition in Arkansas and other southern states. Karr Shannon, *Integration Decision Is Unconstitutional,* is a good statement of the states' rights position upon which the theory of interposition rested. Shannon was the editor of the *Arkansas Democrat* during the period discussed here, and this book is a collection of editorials written during the time of the crisis.

18. *Southern School News,* Feb. 1956, 2, Mar. 1956, 2, Apr. 1956, 8, June 1956, 10, July 1956, 9, Aug. 1956, 3; Faubus, *Down from the Hills,* 113–41.

19. *Southern School News,* Feb. 1956, 11, Apr. 1956, 8. The author first became aware of the connection between politics and the issues of interposition and taxation during interviews with former governor Faubus (July 15, 1980), James Johnson (Sept. 4, 1980), and Marcus Halbrook (via telephone, Jan. 30, 1980). See Faubus, *Down from the Hills,* 113–41, for detailed statements concerning these interconnections.

20. *Southern School News,* Aug. 1956, 3; Nov. 1956, 12; Dec. 1956, 8; Jan. 1957, 8. Faubus, *Down from the Hills,* 11, 55, 93, 125, 146, 148, 152, notes measures favorable to blacks. Pettigrew and Campbell, "Faubus and Segregation," 442, compares black support for Faubus in the 1956 and 1958 Democratic primary elections for governor and shows black support during the governor's second-term bid.

21. The conclusion that in Little Rock there was reluctant but real acceptance of integration is based on Blossom, *It Has Happened Here,* 2; Iggers to author, Sept. 17, 1980; Faubus's own statement to this effect in his proclamation of Sept. 2, 1957, in which he gives his reasons for preventing integration of Central High School; and, of course, the editorials in the *Arkansas Gazette* and *Arkansas Democrat* cited in note 15. Alexander, *Little Rock Recall Election,* 3, also supports this conclusion. The vote in Pulaski County on the Nov. 1956 Resolution of Interposition was 28,038 in favor and 17,808 against. In the state, the pupil assignment measures were also passed in the Nov. election by a divided margin: 214,712 for and 121,129 against. On the school board election,

see *Southern School News,* Apr. 1957, 15; *Aaron v. Cooper,* 243 F. 2d 361 (C.A. 8, 1957). The basis for the NAACP's decision not to appeal is discussed in "Eisenhower Administration, Wiley Branton Interview, 1973," Oral History Research Office, Columbia University, New York, 53.

22. On the interposition enabling legislation, see *Southern School News,* Feb. 1957, 3, Mar. 1957, 13, Apr. 1957, 15; Bates, *Long Shadow of Little Rock,* 53–55. The connection between the interposition legislation and the tax program during the 1957 legislative term became clear in interviews with Governor Faubus (July 15, 1980) and Marcus Halbrook (Jan. 30, 1980). Faubus gives the details of the politics involved in *Down from the Hills,* 157–77, esp. 169.

23. Bates, *Long Shadow of Little Rock,* 57–58; Blossom, *It Has Happened Here,* 30–49. Faubus, *Down from the Hills,* 187–88, 192, 200–201, gives the views of three principals concerning rising tension in Little Rock. Further evidence concerning increased tension is to be found in "Integration in Public Schools in Little Rock," FBI Report 44-12284-933, pp. 19–21, 78, 83. This report was compiled by the FBI at the order of federal district judge Ronald N. Davies during the fall of 1957. The report, never made public, is used here with the permission of Judge Davies and the FBI. References here and in the following paragraph to Upton's and the school board's discussions are based on "Integration in Public Schools in Little Rock," 76–77, 83, 94–95, 98, 103–4, 112–16. These pages include reports of FBI interviews with Blossom, William J. Smith, Harold J. Engstrom, and Upton concerning the discussions with Miller. The substance of these discussions was confirmed in interviews with Smith (Little Rock, Sept. 3, 1980) and Engstrom (Little Rock, June 30, 1980) and in conversation with Upton. The author was unable to speak with Judge Miller (who is over ninety years old), due to his health.

24. In addition to the FBI report and interviews just cited, the sequence of events given in this paragraph was supported by Faubus in an interview with me (July 15, 1980) and by another FBI report, "Integration in Public Schools in Arkansas," 44-12284-937, pp. 17–18, which includes an FBI interview with William F. Rector. The jurisdictional basis of Rector's suit was an Arkansas statute of 1953 giving taxpayers in the Little Rock school district with children in the public schools standing to challenge decisions of the school board. See "Complaint for Declaratory Judgement," 13, in the FBI report just cited. See also Faubus, *Down from the Hills,* 201; *Southern School News,* Sept. 1957, 6, on the suit filed by Rector and the local ministers.

25. *Southern School News,* Sept. 1957, 6; "Memorandum from A. B. Caldwell to Assistant Attorney General Warren Olney III," in FBI Report 44-12284-933, pp. 23–24. Caldwell, an attorney for the U.S. Justice Department, was an Arkansan whom Faubus spoke with in a private conference on Aug. 28, 1957. During the conference, Faubus said that Griffin's speech had changed the mood of Little Rock from reluctant acceptance of integration to opposition. This view is reiterated in Faubus, *Down from the Hills,* 195, and shared by Blossom, *It Has Happened Here,* 54, and Hays, *Southern Moderate Speaks,* 153. See also Bartley, "Looking Back at Little Rock," 109.

26. The connections between Griffin's speech and Faubus's political situation are noted in Hays, *Southern Moderate Speaks,* 187; Blossom, *It Has Happened*

Here, 53–54. The importance of these related themes is developed further in "Caldwell Memorandum," 23–25, and Blossom interview, 83, 97–98, 104, both in FBI Report 44-12284-933. See also Faubus, *Down from the Hills,* 187. In an interview with me (July 15, 1980), Faubus noted his responsibility for enforcing interposition measures until they were declared invalid by the courts; he noted, too, that this obligation placed him in a difficult political situation as Sept. 3 neared.

27. Faubus's meeting with Caldwell is discussed in *Down from the Hills,* 197–98. In his treatment of this meeting, Faubus does not state that he told the Justice Department attorney that he had arranged the chancery court suit; he does admit, however, that it was through his efforts that the suit was filed (*Down from the Hills,* 201). This conclusion is supported further by Faubus's statement at a meeting with the school board (Blossom interview, 96, in FBI Report 44-12284-933). The chancery hearing and the federal court proceedings are discussed in "Caldwell Memorandum," 24–26, and Blossom interview, 96, both in FBI Report 44-12284-933; Blossom, *It Has Happened Here,* 60–62; Bates, *Long Shadow of Little Rock,* 57; Faubus, *Down from the Hills,* 199, 201–3; *Southern School News,* Sept. 1957, 6. The meetings with Faubus's advisers are discussed in interviews with each adviser present: FBI Report 44-12284-933, pp. 43–73. For the private meetings between Faubus and Blossom following the federal court's decision, see Blossom interview, 97–98, 100, in FBI Report 44-12284-933; Blossom, *It Has Happened Here,* 66.

28. See the full text of Faubus's announcement in FBI Report 44-12284-933, pp. 30–40.

29. See Faubus's announcement in FBI Report 44-12284-933. Faubus never gave convincing proof that violence would occur. In *Down from the Hills,* 198–204, 206, Faubus contends that Blossom was his primary source for this perception. The bulk of FBI Report 44-12284-933 is devoted to tracing down rumors concerning possible violence and to determining the validity of Faubus's claims. After an extensive investigation, the FBI report concluded that, other than a few rumors, there was no basis for Faubus's claim. The report shows that even the rumors grew out of a few minor incidents that had no con- nection with integration.

30. Huckaby, *Crisis at Central High,* and Blossom, *It Has Happened Here,* 98–176, describe the events within Central from the school administration's point of view. For the perspective of the black children and the NAACP, see Daisy Bates Papers, State Historical Society of Wisconsin, Madison; Bates, *Long Shadow of Little Rock,* 63–116. For the level of harassment, see also the briefs filed for *Aaron v. Cooper, Petition for Writ of Certiorari to the United States Court of Appeals for the Eighth Circuit, in the Supreme Court of the United States, October Term, 1958.* The author used the briefs of the school board's attorney, Richard C. Butler, with his permission, and those of the NAACP (which are located in the NAACP Legal Defense Fund offices in New York City). Interestingly, most white students remained uninvolved with the black children's plight; see *Arkansas Gazette,* Feb. 1, 2, 1981. The public rationale for the school board's request for delay is worked out in the briefs just cited. For the private justifica- tion for the delay, see the author's interview with Richard C. Butler (Feb. 5,

1980) and "Eisenhower Administration, Richard C. Butler Interview, 1972," Oral History Research Office. See also Bates, *Long Shadow of Little Rock,* 151–55.

31. For Lemley's decision and its appeal, see *Aaron v. Cooper,* 163 F. Supp 13 (E.D. Ark.), *cert. denied,* 357 U.S. 566, *reversed en banc,* 257 F. 2d 33 (8th Cir.), *affirmed,* 358 U.S. 1 (1958).

32. See Alexander, *Little Rock Recall Election,* and Spitzberg, "Racial Politics," esp. 1–19, for Faubus's response to the Supreme Court's decision, for events of 1958–59 school year, and for the special school board election. See also Bates, *Long Shadow of Little Rock,* 155–59; *Cooper v. Aaron,* 358 U.S. 1 (1958).

33. The responsibility of the Supreme Court for the gradualism and delay that grew out of the vagueness of "deliberate speed" is discussed in Hutchinson, "Unanimity and Desegregation," 50–60; Wasby, D'Amato, and Metrailer, *Desegregation from* Brown *to* Alexander, 108–30. See Blossom, *It Has Happened Here,* 29, for the argument that "minimum integration" under the law was what the majority of whites wanted.

34. Blossom, *It Has Happened Here,* 29, notes that the NAACP's suit of 1956 was "unfortunate" because "it attracted undesirable attention to the Little Rock situation at a time when calm, intelligent cooperation was essential for the success of our program."

35. This thesis was developed in Richard C. Butler's argument of *Cooper v. Aaron* before the Supreme Court, given in the transcript of the record in Box 325, Legal (Aug., Special Term), 1958, Case #1, Notes and Memos, Justice Harold H. Burton Papers, Library of Congress, Washington, DC.

36. Bates, *Long Shadow of Little Rock,* 57, suggests that the chancery suit was the result of efforts of the White Citizens' Council. Blossom, *It Has Happened Here,* 60–61, states that Faubus himself announced to the school board on Aug. 26 that he would get his own court order. Olney, "Government Lawyer Looks at Little Rock," 5090–92, relates Caldwell's testimony, given in the FBI interview cited above, that notes the connection between interposition law and the chancery suit. But none of these studies establishes the connection between the Upton-Miller discussions and the politics of interposition.

Orval E. Faubus: Out of Socialism into Realism

1. V. O. Key Jr., *Southern Politics in State and Nation* (New York: Knopf, 1949), 8. Populism was not restricted to the hill country, but, as Key points out, radical politics had a more marked influence in the thin-soiled uplands than in the planter-controlled delta.

2. Bonnie Pace, interview with author, Combs, AR, Nov. 9, 1990.

3. Pace, interview, Nov. 9, 1990; Orval E. Faubus, interview with author, Conway, AR, June 14, 1988.

4. *Madison County Record,* Mar. 9, 1933 (from the Combs news column by "Jimmie Higgins," Sam Faubus's nom de plume); *Madison County Record,* Mar. 16, 1933 (article by Arch Cornett).

5. Orval E. Faubus to author, May 28, 1993.

6. Faubus speech to University of Arkansas Young Democrats, Fayetteville, AR, Apr. 30, 1993.

7. Faubus to author, Feb. 11, 1993.

8. Walt W. Rostow, *The Stages of Economic Growth, A Non-Communist Manifesto* (Cambridge: Cambridge University Press, 1960), 18.

9. *Arkansas Recorder,* Jan. 18, 1957, 8.

10. *Arkansas Recorder,* Oct. 19, 1956, 2.

11. Key, *Southern Politics,* 666.

12. Key, *Southern Politics,* 669. For a discussion of the negative influence of race in shaping the black belt's domination of southern politics, see chaps. 1 and 31.

13. Key, *Southern Politics,* 672.

14. U.S. Bureau of the Census, *Seventeenth Census of the United States, 1950,* vol. 2, *Characteristics of the Population* (Washington, DC: Government Printing Office, 1952), pt. 4, p. 65.

15. Faubus, interview with author, Nov. 29, 1993, Arkansas Educational Television Network, Conway, AR, videocassette.

16. Faubus to John Connally, Mar. 27, 1980, Orval Eugene Faubus Papers (hereafter OEF Papers), Special Collections, University of Arkansas Libraries, Fayetteville; Faubus to author, May 27, 1994.

17. Faubus to Harry Dent, Jan. 10, 1973, OEF Papers.

18. Faubus memorandum to staff, Oct. 11, 1965, OEF Papers.

19. For various perspectives on southern populism and some of its adherents, see W. Scott Morgan, *History of the Wheel and Alliance and the Impending Revolution* (Fort Scott, KS: J. H. Rice & Sons, 1889); Theodore Saloutos, *Farmer Movements in the South, 1865–1933* (Berkeley: University of California Press, 1960); Francis Butler Simkins, *The Tillman Movement in South Carolina* (Durham: Duke University Press, 1926); C. Vann Woodward, *Tom Watson: Agrarian Rebel* (New York: Macmillan, 1938); James Turner, "Understanding the Populists," *Journal of American History* 67 (Sept. 1980): 354-73; Robert C. McMath Jr., *Populist Vanguard: A History of the Southern Farmers' Alliance* (Chapel Hill: University of North Carolina Press, 1975); John D. Hicks, *The Populist Revolt: A History of the Farmers' Alliance and the People's Party* (Minneapolis: University of Minnesota Press, 1931); Bruce Palmer, *"Man over Money": The Southern Populist Critique of American Capitalism* (Chapel Hill: University of North Carolina Press, 1980); Lawrence Goodwyn, *Democratic Promise: The Populist Moment in America* (New York: Oxford University Press, 1976).

20. *Madison County Record,* Mar. 9, 1933.

21. *Madison County Record,* Mar. 16, 1933.

22. For various perspectives on the relative radicalism of southwestern Socialists, see Garin Burbank, *When Farmers Voted Red: The Gospel of Socialism in the Oklahoma Countryside, 1910–1924* (Westport, CT: Greenwood Press, 1976); David A. Shannon, *The Socialist Party of America: A History* (New York: Macmillan, 1955); James R. Green, *Grass-Roots Socialism: Radical Movements in the Southwest, 1894–1943* (Baton Rouge: Louisiana State University Press, 1978);

George Gregory Kiser, "The Socialist Party in Arkansas, 1900–1912" (M.A. thesis, University of Arkansas), 1980.

23. David A. Shannon, *Socialist Party in America,* 3, 35.

24. Kiser, "Socialist Party in Arkansas," 87–88, 110–11.

25. David A. Shannon, *Socialist Party of America,* 266.

Diversity within a Racial Group: White People in Little Rock, 1957–1959

1. Stephen L. Carter, *Reflections of an Affirmative Action Baby* (New York: Basic Books, 1991), 6.

2. Examples abound in mainstream northern, and often southern, liberal opinion. See, e.g., Nathan Glazer and Daniel Patrick Moynihan, *Beyond the Melting Pot: The Negroes, Puerto Ricans, Jews, Indians, and Irish of New York City,* 2nd ed. (Cambridge: MIT Press, 1970), xxii, xxiv, which distinguishes between a "northern" and a "southern" model of race relations: the "southern" is rigid, violent, and intraracially homogeneous. John Howard Griffin, a southern-reared writer whose narrative actually includes a couple of examples of nonracist white southerners, allowed his book, *Black like Me* (New York: Signet, 1961), to be sensationalized into a best-selling oversimplification of southern white attitudes. See esp. Griffin's own preface and the covers of various paperback editions. Griffin's episodes of southern white kindness often resolve into revelations of the not-so-subtle condescension underneath the posture of most southern "liberals." See, e.g., the climatic episodes of the book: 125–27.

Even Dwight Macdonald, who made a career out of drawing fine distinctions elsewhere, lumped all white southerners together in the "brutality" of their racial behavior. See his famous essay distinguishing varying degrees of German responsibility for the Holocaust, "On the Responsibility of Peoples," *Politics* (Feb. 1945), reprinted in Macdonald, *Memoirs of a Revolutionist: Essays in Political Criticism* (New York: Farrar, Straus and Cudahy, 1957), 45–46. Macdonald holds white southerners up as a contrast to the heterogeneity of Hitler-era German attitudes toward Jews. Macdonald seems to have adopted his view wholesale from John Dollard's best-selling sociological study, *Caste and Class in a Southern Town,* 3rd ed. (New Haven: Yale University Press, 1937).

Perhaps the most vivid examples of the stereotype of white southerners are in editorial cartoons. See, e.g., *Washington Post* cartoonist Herbert Block's 1958 cartoon "Nah You Ain't Got Enough Edjiccashun To Vote," reprinted in *Straight Herblock* (New York: Simon and Schuster, 1964); and Richard Q. Yardley, "Vindicated!" (which pictures a mentally retarded–looking "latent mob spirit"), *Baltimore Sun,* Sept. 25, 1957.

For criticism of stereotypes of white southerners, see Harriette Arnow's hillbilly novel, *The Dollmaker* (New York: Macmillan, 1954); and J. Wayne Flynt's scholarly history, *Dixie's Forgotten People: The South's Poor Whites* (Bloomington: Indiana University Press, 1980).

3. White opinion was revealed in three segregationist resolutions approved by Arkansas voters in the Nov. 1956 election; see Record and Record, *Little Rock,*

U.S.A., 27. On southern white opinion in general, see H. H. Hyman and P. B. Sheatsley, "Attitudes toward Desegregation," *Scientific American,* Dec. 1956, 35–39.

4. Examples of this propaganda are in folder 1, box 4, Daisy Bates Papers, Special Collections Division, University of Arkansas Libraries, Fayetteville; and folders 353–355, box 34, Arkansas Council on Human Relations Papers (hereafter ACHR Papers), Special Collections Division, University of Arkansas Libraries, Fayetteville.

5. *Arkansas Gazette,* Sept. 1, 1957.

6. On Ogden and Lorch, see Bates, *Long Shadow of Little Rock,* 64–71, 75, 87, 180, 189–93, 199; Cartwright, "Lesson from Little Rock"; Cartwright, "Improbable Demagogue"; and Cartwright, "Failure in Little Rock," *Progressive,* June 1958, 12–15. See also Cartwright's notes for lectures and sermons on racial issues, ACHR Papers, box 5, folder 48. The Arkansas Council on Human Relations, established in Dec. 1954, was on record supporting the *Brown* decision as "both legally just and morally right." See "The Arkansas Council on Human Relations: An Introduction," ACHR leaflet, July 1955, ser. IV, folder 217, Southern Regional Council Papers (hereafter SRC Papers) (microfilm, University Microfilms International, 1984), reel 141. However, some members of its executive board opposed the NAACP's efforts to press the legal case to speed up desegregation, thinking that was too radical. See Minutes of Executive Committee meeting, July 11, 1955, ser. IV, folder 223, SRC Papers, reel 141.

7. *Arkansas Faith,* May 1956, in Daisy Bates Papers, box 4, folder 1.

8. Different perspectives on Faubus's decision to block desegregation appear in Hays, *Southern Moderate Speaks,* 131–32; Knebel, "Real Little Rock Story," 31–33; and Faubus's own *Down from the Hills,* 191–95. Harris is qtd. in Hays, *Southern Moderate Speaks,* 134.

9. Jim Johnson qtd. in Jack Bass and Walter DeVries, *The Transformation of Southern Politics: Social Change and Political Consequence since 1945* (New York: Basic Books, 1976), 92. Even after this point, Faubus continued to espouse moderation, saying that he had sent the troops to prevent violence, not to prevent integration. He implied that he was protecting the black students from extreme segregationists.

10. Southern Regional Council report, June 27, 1955, ser. III, file 237, SRC Papers, reel 116.

11. Campbell and Pettigrew, *Christians in Racial Crisis,* 26–27, 34.

12. *Southern School News,* May 1956, in Record and Record, *Little Rock, U.S.A,* 16–17.

13. Campbell and Pettigrew, *Christians in Racial Crisis,* 2–3, 17, 37, 65; Christmas Message from Colbert Cartwright, Dec. 14, 1958, ser. IV, folder 215, SRC Papers, reel 141.

14. Reprinted in *Christian Century,* Oct. 2, 1957, ser. IV, file 217, SRC Papers, reel 141.

15. Campbell and Pettigrew, *Christians in Racial Crisis,* 34.

16. Campbell and Pettigrew, *Christians in Racial Crisis,* 69–70, 82–83.

17. Record and Record, *Little Rock, U.S.A.,* 17.

18. They did this by joining the prayer meetings on Columbus Day 1957, which, although many organizers remained noncommittal on the merits of integration, were a gesture of opposition to a rival prayer meeting organized by avowed segregationists (Campbell and Pettigrew, *Christians in Racial Crisis,* 30–33). See also "To the Churches of Little Rock," by the Episcopal bishop of Little Rock, Robert Brown (who initiated the Columbus Day meetings), Sept. 23, 1957, in folder 48, box 5, ACHR Papers.

19. Ministers' statement with list of signers and their churches in *New South* 12 (Oct. 1957): 14; Campbell and Pettigrew, *Christians in Racial Crisis,* 19.

20. Jacoway, "Taken by Surprise," 22.

21. Campbell and Pettigrew, *Christians in Racial Crisis,* 41–42, 47. It should be noted that the students of Hall High themselves voted overwhelmingly (70 percent) in favor of desegregating their school in 1958. See Fred Routh to Harold Fleming, Sept. 23, 1958, ser. IV, folder 220, SRC Papers, reel 141.

22. *Arkansas Gazette,* Sept. 10, 1957.

23. Huckaby, *Crisis at Central High,* 12.

24. Craig Rains qtd. in Hampton and Fayer, *Voices of Freedom,* 43–44.

25. Marcia Webb Lecky qtd. in Hampton and Fayer, *Voices of Freedom,* 50.

26. *Kansas City Star,* Dec. 8, 1957, in Daisy Bates Papers, folder 9, box 12.

27. White student and Blossom qtd. in Record and Record, *Little Rock, U.S.A.,* 59–63; Huckaby, *Crisis at Central High,* 36.

28. Rockefeller qtd. in Fred Routh to Nat Griswold, Apr. 19, 1956, ser. IV, folder 220, SRC Papers, reel 141.

29. Jacoway, "Taken by Surprise," 15–41.

30. Blossom qtd. in Ashmore, *Hearts and Minds,* 257; Potts qtd. in Record and Record, *Little Rock, U.S.A.,* 34. Judge Ronald Davies cited Mayor Mann's testimony that there was no indication there would be any violence resulting from his decision to throw out the injunction requested by the Mothers' League.

31. Ashmore, *Hearts and Minds,* 266; Mann's telegram in Stephen E. Ambrose, in *Eisenhower: The President* (New York: Simon and Schuster, 1984), 419.

32. Profile of WEC members from poll in *Arkansas Gazette,* June 26, 1960. On the origins of the WEC, see Nat Griswold to Henry Alexander, Sept. 16, 1960, in folder 277, box 27, ACHR Papers.

33. Jacoway, "Taken by Surprise," 31. The gender division seems to have functioned differently among lower-class women than among the upper class. Female status did not seem to free lower-class women to take a more explicit or militant position than their husbands. There seemed to be complete congruence between the Mothers' League of Central High and segregationist statements made by men. Women did perhaps strengthen the segregationist appeal, however, by invoking the special authority they had as mothers.

34. Spitzberg, *Racial Politics,* 87.

35. A related advertisement by doctors indicated a strong consensus among professionals against Faubus. See Nat R. Griswold manuscript, June 3, 1959, folder 277, box 27, ACHR Papers.

36. Not a single new industry located in Little Rock in the academic year that the schools were closed; see *New South* 14 (June 1959): 10.

37. *Arkansas Democrat,* May 9, 1959.

38. Jacoway, "Taken by Surprise," 34–36.

39. Chamber of Commerce vote tally and statement in *New South* 14 (June 1959): 8–9; and in Jacoway, "Taken by Surprise," 33.

40. *Arkansas Democrat,* May 9, 1959.

41. Bates, *Long Shadow of Little Rock,* 184–86.

42. Daisy Bates, interview with Elizabeth Jacoway, Oct. 11, 1976, transcript in the Southern Oral History Project, University of North Carolina Library, Chapel Hill, 17–18.

43. Kenneth Clark, "Observations on Little Rock," *New South* 13 (June 1958): 3–8.

44. Bates, interview with Jacoway, Oct. 11, 1976, 60, 54.

Power from the Pedestal: The Women's Emergency Committee and the Little Rock School Crisis

1. Jacoway, "Taken by Surprise"; Bartley, "Looking Back at Little Rock," 104.

2. "Has Arkansas Gone Liberal?" *Chicago Defender,* May 7, 1955, qtd. in McMillen, "White Citizens' Council," 96.

3. Some examples of such works include Bartley, *Rise of Massive Resistance;* Kluger, *Simple Justice;* George R. Metcalf, *From Little Rock to Boston: The History of Desegregation* (Westport, CT: Greenwood Press, 1983); and Wilkinson, *From Brown to Bakke.*

4. These include Bartley, "Looking Back at Little Rock," 101–16; Freyer, "Politics and Law"; McMillen, "White Citizens' Council," 95–122; and Wallace, "Orval Faubus."

5. Alexander, *Little Rock Recall Election.*

6. Jacoway, "Taken by Surprise."

7. Spitzberg, *Racial Politics.*

8. Campbell and Pettigrew, *Christians in Racial Crisis,* 19.

9. Hays, *Southern Moderate Speaks,* 94.

10. *Arkansas Gazette,* Sept. 4, 1957.

11. Spitzberg, *Racial Politics,* 39.

12. Spitzberg, *Racial Politics,* 70.

13. In early Oct. 1957, nearly a month after Faubus had called out the National Guard, the city's most prominent business leaders met in an attempt to resolve the crisis. The "Guy Committee" was composed of the past presidents and current board members of the Little Rock Chamber of Commerce. Meeting secretly, they disagreed on principles and strategy and could agree only to meet with the governor and issue a public statement in favor of law and order. E. Grainger Williams, a participant, described the Guy Committee's activities this way: "We took a picture and that's about it." See Jacoway, "Taken by Surprise," 26–27; E. Grainger Williams, video interview with Arkansas Interfaith Council, n.d.

14. Blossom, *It Has Happened Here,* 118.

15. Campbell and Pettigrew, *Christians in Racial Crisis,* 129.

16. Huckaby, *Crisis at Central High.*

17. Blossom, *It Has Happened Here,* 191; Anthony Lewis, *Portrait of a Decade: The Second American Revolution* (New York: Random House, 1964), 60.

18. In particular, the governor wielded considerable power through his appointments to various regulatory commissions. Commissioners owed their appointments to Faubus and were reluctant to grant licenses or favors to businessmen who opposed him on this issue. Moreover, Witt Stephens was one of Faubus's closest advisors, and his business interests included natural gas, banking, and bond issues (Spitzberg, *Racial Politics,* 72).

19. Harry S. Ashmore, preface to Huckaby, *Crisis at Central High,* xii.

20. Mary Jane Gates, interview with author, Little Rock, Jan. 5, 1993.

21. Mary Jane Gates, interview, Jan. 5, 1993.

22. Vivion Brewer, "The Embattled Ladies of Little Rock," manuscript, p. 5, Vivion Brewer Papers, Sophia Smith Collection, Smith College, Northampton, MA.

23. Like the women who had worked in the antilynching campaigns, Terry believed that women could be most effective by educating community members in racial tolerance. However, as C. Vann Woodward and others have shown, their view of segregation as a relic of the Old South perpetuated by the ignorance of poor whites denied the reality that segregation had been created in the early twentieth century and sustained by each succeeding generation of white leaders, including Terry's peers. See Brewer, "Embattled Ladies," 7; Jacquelyn Dowd Hall, *Revolt against Chivalry: Jessie Daniel Ames and the Women's Campaign against Lynching* (New York: Columbia University Press, 1979), 213; C. Vann Woodward, *The Strange Career of Jim Crow,* 3rd ed. (Oxford: Oxford University Press, 1974).

24. Jane Mendel, interview with author, Little Rock, Jan. 4, 1993.

25. One example of her unique prominence occurred in 1958 after Faubus launched a particularly vicious attack against her. Dozens of the city's most prominent citizens rallied to her defense, flooding the local papers with letters of support. See ser. 2, box 5, file 2, Fletcher-Terry Papers.

26. Maurice Mitchell, interview with author, Little Rock, Jan. 7, 1993.

27. Brewer, "Embattled Ladies," 7.

28. Minutes of WEC meetings, Sept. 23, 1958, through May 5, 1959, box 2, file 1, WEC Papers, Arkansas History Commission, Little Rock.

29. Information related to the membership survey can be found in box 1, file 6, WEC Papers. Brewer also included a copy of survey results in the appendix of her manuscript.

30. Interestingly, only 65 percent of the respondents said that they had actually volunteered for the WEC; the others had apparently just given money. Moreover, though membership climbed throughout the year, attendance at monthly meetings remained steady at sixty to one hundred members.

31. U.S. Bureau of the Census, *The Statistical History of the United States, from Colonial Times to the Present* (New York: Basic Books, 1976), 297, 380, 381.

32. Although 15 percent of the members were from outside the city or state, most of these members provided only financial support, and the survey refuted

the primary accusation that the WEC members were northerners (membership files, WEC Papers).

33. Alexander, *Little Rock Recall Election,* 26.

34. Alexander, *Little Rock Recall Election;* Spitzberg, *Racial Politics,* 23.

35. Preliminary survey results, Sept. 28, 1960, box 1, file 6, WEC Papers.

36. Sara Evans, *Personal Politics: The Roots of Women's Liberation in the Civil Rights Movement and the New Left* (New York: Knopf, 1979), 28.

37. Jean Gordon, interview; Mary Sandlin Fletcher Worthen, interview; Kathryn Lambright, interview; Pat House, interview; Dottie Morris, interview, all Oral History Collection (hereafter OHC), University of Arkansas at Little Rock.

38. Worthen, interview, OHC; Lambright, interview, OHC.

39. Irene Samuel, interview with author, Little Rock, Jan. 5, 1993.

40. Lambright, interview, OHC, 15, 41–42.

41. Most scholars describe women reformers as middle class. Generally, the women they refer to did not have to work outside the home. Thus, for the purposes of this essay, I will refer to middle-class and upper-class women as members of the leisure class, as compared with women of the working class.

42. Sara Evans, *Born for Liberty: A History of Women in America* (New York: Free Press, 1989), esp. chaps. 4, 6. However, labor unions were a major exception to this rule. Women in labor unions were predominantly working class. Middle- and upper-class women generally avoided labor unions in favor of less radical associations.

43. Evans, *Born for Liberty,* 140; Nancy Woloch, *Women and the American Experience* (New York: Knopf, 1984), 270; Evans, *Personal Politics,* 27.

44. Pat House, interview with author, Little Rock, Jan. 9, 1993.

45. The husbands of most WEC members faced virtually no economic repercussions, but the leaders' husbands were subject to serious reprisals. Irene Samuel's husband was an obstetrician, and as a result of her actions, nearly all of his patients chose another doctor. Vivion Brewer's husband lost his job with the Veterans' Administration Hospital during this period, and Brewer was convinced it was the result of her work with the WEC. Other sources have since disputed that notion, but it is clear that the leaders' husbands were targeted economically, while the husbands of less prominent members were not held financially responsible for their wives' actions.

46. Samuel, interview, Jan. 7, 1993.

47. Adolphine Fletcher Terry, "Life Is My Song, Also," manuscript, Charlie May Simon Papers, Archives and Special Collections, Ottenheimer Library, University of Arkansas at Little Rock, 240.

48. Membership survey data, box 1, file 6, WEC Papers.

49. House, interview, Jan. 9, 1993; Mendel, interview, Jan. 4, 1993; Sara Murphy, interview with author, Little Rock, Jan. 4, 1993; Samuel, interview, Jan. 7, 1993.

50. Membership lists, box 1, file 2, WEC Papers.

51. Membership survey, box 1, file 6, WEC Papers.

52. Samuel, interview, Jan. 7, 1993.

53. Membership lists, box 1, file 2, WEC Papers.

54. Samuel, interview, Jan. 7, 1993.

55. Vivion Brewer, interview, Southern Oral History Project.

56. Mary Jane Gates, interview, Jan. 5, 1993.

57. Mendel, interview, Jan. 4, 1993.

58. Samuel, interview, Jan. 7, 1993.

59. Sara Murphy, interview, Jan. 4, 1993.

60. Sara Murphy, interview, Jan. 4, 1993.

61. Adolphine Fletcher Terry, "Life Is My Song, Also," 231.

62. Edwin Dunaway, interview with author, Little Rock, Jan. 5, 1993.

63. Membership survey data, box 1, file 6, WEC Papers.

64. Samuel, interview, Jan. 7, 1993.

65. In recent interviews, WEC members and local businessmen claim that the WEC leaders were more integrationist than the general members. In their analyses of the school crisis, both Jacoway and Spitzberg assert this as fact. However, the evidence is inconclusive. Archival sources offer little information about the attitudes of general members toward issues of race, and recent interviews with WEC leaders are colored by the passage of time.

66. Membership survey data, box 1, file 6, WEC Papers.

67. Brewer, "Embattled Ladies," 8.

68. Brewer, "Embattled Ladies," 7–8.

69. Although I think Jacoway overstates the founders' original commitment to social justice, her description of that first meeting is otherwise very apt ("Taken by Surprise," 31).

70. Brewer, "Embattled Ladies," 9.

71. Brewer, "Embattled Ladies," 11.

72. Jacquelyn Dowd Hall, *Revolt against Chivalry*, 181.

73. The WEC Papers include files of secondary material that were part of the WEC library on issues of racial tolerance. Moreover, the minutes of nearly every meeting include references to a speaker or film educating the group on racial issues (boxes 2, 17, 18, 20–23, WEC Papers).

74. Brewer, "Embattled Ladies," 8.

75. "Once More a Showdown," *Newsweek*, Oct. 6, 1958.

76. Minutes of WEC meeting, Sept. 23, 1958, WEC Papers; Brewer, "Embattled Ladies," 1–33.

77. The only other white opposition came over the issue of football. Furious at the effect closed schools would have on the football season, citizens had quickly forced the governor to restore football practice at the closed high schools. But no civic leaders organized to protest the effect closed schools would have on education or the economic health of the community.

78. Spitzberg, *Racial Politics*, 87.

79. Brewer, "Embattled Ladies," 20–21.

80. Samuel, interview, Jan. 7, 1993.

81. Brewer, "Embattled Ladies," 18.

82. Brewer, "Embattled Ladies," 21.

83. Dunaway, interview, Jan. 5, 1993.

84. Minutes of WEC meeting, Oct. 7, 1958, WEC Papers.

85. Mendel, interview, Jan. 4, 1993.

86. House, interview, Jan. 9, 1993.

87. Samuel, interview, Jan. 7, 1993.

88. Spitzberg, *Racial Politics*, 87.

89. Brewer, "Embattled Ladies," 13.

90. Spitzberg, *Racial Politics*, 87.

91. Mendel, interview, Jan. 4, 1993.

92. Alford and Alford, *Case of the Sleeping People*, 100–108.

93. WEC member Margaret Stephens ran for school board position II against segregationist candidate Robert Laster. Laster, a municipal traffic judge, defeated Stephens (Brewer, "Embattled Ladies," 45).

94. Minutes of WEC meeting, Dec. 2, 1958, WEC Papers.

95. *Crisis in the South*, 99.

96. Brewer, "Embattled Ladies," 46.

97. *Arkansas Gazette*, Nov. 27, 1958.

98. E. Grainger Williams Papers, Archives and Special Collections, Ottenheimer Library, University of Arkansas at Little Rock.

99. Spitzberg, *Racial Politics*, 105.

100. Spitzberg, *Racial Politics*, 106; E. Grainger Williams Papers.

101. E. Grainger Williams, interview with author, Little Rock, Jan. 6, 1993.

102. In recent interviews, Samuel and Morris have asserted that there was no membership list at all, and thus they were not lying to the city authorities when they denied keeping such records. Vivion Brewer, in her memoir, wrote not only of having a list but of keeping it at a different woman's house each night to protect the identity of the WEC members. It seems likely that Morris and Samuel were correct in asserting that there was no membership list and that Brewer was talking about the mailing lists that were kept. The difference between a membership list and a mailing list seems to be only semantic, however, as the mailing lists that remain in the WEC archives divide the members into anonymous members, night members, etc. Dottie Morris, interview with author, Little Rock, Jan. 5, 1993; Samuel, interview, Jan. 7, 1993.

103. Letter from Mrs. Woodbridge Morris, secretary, to Little Rock city clerk, Apr. 1, 1959 (including enclosures), box 2, file 2, WEC Papers.

104. Letter from Letcher Langford to Morris, Apr. 26, 1959, box 2, file 2, WEC Papers.

105. John Pagan, "Orval Eugene Faubus and the Politics of Racism," manuscript, John Pagan Personal Files, 81.

106. *Arkansas Gazette*, May 7, 1959.

107. Alexander, *Little Rock Recall Election*, 15.

108. The membership of STOP drew so heavily from the husbands of WEC members that two membership lists were kept—those whose wives were WEC members and those whose wives were not (box 7, file 5, WEC Papers).

109. Dunaway, interview, Jan. 5, 1993; Mitchell, interview, Jan. 7, 1993; E. Grainger Williams, interview, Jan. 6, 1993. Spitzberg, *Racial Politics*, 18, cites other interviews that support this claim.

110. Spitzberg, *Racial Politics,* 18.

111. Mitchell, interview, Jan. 7, 1993.

112. Mitchell, interview, Jan. 7, 1993.

113. E. Grainger Williams, interview, Jan. 6, 1993.

114. Brewer, "Embattled Ladies," 125–26.

115. House, interview, Jan. 9, 1993; Sara Murphy, interview, Jan. 4, 1993; Samuel, interview, Jan. 7, 1993.

116. Sara Murphy, interview, Jan. 4, 1993.

117. House, interview, Jan. 9, 1993.

118. Mendel, interview, Jan. 4, 1993.

119. Mitchell, interview, Jan. 7, 1993.

120. Brewer, "Embattled Ladies," 126.

121. Interviews with participants, Brewer's manuscript, and papers in the WEC collection all attest to the organization of the WEC and the work the women performed (Sara Murphy, interview, Jan. 4, 1993; Samuel, interview, Jan. 7, 1993; Brewer, "Embattled Ladies," 125–33; box 7, WEC Papers; Spitzberg, *Racial Politics,* 21–22).

122. Brewer, "Embattled Ladies," 131. Newspapers and magazines across the nation hailed Little Rock's moderate victory and portrayed STOP leaders as heroes of their community. Few even mentioned the work of the WEC. An article in the *Progressive* listed the WEC along with the PTA and "other organizations [that] voiced protests." A *Time* article omitted any reference to the WEC but mentioned that "to STOP's support came an overwhelming majority of Little Rock's 13,000 member PTA council" (Cartwright, "HOPE Comes to Little Rock," 7–9; "Counter-Revolution," *Time,* May 25, 1959, 69).

123. *Arkansas Gazette,* May 27, 1959.

124. Spitzberg, *Racial Politics,* 118.

125. "Taps," *Pine Bluff Commercial,* Nov. 5, 1963.

126. Bartley, "Looking Back at Little Rock," Jacoway, "Taken by Surprise," and Spitzberg, *Racial Politics,* provide the most extensive analyses of this abdication of civic leadership.

127. Spitzberg, *Racial Politics,* 95.

The Little Rock Crisis and Postwar Black Activism in Arkansas

1. Charles M. Payne, *I've Got the Light of Freedom: The Organizing Tradition and the Mississippi Freedom Struggle* (Berkeley: University of California Press, 1995), 424.

2. Eisenhower, *White House Years;* Hays, *Southern Moderate Speaks* and *Politics Is My Parish;* Faubus, *Down from the Hills* and *Down from the Hills, II;* Blossom, *It Has Happened Here;* Mann, "Truth about Little Rock"; Ashmore, *Negro and the Schools, Epitaph for Dixie,* and *Hearts and Minds;* Alford and Alford, *Case of the Sleeping People;* Huckaby, *Crisis at Central High;* Sara Murphy, *Breaking the Silence.*

3. Roy Reed, *Faubus;* Sherrill, "Orval Faubus"; Wallace, "Orval Faubus"; Bartley, "Looking Back at Little Rock"; McMillen, "White Citizens' Council";

Campbell and Pettigrew, *Christians in Racial Crisis;* Lorraine Gates, "Power from the Pedestal"; Jacoway, "Taken by Surprise"; Peltason, *Fifty-Eight Lonely Men;* and Freyer, *Little Rock Crisis.*

4. Bates, *Long Shadow of Little Rock.*

5. Tom Dillard, "Scipio A. Jones," *AHQ* 31 (Autumn 1972): 201–19; Dillard, "To the Back of the Elephant: Racial Conflict in the Arkansas Republican Party," *AHQ* 33 (Spring 1974): 3–15.

6. On ANDA, see John A. Kirk, "Dr. J. M. Robinson, the Arkansas Negro Democratic Association and Black Politics in Little Rock, Arkansas, 1928–1952," pt. 1, *Pulaski County Historical Review* 41 (Spring 1993): 2–16, and pt. 2, 41 (Summer 1993): 39–47.

7. August Meier and John H. Bracey Jr., "The NAACP as a Reform Movement, 1909–1965: 'To Reach the Conscience of America,'" *Journal of Southern History* 59 (Feb. 1993): 13–30; Richard C. Cortner, *A Mob Intent on Death: The NAACP and the Arkansas Riot Cases* (Middletown, CT: Wesleyan University Press, 1988).

8. Telegram from William Pickens to Carrie Sheppherdson, Jan. 5, 1925, pt. 12, selected branch files, box G-12, Papers of the NAACP (hereafter NAACP [branch] Papers) (microfilm, University Publications of America, 1982), reel 4, frame 0879.

9. Mrs. H. L. Porter to Roy Wilkins, Nov. 14, 1933, NAACP (branch) Papers, reel 4, frames 0039–41.

10. On the white primary cases across the South, see Darlene C. Hine, *Black Victory: The Rise and Fall of the White Primary in Texas* (Millwood, NY: KTO Press, 1979).

11. Hine, *Black Victory,* 97.

12. Walter White to Arthur Spingarn, Nov. 7, 1929, misc. correspondence, NAACP, Little Rock, Special Collections Division, University of Arkansas Libraries, Fayetteville.

13. Harvard Sitkoff, *A New Deal for Blacks: The Emergence of Civil Rights as a National Issue* (New York: Oxford University Press, 1978), provides an excellent overview of the plight of blacks in the 1930s. On the displacement of agricultural workers due to New Deal policies, see Pete Daniel, "The Legal Basis of Agrarian Capitalism: The South since 1933," in *Race and Class in the American South since 1890,* ed. Melvyn Stokes and Rick Halpern (Oxford: Berg Publishers, 1994), 79–102. For local developments, see *Survey of Negroes in Little Rock and North Little Rock* (Little Rock: Urban League of Greater Little Rock, 1941). The best collection of primary materials concerning the effects of the New Deal in Arkansas is the Floyd Sharp scrapbooks, 1933–43, Arkansas History Commission, Little Rock. Sharp was coordinator of the WPA in the state.

14. On wartime developments in Arkansas, see C. Calvin Smith, *War and Wartime Changes: The Transformation of Arkansas, 1940–1945* (Fayetteville: University of Arkansas Press, 1986).

15. William Pickens to W. H. Flowers, May 10, 1940, group 2, ser. c, box 10, "Pine Bluff, Ark., 1940–1947," NAACP Papers (hereafter NAACP [LC] Papers), Library of Congress, Washington, DC. For a more extensive account of W. H.

Flowers and the CNO, see John A. Kirk, "'He Founded a Movement': W. H. Flowers, the Committee on Negro Organizations, and the Origins of Black Activism in Arkansas," in *The Making of Martin Luther King and the Civil Rights Movement,* ed. Brian Ward and Tony Badger (New York: New York University Press, 1996), 29–44.

16. W. H. Flowers to Walter White, Oct. 31, 1938; Charles Houston to Flowers, Nov. 22, 1938; Thurgood Marshall to Flowers, Apr. 14, 1939, all in W. H. Flowers Papers (hereafter WHF Papers), Pine Bluff, AR. The W. H. Flowers Papers are unprocessed and uncollected at his law offices in Pine Bluff and are as Flowers left them at the time of his death in 1990. Research was conducted with the kind permission of his daughter, Stephanie Flowers.

17. *CNO Spectator,* July 1, 1940. On the Democratic Party of Arkansas, see Key, *Southern Politics,* 183–204.

18. *CNO Spectator,* July 1, 1940; press release, Oct. 12, 1940, WHF Papers. Accounts of the meeting appeared in various black newspapers throughout the country, most notably the *Pittsburgh Courier;* see W. H. Flowers to William H. Nunn, Oct. 5, 1940, WHF Papers.

19. Press release, Sept. 11, 1941, WHF Papers.

20. *Arkansas State Press,* Mar. 6, 1942.

21. Thomas E. Patterson, *History of the Arkansas Teachers Association* (Washington, DC: National Education Association, 1981), 89–91.

22. Mrs. H. L. Porter to Walter White, group 2, ser. c, box 9, "Little Rock, Arkansas, 1940–1947," NAACP (LC) Papers.

23. W. H. Flowers to Ella Baker, Aug. 18, 1945, group 2, ser. c, box 11, "Arkansas State Conference, April 1945–December 1948," NAACP (LC) Papers.

24. *Arkansas Gazette,* Mar. 26, 1942.

25. *Arkansas State Press,* Mar. 27, 1942.

26. *Arkansas State Press,* Mar. 27, 1942; *Arkansas Gazette,* Mar. 24, 1942.

27. *Arkansas State Press,* Mar. 27, Apr. 5, 1942.

28. *Arkansas State Press,* Apr. 10, 24, May 1, 8, 1942.

29. *Arkansas State Press,* Aug. 21, 1942; *Arkansas Gazette,* Aug. 19, 1942.

30. Charles Bussey, interview with author, Dec. 4, 1992, Pryor Center.

31. *Arkansas Gazette,* Nov. 21, 1949.

32. Griffin Smith Jr., "Localism and Segregation: Racial Patterns in Little Rock, Arkansas, 1945–1954" (M.A. thesis, Columbia University, 1965), 52–53, 80, 94–95.

33. *Arkansas State Press,* Sept. 17, 1948, Dec. 16, 1949, Dec. 29, 1950, Nov. 30, 1951.

34. *Arkansas Gazette,* May 13, 1950.

35. *Arkansas Gazette,* June 4, 1950.

36. *Arkansas Democrat,* June 7, 1950; *Arkansas Gazette,* June 8, 1950.

37. *Arkansas Democrat,* June 16, July 6, 1950.

38. *Arkansas Gazette,* Sept. 23, 1950.

39. Guerdon D. Nichols, "Breaking the Color Barrier."

40. Wiley A. Branton, speech, Apr. 28, 1957, qtd. in Bennie W. Goodwin, "Silas Hunt—The Growth of a Folk Hero," 18–19, Special Collections Division, University of Arkansas Libraries, Fayetteville.

41. Guerdon D. Nichols, "Breaking the Color Barrier," 18–19; Christopher C. Mercer, interview with author, Apr. 19, 1993, Pryor Center.

42. *State Press,* Aug. 27, 1948; "Arkansas Med School Opens Its Doors," *Ebony,* Jan. 1949; A. Stephen Stephan, "Desegregation of Higher Education in Arkansas," *Journal of Negro Education* 27 (Summer 1958): 243–52; M. A. Jackson, interview with author, Feb. 10, 1993, Pryor Center.

43. Marcus Taylor to Ella Baker, Dec. 4, 1945, group 2, ser. c, box 9, "Little Rock, Arkansas, 1940–1947," NAACP (LC) Papers.

44. Gloster B. Current to Thurgood Marshall, memorandum, n.d., group 2, ser. c, box 11, "Arkansas State Conference, April 1945–December 1948," NAACP (LC) Papers.

45. Lucille Black to W. H. Flowers, Jan. 15, 1948, group 2, ser. c, box 10, "Pine Bluff, Ark., 1948–1955," NAACP (LC) Papers.

46. Donald Jones to Gloster B. Current, memorandum, n.d., group 2, ser. c, box 11, "Arkansas State Conference, April 1945–December 1948," NAACP (LC) Papers.

47. Donald Jones to Gloster B. Current, Feb. 24, 1949, group 2, ser. c, box 10, "Arkansas State Conference 1949–1950," NAACP (LC) Papers.

48. Walter White to Pine Bluff NAACP, Feb. 25, 1949; Roy Wilkins to Arkansas branches of the NAACP, May 10, 1949, both group 2, ser. c, box 10, "Pine Bluff, Ark., 1948–1955," NAACP (LC) Papers.

49. Lulu B. White to Gloster B. Current, Nov. 1, 1950, group 2, ser. c, box 11, "Arkansas State Conference, 1949–1950," NAACP (LC) Papers.

50. Gloster B. Current, "Memorandum to the Staff, Branches and Regional Offices," Aug. 7, 1951, group 2, ser. c, box 11, "Arkansas State Conference, 1951–1952," NAACP (LC) Papers.

51. U. Simpson Tate to Gloster B. Current, Aug. 20, 1952, group 2, ser. c, box 11, "Arkansas State Conference, 1951–1952," NAACP (LC) Papers.

52. *Arkansas State Press,* Dec. 17, 1948, Nov. 18, 1949.

53. *Arkansas State Press,* Jan. 14, July 15, 1949; *Arkansas Gazette,* July 31, 1988.

54. *Arkansas State Press,* Oct. 26, Dec. 14, 1951, Mar. 7, 1952.

55. On the Supreme Court, the NAACP, and higher-education suits, see Mark Tushnet, *The NAACP's Legal Strategy against Segregated Education, 1925–1950* (Chapel Hill: University of North Carolina Press, 1987). For a comprehensive discussion of the background of *Brown,* see Kluger, *Simple Justice.*

56. Bates, *Long Shadow of Little Rock,* 47–48.

57. Edwin E. Dunaway, interview with author, May 5, 1993, Pryor Center.

58. *Southern School News,* Apr. 1955, 3, Aug. 1956, 3, July 1956, 9.

59. *Southern School News,* Apr. 1957, 15.

60. Rufus King Young, interview with author, Feb. 16, 1993, Pryor Center.

61. Georg C. Iggers to Tony Freyer, Sept. 17, 1980, courtesy Georg Iggers.

62. Iggers, "Arkansas Professor," 285.

63. Blossom, *It Has Happened Here,* 11–13.

64. Iggers, "Arkansas Professor," 286.

65. Iggers, "Arkansas Professor," 286–87.

66. *Southern School News,* July 1955, 3; Iggers, "Arkansas Professor," 287.

67. *Southern School News,* Sept. 1955, 10, July 1955, 3, Aug. 1955, 15, Sept. 1955, 10.

68. Iggers, "Arkansas Professor," 289.

69. *Southern School News,* Mar. 1956, 4.

70. Iggers, "Arkansas Professor," 290; *Southern School News,* Apr. 1957, 15, May 1957, 2. For an account of pre-1957 issues in *Aaron v. Cooper,* see Freyer, *Little Rock Crisis,* chap. 2.

71. Cothran and Phillips, "Negro Leadership in a Crisis Situation," 111.

72. For a more expansive account of black activism and race relations during the postwar period, see John A. Kirk, *Redefining the Color Line: Black Activism in Little Rock, Arkansas, 1940–1970* (Gainesville: University Press of Florida, 2002).

International Pressure and the U.S. Government's Response to Little Rock

1. *To Secure These Rights: The Report of the President's Committee on Civil Rights* (Washington, DC: Government Printing Office, 1947), 146–48. Mary L. Dudziak explores the link between civil rights policy and foreign policy in the Truman years in "Desegregation as a Cold War Imperative," *Stanford Law Review* 41 (Nov. 1988): 61–120.

2. Secretary of State Dean Acheson to Attorney General James P. McGranery, Dec. 2, 1952, Records of the Department of State, Record Group 59 (hereafter RG 59), National Archives and Records Administration, College Park, MD.

3. Brief for the United States as *Amicus Curiae, Brown v. Board of Education,* 374 US 483 (1954), 6.

4. Richard Dalfiume, qtd. in Donald R. McCoy, Richard T. Ruetten, and J. R. Fuchs, eds., *Conference of Scholars on the Truman Administration and Civil Rights, April 5–6, 1968* (Independence, MO: Harry S. Truman Library Institute for National and International Affairs, 1968), 21.

5. Of all the unjust court rulings against African Americans, the Jimmy Wilson case received the most overseas publicity. In 1958, an Alabama court sentenced Wilson to death for stealing $1.95 from a white woman. Appeals on his behalf came from the six continents. Leaders such as Prime Minister Nkrumah of Ghana contacted Eisenhower. Secretary of State John Foster Dulles told Alabama governor James Folsom that U.S. diplomatic missions around the world had reported widespread anger over the Wilson sentence. The governor, who said he received one thousand letters daily on the issue, mostly from abroad, commuted Wilson's sentence. There are several folders in the State Department records on the Jimmy Wilson case. See, e.g., John Foster Dulles to James Folsom, telegram, Sept. 4, 1958, and Folsom to Dulles, Sept. 5, 1958, both RG 59.

6. In the wake of Eisenhower's intervention in Little Rock, Senator Herman Talmadge, a Georgia Democrat, played on the fears of anticommunists: "We still mourn the destruction of the sovereignty of Hungary by Russian tanks and

troops in the streets of Budapest. We are now threatened with the spectacle of the President of the United States using tanks and troops in the streets of Little Rock to destroy the sovereignty of the state of Arkansas" (*U.S. News and World Report,* Oct. 4, 1957).

7. John Foster Dulles told Paul Robeson in 1946 that the reason the United States could not take a stronger stand against South Africa was that he did not "feel that the United States, in view of its own record, was justified in adopting a holier-than-thou attitude" (Brenda Gayle Plummer, *Rising Wind: Black Americans and U.S. Foreign Affairs, 1935–1960* [Chapel Hill: University of North Carolina Press, 1996], 154).

8. "Opinion about U.S. Treatment of Negroes," report 38, July 24, 1956, Office of Research, Public Opinion Barometer Reports, 1955–1956, Records of the United States Information Agency, Record Group 306 (hereafter RG 306), National Archives and Records Administration.

9. *New York Times,* Apr. 29, 1956.

10. In his memoir, Chief Justice Earl Warren recalled a talk with Eisenhower: "The President . . . took me by the arm and, as we walked along, speaking of the Southern states in the segregation cases, he said, 'These are not bad people. All they are concerned about is to see that their sweet little girls are not required to sit in school alongside some big overgrown Negroes.' Shortly thereafter, the *Brown* case was decided, and with it went our cordial relations" (Earl Warren, *Memoirs of Earl Warren* [Garden City, NY: Doubleday, 1977], 291).

11. A day after the crisis broke out, Eisenhower stated that he did not intend to propose federal intervention in southern school disputes.

12. The act empowered the federal government to seek court injunctions against obstruction or deprivation of voting rights, among other things.

13. Little Rock occupied front-page space "usually reserved for major domestic news" (Dispatch 151, American Embassy, Canberra, Australia, to Department of State, Oct. 1, 1957, RG 59).

14. Dispatch 188, American Embassy, Djakarta, Indonesia; USIA to Department of State, Oct. 7, 1957, both RG 59.

15. Dispatch 141, American Embassy, Tripoli, Libya, to Department of State, Oct. 22, 1957, RG 59.

16. Dispatch 111, American Consulate, São Paolo, Brazil, to Department of State, Sept. 23, 1957, RG 59. In Ecuador, leading papers carried editorials of condemnation. See Dispatch 256, American Embassy, Quito, Ecuador, to Department of State, Oct. 19, 1957, RG 59.

17. Letter to Eisenhower from Buenos Aires, Argentina, Sept. 16, 1957; Federation of Free Students of Argentina to the students of the United States, Oct. 19, 1957, both RG 59.

18. "Public Reactions to Little Rock in Major World Capitals," Special Report Series SR-8, Oct. 29, 1957, RG 306.

19. Telegram 31 from Copenhagen, Denmark, to secretary of state, Sept. 5, 1957, RG 59.

20. Dispatch 255, American Embassy, Stockholm, Sweden, to Department of State, Sept. 10, 1956, RG 59.

21. Telegram from Bern, Switzerland, to secretary of state, Sept. 12, 1957, RG 59.

22. Dispatch 45, U.S. Consulate General, Amsterdam, the Netherlands, to secretary of state, Sept. 12, 1956, RG 59. *De waarheid* continued, "Neither President Eisenhower nor Adlai Stevenson are [*sic*] endeavoring to halt American colonialism—the 7th Fleet's operations against Syria and the actions of the Arkansas militia against the Negro are but different sides of the same policy."

23. Dispatch 45, U.S. Consulate General, Amsterdam, to secretary of state, Sept. 12, 1956, RG 59. A Dutch news editorial entitled "Just the Same as the Actions of the Little Bastards of the Hitler Jugend . . . Shame on America" asked whether there was "no one in the USA who can tell these boys full of hate that some 150 years ago their ancestors fetched Negroes as slaves from Africa, making big money on those cargoes of human flesh. These people do great harm to American friendship. What dirty minds."

24. Dispatch 115, American Embassy, Dublin, Ireland, to Department of State, Sept. 23, 1957, RG 59.

25. Dispatch 64, American Embassy, Luxembourg, to Department of State, Sept. 24, 1957, RG 59.

26. Dispatch 69, American Embassy, Luxembourg, to Department of State, Sept. 30, 1957, RG 59.

27. Dispatch 401, American Embassy, Brussels, Belgium, to Department of State, Oct. 8, 1957, RG 59.

28. *New York Post,* May 8, 1958.

29. Dispatch 462, American Embassy, Vienna, Austria, to State Department, Nov. 5, 1958, RG 59.

30. Telegram 23 from American Embassy, Paris, France, to Department of State, Sept. 26, 1957, RG 59.

31. Telegram from Bonn, West Germany, to USIA, Oct. 5, 1957, RG 59.

32. Dispatch 86, American Consulate, Dar es Salaam, to Department of State, Sept. 28, 1957, RG 59. In African countries, coverage of Little Rock was somewhat limited. In Ghana, e.g., USIA and embassy officials reported that "the media are not so good and have limited circulation; at the same time Ghanaians are preoccupied with domestic matters" (Dispatch 170, American Embassy, Accra, Ghana, to Department of State, Nov. 15, 1957, RG 59). Nevertheless, upon his return from Ghana's independence celebrations, Vice President Richard M. Nixon told President Eisenhower that American officials could not talk about equality to the people of Ghana or Africa or Asia while "we practice inequality in the United States." Nixon recommended that "in the national interest . . . we must support the necessary steps which will assure orderly progress toward the elimination of discrimination in the United States" (*Department of State Bulletin,* Apr. 22, 1957, 43). During Nixon's visit to Ghana, a story circulated that Nixon had asked a man in Ghana how it felt to be free. The man replied, "I would not know. I am from Alabama" (Hugh Tinker, *Race, Conflict, and the International Order: From Empire to United Nations* [New York: St. Martin's, 1977], 84).

33. Dispatch 31, American Consulate, Kampala, Uganda, to Department of State, Oct. 4, 1957, RG 59.

34. Dispatch 37, American Consulate, Kampala, to Department of State, Oct. 3, 1957, RG 59.

35. Dispatch 31, American Consulate, Kampala, to Department of State, Oct. 4, 1957, RG 59.

36. Dispatch 115, American Consulate, Lagos, Nigeria, to Department of State, Oct. 14, 1957, RG 59.

37. Dispatch 155, American Consulate, Lagos, to Department of State, Nov. 29, 1957, RG 59.

38. Dispatch 59, American Consulate, Lourenço Marques, Mozambique, to Department of State, Sept. 30, 1957, RG 59.

39. Dispatch 96, American Consulate, Nairobi, Kenya, to Department of State, Oct. 2, 1957, RG 59.

40. Dispatch 59, American Consulate, Lourenço Marques, to Department of State, Sept. 30, 1957, RG 59.

41. Dispatch 11, American Consulate, Port Elizabeth, South Africa, to Department of State, Nov. 13, 1957, RG 59.

42. Dispatch 113, American Consulate, Johannesburg, South Africa, to Department of State, Dec. 5, 1957, RG 59.

43. *Public Papers of the Presidents of the United States: Dwight D. Eisenhower, 1957* (Washington, DC: Government Printing Office), 694.

44. For positive responses, see Dispatch 70, American Embassy, Luxembourg, to Department of State, Oct. 1, 1957; Dispatch 59, American Consulate, Lourenço Marques, to Department of State, Sept. 30, 1957; Dispatch 401, American Embassy, Brussels, to Department of State, Oct. 8, 1957; Dispatch 96, American Consulate, Nairobi, to Department of State, Oct. 2, 1957; Dispatch 31, American Consulate, Kampala, to Department of State, Oct. 4, 1957; Dispatch 313, American Embassy, Bogota, Colombia, to Department of State, Oct. 7, 1957; Department of State, Instruction 1565 to American Embassy in London, Nov. 17, 1957. The quotation is in Dispatch 69, American Embassy, Luxembourg, to Department of State, Sept. 30, 1957, and the accusation concerning civil rights legislation is in Dispatch 16, American Consulate, Cardiff, Wales, to Department of State, Sept. 27, 1957. All are in RG 59.

45. Telegram 43 from Stockholm, Sweden, to Secretary of State, Sept. 25, 1957, RG 59.

46. Telegrams 527, 532, The Hague to Secretary of State, Sept. 26, 1957, RG 59.

47. Telegram, Quito, Ecuador, to Secretary of State, Sept. 28, 1957, RG 59.

48. Dispatch 99, American Consulate, Dakar, French West Africa, to Department of State, Oct. 30, 1957, RG 59.

49. Dispatch 218, American Embassy, San José, Costa Rica, to Department of State, Oct. 4, 1957, RG 59.

50. Telegram 415, joint USIA-State, Rio de Janeiro, Brazil, to Secretary of State, Sept. 26, 1957, RG 59.

51. Communication 504 from U.S. United Nations Mission, New York, to Department of State, Dec. 9, 1957, RG 59.

52. Office memorandum, July 18, 1958, USIA Office of Research, special reports 1953–63, RG 306.

53. "Post–Little Rock Opinion on the Treatment of Negroes in the U.S.," Program and Media Series, Jan. 1958, RG 306.

54. *New York Post,* June 4, 1958.

55. *Report of the United States Commission on Civil Rights* (Washington, DC: Government Printing Office, 1959), 548.

56. Clayborne Carson, *In Struggle: SNCC and the Black Awakening of the 1960s* (Cambridge: Harvard University Press, 1981), 16.

57. Martin Luther King Jr., *Why We Can't Wait* (New York: Harper & Row, 1964), 9–10.

After 1957: Resisting Integration in Little Rock

The author wishes to thank Ernest Dumas for his insightful reading of this essay.

1. Adolphine Fletcher Terry to William H. McLean, Mar. 9, 1970, ser. 1, box 2, file 6, Fletcher-Terry Papers, Special Collections, Ottenheimer Library, University of Arkansas at Little Rock; *Arkansas Gazette,* Mar. 11, 1970.

2. *Arkansas Gazette,* May 12, 13, 1965.

3. *LRSD v. PCSSD,* 584 F. Supp. 328 (U.S. Dist., 1984).

4. Jeannie Whayne et al., *Arkansas: A Narrative History* (Fayetteville: University of Arkansas Press, 2002), 301–2; Carl Moneyhon, *Arkansas and the New South, 1874–1929* (Fayetteville: University of Arkansas Press, 1997), 107–8; Calvin R. Ledbetter Jr., *Carpenter from Conway: George Washington Donaghey as Governor of Arkansas, 1909–1913* (Fayetteville: University of Arkansas Press, 1993), 130–32; Raymond Arsenault, *The Wild Ass of the Ozarks: Jeff Davis and the Social Bases of Southern Politics* (Knoxville: University of Tennessee Press, 1984), 88–92, 145–46, 214; John Graves, *Town and Country: Race Relations in an Urban-Rural Context, Arkansas, 1865–1905* (Fayetteville: University of Arkansas Press, 1990), 194–96; Kenneth C. Barnes, *Journey of Hope: The Back-to-Africa Movement in Arkansas in the Late 1800s* (Chapel Hill: University of North Carolina Press, 2004), 84–85; Ben F. Johnson III, *Fierce Solitude: A Life of John Gould Fletcher* (Fayetteville: University of Arkansas Press, 1994), 12–15.

5. Adolphine Fletcher Terry, "Life Is My Song, Also," 130–31; Peggy Harris, "Adolphine Fletcher Terry," in *Arkansas Biography,* ed. Nancy Williams (Fayetteville: University of Arkansas Press, 2000), 283–84; Harris, "'We Would Be Building': The Beginning of the Phyllis Wheatley YWCA in Little Rock," *Pulaski County Historical Review* 43 (Winter 1995): 70–86; Frances M. Ross, "The New Woman as Club Woman and Social Activist in Turn of the Century Arkansas," *AHQ* 50 (Winter 1991): 342–43; A. Elizabeth Taylor, "The Women's Suffrage Movement in Arkansas," *AHQ* 15 (Spring 1956): 17–52.

6. Black voters in the neighborhoods slated for clearance voted against the housing bond issue, however. See *Arkansas Gazette,* Jan. 5, 6, May 10, 1950; Sara Murphy, *Breaking the Silence,* 20–22; George B. Tindall, *The Emergence of the New South, 1913–1945* (Baton Rouge: Louisiana State University Press, 1967), 485–86,

636–37; John Egerton, *Speak against the Day: The Generation before the Civil Rights Movement in the South* (Chapel Hill: University of North Carolina Press, 1994), 91–104, 154–67, 185–97.

7. Kirk, "Massive Resistance and Minimum Compliance," 90–91; Spitzberg, *Racial Politics,* 38–42; Jason Sokol, *There Goes My Everything: White Southerners in the Age of Civil Rights, 1945–1975* (New York: Knopf, 2006), 13–15, 33–35, 43, 46, 53–54; Earl Black and Merle Black, *Politics and Society in the South* (Cambridge: Harvard University Press, 1987), 76–86; Kirk, *Redefining the Color Line,* 64; Berna J. Love, *End of the Line: A History of Little Rock's West Ninth Street* (Little Rock: Center for Arkansas Studies, 2003), 19, 36–37; Ben F. Johnson III, *Arkansas in Modern America: 1930–1999* (Fayetteville: University of Arkansas Press, 2000), 61–65; C. Calvin Smith, *War and Wartime Changes,* 127–29.

8. *Arkansas Gazette,* Aug. 29, 1952; Kirk, "'Study in Second Class Citizenship,'" 278–79; Sara Murphy, *Breaking the Silence,* 23–24.

9. *Arkansas State Press,* Jan. 30, 1953, qtd. in Sara Murphy, *Breaking the Silence,* 24. Harry Bass, head of the Little Rock Urban League, was apparently among those leaders upbraided by Bates; see *LRSD v. PCSSD,* 778 F.2d 404 (8th Circuit, 1985).

10. Everett Tucker Jr. to Virgil Blossom, Mar. 15, 1957, ser. 1, box 1, file 10, Virgil Blossom Papers, Special Collections Department, University of Arkansas Libraries, Fayetteville; Spitzberg, *Racial Politics,* 51–52; Blossom, *It Has Happened Here,* 12–19.

11. Tony Badger, "*Brown* and Backlash," in Webb, *Massive Resistance,* 45–47; Karen S. Anderson, "Massive Resistance and Southern Social Relations," in Webb, *Massive Resistance,* 206–9; C. Fred Williams, "Class: The Central Issue in the 1957 Little Rock Crisis," *AHQ* 56 (Autumn 1997): 341–44; Roy, *Bitters in the Honey,* 24–25, 149; Sokol, *There Goes My Everything,* 216–18.

12. Cope, "'Honest White People'"; Cope, "'Marginal Youngsters'"; Cope, "'Thorn in the Side'?"; Roy Reed, *Faubus,* 207, 213, 217, 225–26, 240, 244; McMillen, "White Citizens' Council"; David R. Goldfield, *Black, White, and Southern: Race Relations and Southern Culture, 1940 to the Present* (Baton Rouge: Louisiana State University Press, 1990), 81–84.

13. Bates, *Long Shadow of Little Rock,* 94–97, 111, 176; Stockley, *Daisy Bates,* 115, 122, 145–46, 181, 202, 204; Jacoway, *Turn Away Thy Son,* 183–94; Kirk, *Redefining the Color Line,* 158–59; Badger, "*Brown* and Backlash," 51; Roy Reed, *Faubus,* 203, 233; Jacoway, "Taken by Surprise," 28.

14. Roy Reed, *Faubus,* 245–46; Jacoway, *Turn Away Thy Son,* 268–74; Kilpatrick, "Wiley Austin Branton"; Jacoway, "Richard C. Butler"; Freyer, *Little Rock Crisis,* 139–58.

15. Miller, "Challenging the Segregationist Power Structure"; Brewer, *Embattled Ladies,* 8–11, 29–41, 48; Lorraine Gates, "Power from the Pedestal"; Jacoway, "Down from the Pedestal"; Adolphine Fletcher Terry diary (undated prefatory material, quotation), Feb. 27, Mar. 31, Apr. 11, 17, 18, 1958, Fletcher-Terry Papers.

16. Roy Reed, *Faubus,* 196; Jacoway, *Turn Away Thy Son,* 297; Brewer, *Embattled Ladies,* 60–61; Sara Murphy, *Breaking the Silence,* 106–9; Lorraine Gates, "Power from the Pedestal," 47–54; *Arkansas Gazette,* May 12, 1975.

17. *Arkansas Gazette,* Mar. 25, 31, 1959; *Acts of Arkansas* (1959), 1827. In Nov. 1956, Arkansas voters had approved an initiated pupil placement act that had been advanced by Faubus to counter the more radical measures proposed by Jim Johnson. This act was in peril after the Virginia statute on which it had been modeled was overturned by the U.S. Supreme Court. The *Arkansas Gazette* reported that the Chamber of Commerce advertisement referred to the 1956 law rather than the one just approved by the legislature. The governor had not yet signed the bill when the ad was published, but the chamber's reference to a pupil assignment law "upheld by the United States Supreme Court" suggests that the businessmen were already placing their hopes on the 1959 version. See Roy Reed, *Faubus,* 177–78; Wilkinson, *From* Brown *to* Bakke, 84.

18. Ashmore, *Hearts and Minds,* 282; Sara Murphy, *Breaking the Silence,* 174–83; Brewer, *Embattled Ladies,* 156–67; Roy Reed, *Faubus,* 252–56; Kirk, *Redefining the Color Line,* 134–36.

19. *Arkansas Gazette,* June 21 (editorial quotation), 26, 28, 1959; *New York Times,* June 12, Aug. 17 (Tucker quotation), 1959; Spitzberg, *Racial Politics,* 111, 115–16.

20. Rector letter of Mar. 16, 1960, qtd. in "Letter to My Friends," ser. 1, box 2, file 6, Fletcher-Terry Papers; Sara Murphy, *Breaking the Silence,* 108, 185–86; Brewer, *Embattled Ladies,* 235–37.

21. Kirk, *Redefining the Color Line,* 151–58; Johnson, *Arkansas in Modern America,* 152; Bill Terry, "Little Rock's Most Crucial Election: The Thorny and Contrary Issue of How Does Your City Grow," *Arkansas Times* (Oct. 1976): 8–30.

22. *LRSD v. PCSSD* (1984); *Arkansas Gazette,* Mar. 29, 1959, June 27, 1971 (quotations from commission investigation); Martha Walters, "Little Rock Urban Renewal," *Pulaski County Historical Review* 24 (Mar. 1976): 12–16; Margaret Arnold, "Little Rock's Vanishing Black Communities," *Arkansas Times* (June 1978): 36–43; Raymond Rebsamen, "Urban Renewal: Progress on a Timetable," *Arkansas Economist* 4 (Fall 1961): 1–8; Kirk, *Redefining the Color Line,* 173–74. Although the Eighth Circuit Court of Appeals did not accept Judge Woods's remedy to consolidate the three county districts to provide relief for Little Rock, the appeals judges found no errors in the district court's findings on residential segregation: "The district court also found that the Little Rock Housing Authority accentuated segregation in public housing and, thus, in schools, by razing black neighborhoods (which bordered on white areas) and relocating the uprooted blacks in housing projects in eastern Little Rock. White residents, whose neighborhoods were more selectively cleared, were relocated to western Little Rock. The district court found that these decisions were part of 'a deliberate policy of the Little Rock Housing Authority and other governmental bodies to maintain a residential racial segregation'" (*LRSD v. PCSSD* [1985]).

23. *Clark v. Board of Education,* 369 F.2d 661 (8th Circuit, 1966); *Arkansas Gazette,* Apr. 23, May 5, May 18, May 23, Sept. 18, 1965; Kirk, *Redefining the Color Line,* 174–76; James T. Patterson, Brown v. Board of Education: *A Civil Rights Milestone and Its Troubled Legacy* (New York: Oxford University Press, 2001), 100–101. Although the district judge did not toss out the freedom-of-choice plan, he did order the district to enroll the Clark children in the predominantly white school near their home.

24. Spitzberg, *Racial Politics*, 153–54, 160–61; Kirk, *Redefining the Color Line*, 150–53; Sara Murphy, *Breaking the Silence*, 235–48; Johnson, *Arkansas in Modern America*, 154–55. In the so-called Oregon report discussed below, the authors identified as "liberal pressure groups," in addition to COCA, the Special Committee on Public Education, the Arkansas Council on Human Relations, and the NAACP and noted the "overlap in membership" of "middle-class Negroes and members of the white middle and upper-classes" (Bureau of Education Research, University of Oregon, "A Report to the Board of the Directors of the Little Rock School District," May 1967, 46, Special Collections, Ottenheimer Library, University of Arkansas at Little Rock).

25. Bureau of Education Research, "Report," 43, 46, 102. The conclusions of the report were covered in a series of articles: *Arkansas Gazette*, June 12–14, 1967. Also see *Arkansas Gazette*, Aug. 30, 1966, June 21, July 13, 1971.

26. Edwin N. Barrow, a school board member, objected to the Oregon report by asserting, "We are not a Board to create sweeping sociological change in this city" (*Arkansas Gazette*, June 21, 1967). When Superintendent Floyd Parsons later revealed his opposition to the Oregon report, he acknowledged that integration improved education in a "sociological sense," but not in a "strictly academic sense." Audience members attending the school board meeting booed a board member who disagreed with Parsons' assertion (*Arkansas Gazette*, July 13, 1967). Little Rock was not unique in experiencing the shift of those supporting open schools to opposition to suburban integration, as is revealed in an excellent and provocative recent study that shaped my thinking on this matter: Matthew D. Lassiter, *The Silent Majority: Suburban Politics in the Sunbelt South* (Princeton: Princeton University Press, 2006). Lassiter's book, however, does not cover the events in Little Rock.

27. *Arkansas Gazette*, Mar. 14, 1968.

28. *Arkansas Gazette*, July 28, Sept. 24–27, Dec. 19 (quotation), 1967.

29. *Arkansas Gazette*, Sept. 1, Dec. 29–30, 1967, Jan. 5, 1968.

30. *Arkansas Gazette*, Jan. 15, Mar. 2, 8, 10 (ad quotation), 11, 13, 14 (editorial quotation), 1968. Dr. John A. Harrell, board president, and Mrs. Frank N. Gordon, vice president, lost their seats to Jim L. Jenkins (whose daughter attended the private school) and Charles A. Brown.

31. Wilkinson, *From Brown to Bakke*, 108–18.

32. Terry to Tucker, Mar. 1970, ser. 1, box 2, file 6, Fletcher-Terry Papers. In a letter to William McLean, Mar. 9, 1970, Terry wrote: "The apartment buildings at 2016 Wright Avenue had always had white tenants, until about two years ago when Rector's firm took over the management and replaced the white occupants with blacks. The whites were well satisfied; had no desire to move. The down-town district has been completely surrounded by a broad band of blacks, the group with the least purchasing power of any in the community" (Fletcher-Terry Papers, ser. 1, box 2, file 6).

33. "To My Friends," Mar. 3, 1970, Fletcher-Terry Papers, ser. 1, box 2, file 6; *Arkansas Gazette*, Feb. 20, Mar. 3, 6, 11, 1970.

34. *Clark v. Board of Education*, 328 F. Supp. 1205 (U.S. Dist., 1971); *Arkansas Gazette*, July 10, 17, Aug., 7, Sept. 5, 9, 1970; Wilkinson, *From Brown to Bakke*, 134–39.

35. *Arkansas Democrat-Gazette,* Oct. 26, 2003; *Arkansas Gazette,* June 30 (quotation), July 2, Sept. 15, 23, 1971; Johnson, *Arkansas in Modern America,* 202.

36. Both historians and interested observers have emphasized that authentic integration has been stymied by tradition, the failure of personal reconciliation, and a legal impasse based on self-interest. Elizabeth Jacoway concludes her study by noting: "Segregationist thinking was 'deeply written on the heart of [the] culture,' and it could not be changed by force, no matter how worthy or urgent the compelling motives. . . . Sadly, the story of changing attitudes is one that remains unfinished fifty years after the crisis at Central High" (*Turn Away Thy Son,* 362). Grif Stockley observes that Daisy Bates and L. C. Bates "had believed that integration of the schools would be the key to racial progress, not its battleground. At the beginning of the 2004–05 school year, most of Little Rock's schools were substantially black. Though genuine friendships between African Americans and whites are evident in the state of Arkansas, there remains deep distrust between the races, but it is not a subject that attracts a great deal of public discussion" (*Daisy Bates,* 296–97). In his speech on the fortieth anniversary of the school crisis, Arkansas governor Mike Huckabee insisted: "Let me remind us: Government can do some things, but only God can change people's hearts. Government can put us in the same classrooms, but government can't make classmates go home and be friends when school is out. Government can make sure that the doors of every public building are open to everyone. Government can ensure that we share schools and streets and lunch counters and buses and elevators and theaters. But let us never forget that only God can give us the power to love each other and respect each other and share life, liberty and the pursuit of happiness with every American, regardless of who he or she is" (*Arkansas Democrat-Gazette,* Sept. 25, 1997).

37. "William Field 'Billy' Rector," Arkansas Business.com, http://www.arkansasbusiness.com/people_hall_fame.asp?id=30 (accessed Sept. 28, 2006).

38. *LRSD v. PCSSD,* (E.D. Ark. 2007); *Arkansas Democrat-Gazette,* Feb. 24, 2007.

Contributors

John A. Kirk is professor of U.S. history at Royal Holloway, University of London. He is the author of *Redefining the Color Line: Black Activism in Little Rock, Arkansas, 1940–1970* (2002), *Martin Luther King Jr.* (2005), and *Beyond Little Rock: The Origins and Legacies of the Central High Crisis* (2007), and editor of *Martin Luther King, Jr. and the Civil Rights Movement: Controversies and Debates* (2007).

Numan V. Bartley (1934–2004) was, at the time of his death, the E. Merton Coulter Professor of History Emeritus at the University of Georgia. His books include *The Rise of Massive Resistance: Race and Politics in the South in the 1950's* (1969) and *The New South, 1945–1980* (1995).

Neil R. McMillen is professor of history emeritus at the University of Southern Mississippi. He is the author of *The Citizens' Council: Organized Resistance to the Second Reconstruction, 1954–64* (1971) and *Dark Journey: Black Mississippians in the Age of Jim Crow* (1989).

Tony A. Freyer is University Research Professor of History and Law at the University of Alabama. His books include *The Little Rock Crisis: A Constitutional Interpretation* (1984) and *Little Rock on Trial:* Cooper v. Aaron *and School Desegregation* (2007).

Roy Reed, who reported for the *Arkansas Gazette* and the *New York Times* during the civil rights era, is emeritus professor of journalism at the University of Arkansas, Fayetteville. He is the author of *Faubus: The Life and Times of an American Prodigal* (1997) and *Looking for Hogeye* (1986).

David L. Chappell is the Irene and Julian J. Rothbaum Professor of History at the University of Oklahoma. He is the author of *Inside Agitators: White Southerners in the Civil Rights Movement* (1994) and *A Stone of Hope: Prophetic Religion and the Death of Jim Crow* (2004).

Lorraine Gates Schuyler is chief of staff to the president, University of Richmond. She is the author of *The Weight of Their Votes: Southern Women and Political Leverage in the 1920s* (2006).

Azza Salama Layton is associate professor of political science at DePaul University. She is the author of *International Politics and Civil Rights Policies in the United States, 1941–1960* (2000).

Ben F. Johnson III is dean of the College of Liberal and Performing Arts and professor of history at Southern Arkansas University. He is the author of *Fierce Solitude: A Life of John Gould Fletcher* (1994), *Arkansas in Modern America: 1930–1999* (2000), and *John Barleycorn Must Die: The War against Drink in Arkansas* (2005).

Index